TEST ACCOMMODATIONS FOR STUDENTS WITH DISABILITIES

ABOUT THE AUTHOR

Edward Burns received his Ph.D. from the University of Michigan in 1971. He is currently a Professor at the State University of New York at Binghamton, and the Director of the Division of Education. He has written several books and numerous articles relating to educational statistics, testing, educational research in special education, and augmentative communication (viz., single-switch software applications).

TEST ACCOMODATIONS FOR STUDENTS WITH DISABILITIES

By

EDWARD BURNS

State University of New York at Binghamton
Binghamton, New York

CHARLES C THOMAS • PUBLISHER, LTD.
Springfield • Illinois • U.S.A.

T 75873

Published and Distributed Throughout the World by

CHARLES C THOMAS · PUBLISHER, LTD.
2600 South First Street
Springfield, Illinois 62794-9265

*With THOMAS BOOKS careful attention is given to all details of manufacturing
and design. It is the Publisher's desire to present books that are satisfactory as to their
physical qualities and artistic possibilities and appropriate for their particular use.
THOMAS BOOKS will be true to those laws of quality that assure a good name and
good will.*

Printed in the United States of America
MS-R-3

Library of Congress Cataloging in Publication Data

Burns, Edward, 1943-
     Test accommodations for students with disabilities / by Edward
Burns.
          p.   cm.
     Includes bibliographical references (p.   ).
     ISBN 0-398-06844-5 (cloth). -- ISBN 0-398-06845-3 (paper)
     1. Handicapped children--United States--Ability testing.
2. Handicapped children--Education--Law and legislation--United
States. 3. Examinations--United States--Design and construction.
States--Scoring.   I. Title.
LB3051.B7953   1998
371.27 ' 1--dc21

PREFACE

Identifying and implementing valid test accommodations involves the interaction of several important legal, practical and theoretical considerations. How test accommodations are conceptualized, and when and if accommodations are implemented depends on how each of these components is viewed. The purpose of *Test Accommodations for Students with Disabilities* is to consider legal questions, theoretical issues, and practical methods for meeting the assessment needs of students with disabilities. This book is comprised of 10 chapters and includes test accommodation topics relating to Federal and State regulations (including the IDEA Amendments Act of 1997), problems concerning reliability and validity, and practical strategies for planning test accommodations and adapting and modifying tests. In Chapter 1 (REGULATIONS AND ACCOMMODATIONS), a general foundation for making test accommodations is provided, and in Chapter 2 (TEST ACCOMMODATION RELIABILITY AND VALIDITY), important issues relating to the reliability and validity of test accommodations are presented. In Chapter 3, the need for general test accommodation planning is discussed, and Chapter 4 deals primarily with Individualized Education Programs (IEP) designated test accommodations. Chapter 5 (TEST ADAPTATIONS), Chapter 6 (TEST FORMAT MODIFICATIONS), Chapter 7 (SCHEDULING AND TIME MODIFICATIONS) and Chapter 8 (RESPONSE MODIFICATIONS) are concerned with problems, techniques and strategies relating to test accommodations. In Chapter 9 (TEST SCORE ACCOMMODATIONS), methods for interpreting test scores are discussed, and in Chapter 10 (TEST SCORE COMPARISONS), techniques used to compare test scores (and thus the need for special education, related services, and test accommodations) are examined.

This book is intended for psychologists, special educators, reading and speech specialists, regular education teachers, multidisciplinary and IEP team members, parents, and professionals involved in educational decision-making. Every area can benefit from collaboration, but a team approach is essential for the effective identification, planning and implementation of test accommodations. To this end, the ultimate goal of this book is to consider a variety of concerns and to provide several ideas for conceptualizing and implementing valid test accommodations.

EDWARD BURNS

CONTENTS

TEST ACCOMMODATIONS FOR STUDENTS WITH DISABILITIES

Chapter 1

REGULATIONS AND ACCOMMODATIONS

Nondiscriminatory Assessment

Federal regulations provide a firm foundation for administering tests which are nondiscriminatory and which assess what they are intended to assess; that is, tests should be fair and valid. For a student with a disability a test is discriminatory if the test measures the student's disability rather than ability. For example, if a student is classified as learning disabled because of a severe reading problem, testing the student in a content area such as social studies or science by means of a reading-based test would measure, to some extent, the student's reading performance rather than content ability. If the purpose of the test is to measure social studies or science content and not reading, the test would be discriminatory for this student.

If a test measures a student's disability rather than ability, unless the disability is the focus of measurement, the test is discriminatory. However, the corrective task is not simply to modify the test so that the test no longer reflects the student's disability, but to modify the test so that "the test results accurately reflect the student's aptitude or achievement level or whatever other factors the test purports to measure."[1] If a test is modified to the extent that it no longer measures what it was originally designed to measure, the test might no longer be discriminatory (at least on the surface), but the test would no longer be valid. If a reading test is read to a student, this modification might obviate the reading disability, but would also make the test invalid because the test would no longer measure what it was designed to measure.

Testing should be fair and valid, but the many issues which accompany the various regulations and guidelines are not always straightforward and are at times in conflict with one another. The regulations require that tests be valid and used for the purpose for which they were designed, yet there is a distinct legislative charge to test a student's ability rather than disability. In order to achieve the latter (i.e., to test ability), the former (i.e., maintaining validity) can be compromised or at least subject to question.

If a test is changed or modified to test a student's ability rather than disability, the modification will probably change, to some degree, what the test was originally designed to measure. For standardized tests, every departure from how the test was originally standardized will alter to some degree, the interpretation of a student's standardized test performance. Obviously, the goal of every test accommodation is to minimize the magnitude of the accommodation in order to minimize the impact of the accommodation on test validity.

For the most part, the regulations relating to nondiscriminatory and valid assessment are governed by Section 504 of the 1973 Vocational Rehabilitation Act, Public Law 101-476 (the Individuals with Disabilities Education Act or IDEA) which is a reauthorization of the Education of the Handicapped Act or P.L. 94-142, the IDEA Amendments of 1997 (P.L. 105-17) and P.L. 101-336 the 1990 American with Disabilities Act (ADA).

Although legal guidelines can sometimes confuse rather than clarify, Section 504 of the Rehabilitation Act of 1973 is uncharacteristically clear concerning the need for nondiscrimination and provides the basis for much of the legislation involving students with disabilities:

Nondiscrimination Under Federal Grants and Programs

No otherwise qualified individual with a disability in the United States, as defined in section 706(8) of this title shall, solely by reason of his or her disability, be excluded from the participation in, be denied benefits of, or be subjected to discrimination under any program or activity receiving Federal financial assistance.[1,2]

Section 504,[4] IDEA, and ADA each has a unique place in the historical development of special education regulations. Section 504 is essentially civil rights legislation and emphasizes the need for nondiscrimination; IDEA regulations[5] provide considerable detail for interpreting the law relating to special education and related services and is tied to funding; and the ADA regulations emphasizes employment-related nondiscrimination. A violation of Section 504 can result in the termination of Federal financial assistance. However, as noted by Rothstein (1990),

EAHCA[6] "goes beyond a mere nondiscrimination mandate and requires special education and related services to be provided to all children with handicaps in the least restrictive appropriate setting at no cost" (p. 38). A summary of the statutes and regulations relating to special education and nondiscrimination is presented in Table 1.1.

Most recently, IDEA has been improved and reauthorized as the Individuals with Disabilities Education Act Amendments of 1997 (P.L. 105-17[7]). Several notable changes of this reauthorization of IDEA relating to test accommodations involve the inclusion of students with disabilities in assessment programs with accommodations, guidelines for the participation of students with disabilities in alternate assessments,[8] a statement in the IEP of any modifications to State and districtwide assessments which are needed for a student to participate in the assessments, and the reason when a student is not able to participate in these assessments.[9]

Table 1.1 Federal Laws and Regulations Relating to Special Education.[10]

Statute	Public Law	Date	U.S.C.[11]	Regulations[12]
Section 504 of the Rehabilitation Act	P.L. 93-112	1973	29 U.S.C. §794	34 C.F.R. §§104.1-.61, Appendix A & B
Individuals with Disabilities Education Act	P.L. 101-476 P.L. 105-17[a]	1990	20 U.S.C. §§1400-1485	34 C.F.R. §§300.1-.754, Appendix C
American with Disabilities Act	P.L. 101-336	1990	42 U.S.C. §§12101-12213	see 28 C.F.R. §§35.101-.190, Appendix A

Although generic modifications in the form of supplementary aids and services must be provided to ensure regular education participation,[13] there is no specific law or regulation which states that a test must be adapted or modified, or if adapted or modified, what the form of the adaptation or modification should be. The intent of the laws and regulations which relate to testing is to ensure that, as much as possible, the student's ability rather than disability is tested, and that students are given a fair opportunity to demonstrate that ability. The path, however, which leads to a fair and valid assessment is bordered by testing the disability rather than ability[14] on one side and test invalidity[15] on the

---

[a]P.L. 101-476 is a reauthorization of the P.L. 94-142 or the Education of All Handicapped Children Act (EAHCA) of 1975. P.L. 105-17 is entitled the Individuals with Disabilities Education Act Amendments Act of 1997 or IDEA Amendments of 1997 and was signed into law June 4, 1997.

other. That is, not providing a test accommodation might result in measuring the disability, while implementing a test accommodation which significantly changes what the test measures can invalidate the test and result in dubious or misleading test scores. Interestingly enough, both situations can result in discrimination. Not providing a necessary test accommodation obviously discriminates if actual ability is incorrectly assessed, and an overzealous test accommodation which significantly changes what the test measures might preclude necessary services. For example, a student is not tested in reading (or the test is modified so that reading is no longer measured) in order to accommodate the disability. Because the student is not tested, reading services are not provided; and because reading services are not provided, the student does not develop skills in reading even if the student had the ability to develop such skills.

One purpose of a test accommodation is to eliminate discriminatory testing, but the accommodation itself can prove to be just as discriminatory as the effects of the disability it is designed to mitigate. Allowing a student to use a calculator to answer primary fact questions, reading reading-test items, using a computer spell-check for spelling when spelling is being evaluated, and signing reading-test items are all examples of test accommodations that obviate the "skill...that the test purports to measure." These test accommodations not only invalidate the test, but can actually serve to discriminate against a student by not evaluating "specific areas of educational need,"[16] by not allowing the student to demonstrate his or her ability, achievement or whatever else the test purports to measure, or by withholding services.

Testing Ability Rather Than Disability

If a student's disability prevents or distorts the assessment of the skill or knowledge being measured, four possibilities exist for dealing with this situation: (1) providing no modifications to either the test or test situation, (2) making accommodations so that the test measures the individual's ability rather than disability, (3) using an alternative test, or (4) not testing or providing a test exemption.

In order to determine to what extent a student can participate in regular assessment, a test might be given with no accommodations. A state agency might believe that any accommodation might deprive a student of a fair opportunity to participate in regular classroom testing.

And, as was mentioned above, if the student's disability involves the ability being tested (e.g., a reading test is given to a student with a reading disability), not providing test accommodations would be necessary in order to determine the magnitude of the disability, needed remediation, and the extent of progress as a result of remediation.

If a test measures an individual's disability rather than ability, an accommodation might be made to adapt or modify the conditions for testing, the test, or how the test is interpreted. Often a test accommodation provides a reasonable solution to the problem of meeting an individual's right to a fair assessment, and providing a valid assessment of the skill or trait in question.

If a test is inappropriate, an alternative test might be available. For example, if a school uses an achievement test which is not available in large print, and a student uses large print to read, an alternative test available in large print might be used. There will be some differences in content, standardization procedures, and norms between the two tests but an alternative test might be a fair and reasonable solution.

Finally, if a test is inappropriate because it measures a student's disability rather than ability, the simplest solution is not to test at all. Because this might limit an individual's educational opportunities, care must be taken to ensure that the test cannot be modified or that an alternative test is not available. The student must always be given the benefit of the doubt when there is a question about the appropriateness or usefulness of a test. Nonetheless, the need to provide a fair opportunity does not exclude the need to exercise a modicum of common sense. For a 16-year-old student with a severe developmental disability who is functioning at a readiness level, attempting to administer an age-appropriate state competency test would probably have limited educational value.

The Mandate

Federal regulations direct that tests must be valid, must measure ability rather than disability, and must not be discriminatory:

> Tests are selected and administered so as best to ensure that when a test is administered to a child with impaired sensory, manual, or speaking skills, the test results accurately reflect the child's aptitude or achievement level or whatever other factors the test purports to measure, rather than reflecting the child's impaired sensory, manual, or speaking skills (except where those skills are the factors that the test purports to measure);[17]

The Section 504 regulation is essentially the same as IDEA other than Section 504 uses "student" in place of "child."[18]

The basic form of this mandate *to test ability rather than disability except where the ability is the factor being measured* is used by various agencies. In Ohio (Ohio Department of Education, 1996) the regulations require that tests

> are selected and administered to obtain results that accurately reflect the aptitude, achievement level, and/or other factor purportedly being measured of a learner with impaired sensory, manual, or speaking skills, and that do not reflect such learner's impaired sensory, manual, or speaking skills except in the case where the test or other evaluation purports to measure those skills;[19]

The ADA regulation uses similar wording as IDEA and Section 504 but introduces the concept of testing disability rather than ability as a form of discrimination:

> As used in subsection (a), the term discriminate" includes...(7) failing to select and administer tests concerning employment in the most effective manner to ensure that, when such test is administered to a job applicant or employee who has a disability that impairs sensory, manual, or speaking skills, such test results accurately reflect the skills, aptitude, or whatever other factor of such applicant or employee that such test purports to measure, rather than reflecting the impaired sensory, manual, or speaking skills of such employee or applicant (except where such skills are the factors that the test purports to measure);[20]

The regulations emphasize the need to "select and administer tests" to ensure/obtain nondiscriminatory results but there are few guidelines for how this should be accomplished. Section 504 directs that

> in its course examinations or other procedures for evaluating students' academic achievement in its program, a recipient to which this subpart applies shall provide such methods for evaluating the achievement of students who have a handicap that impairs sensory, manual, or speaking skills as will best ensure that the results of the evaluation represents the student's achievement in the course... [21]

Although there is a directive to use "such methods" to evaluate students "which best represents the student's achievement in the course," the exact method depends on the student, the disability, the test, and how the test is used.

The Exception

The mandate for testing and for test accommodations is evident: A test should reflect a student's ability rather than the student's disability. However, IDEA regulations (as do Section 504 and ADA regulations) contain an important and sometimes ignored proviso: "... except where those skills are the factors that the test purports to measure."[22] There are occasions when the disability itself might be the focus of assessment. When this is the case, attempting to minimize the disability might serve to limit growth and opportunity. If a student has a severe learning disability and achieves at a very low level on standardized tests, one solution might be to not use standardized tests. Unfortunately, if this is done, the ability to measure achievement or, consistent with IDEA regulations, assess present levels of performance, plan a meaningful program, and evaluate progress is limited. For a student who is achieving below grade level, a specific test may or may not be appropriate, and an accommodation may or may not be possible. However, eliminating the assessment of achievement limits the ability of the individual to demonstrate achievement.

This interpretation seems to suggest that a normative evaluation of ability or achievement is the only viable form of assessment. In actuality, curriculum-based and qualitative assessment techniques will probably provide better direction as to needed remedial efforts rather than a strictly normative interpretation of performance. However, a normative evaluation of performance is necessary when such indices are used to evaluate the performance of students who are not disabled and thus ensure "that to the maximum extent appropriate, children with disabilities...are educated with children who are not disabled."[23]

Concerning employment, the ADA provides the same directive as IDEA and Section 504 regulations (to test ability rather than disability), but includes the same proviso "except where such skills are the factors that the test purports to measure."[24] The exception is also cited in conjunction with the use of employment tests to screen individuals with disabilities, unless the test is job-related:

> using qualification standards, employment tests or other selection criteria that screen out or tend to screen out an individual with a disability or a class of individuals with disabilities unless the standard or other selection criteria, as used by the covered entity, is shown to be job-related for the position in question and is consistent with business necessity;"[25]

Defining Test Accommodations

Federal and Statewide Guidelines

The intent of federal regulations to measure ability rather than disability is abundantly clear, but they are somewhat vague with respect to specific test accommodations, allowable accommodations, or guidelines for implementing accommodations. This is understandable considering that the use of test accommodations requires a balance between meeting individual needs while maintaining test validity. The need to test ability rather than disability does direct that tests be "selected and administered so as best to ensure that when a test is administered"[26] this goal is achieved. Thus, an accommodation might involve either test selection (e.g., selecting an alternative test) or test administration which includes any and all adaptations and modifications. In this respect the need for a test accommodations is implicit in the regulations: If a test measures a student's disability rather than ability, don't test, use a different test, or somehow adapt or modify the test which is being used without compromising the test's validity.[27]

Service and aids. The purpose of a test accommodation is to eliminate the discriminatory aspects of a test without jeopardizing test validity. No matter where testing takes place, in a special education setting or in a regular classroom, or whether the test reference group is disability- or regular education-based, testing should be nondiscriminatory and valid. Depending on the severity of the disability, test accommodations might go hand in hand with *special education services*. For example, a "specially designed" program might be necessary to meet the instructional and assessment needs of a student with a severe motor, visual or learning disability.[28] For some students *related services* might be necessary to benefit from special education so that in addition to a special education program, other services are provided (e.g., professionals other than the classroom teacher are used to administer and interpret tests).

Because statewide and school testing can be critical for a student to be eligible for an appropriate education, test accommodations can be an essential ingredient for the participation of students with disabilities in the regular school program. In this respect a "modification" can be any *supplementary aid or service* "to the regular education program...necessary to ensure the child's participation in that program."[29]

Section 504 refers to *auxiliary aids* which "may include taped texts, interpreters or other effective methods for making orally delivered materials available to students with hearing impairments, readers in libraries for students with visual impairments, classroom equipment adapted for use by students with manual impairments, and other similar services and actions."[30] The items mentioned here suggest possible types of modifications, but the actual appropriateness of a modification is based on the need to test a student's ability and the need to maintain, as much as possible, test validity.

The term *Section 504 Accommodation* suggests that Section 504 is specifically designed to deal with test accommodations, but this is an informal designation and there is no difference in the type or quality of accommodations provided under Section 504 and IDEA. IDEA regulations[31] provide special education and related services for students identified as having a disability as defined by IDEA; that is, students who meet the criteria for one of the IDEA disability categories and have a need for special education and related services.[32] For students who are covered by IDEA, test accommodations are integrated into special education and related services and are therefore included in the student's IEP. For students not covered by IDEA but by Section 504, "regular or special education and related services that (1) are designed to meet individual education needs"[33] must be provided. As a result, a section 504 Accommodation generally refers to a student who is covered by the much broader definition of a disability in the Section 504 regulations, and who requires a test accommodation.

The term *accommodation* in IDEA and Section 504 is used to signify a *reasonable accommodation* which refers to an accommodation "to the known physical or mental limitations of an otherwise qualified handicapped applicant or employee...".[34] Examples of reasonable accommodations include "(1) making facilities used by employees readily accessible to and usable by handicapped persons, and (2) job restructuring, part-time or modified work schedules, acquisition or modification of equipment or devices, the provision of readers or interpreters, and other similar actions." For employment purposes, a qualified handicapped person is someone who can, with or without a reasonable accommodation, perform the essential job functions in question. For school age students, a "qualified" person with a disability is anyone who is entitled to receive a free appropriate public education (FAPE).

There is an important distinction between the statutory term *otherwise qualified*[35] which is used in the wording of Section 504 ("...no otherwise qualified handicap individual with a disability...," and the term "qualified" which is used in the regulations.[36] The term *otherwise qualified* focuses on the disability and not the effect of the disability on other activities; the term *qualified* suggests that a person is able to perform "essential functions" with "reasonable accommodation."[37] An individual who is blind would not be qualified to drive a car even when the disability is accommodated. Citing case law Phillips (1993) reported that "when the disability itself prevents the person from demonstrating the required skills, the person is not otherwise qualified" (p. xxv). At the postsecondary and vocational level "a handicapped person who meets the academic and technical standards requisite to admission or participation"[38] is qualified. All school age students who require a free appropriate public education are qualified and entitled to suitable test accommodations, "except where those skills are the factors that the test purports to measure."[39]

At the preschool and school level, *qualified* indicates that all students are entitled to special education and related services. Just as for employment, this does not signify that a student with a disability is qualified for an age-appropriate regular education, but an "appropriate" education based on the least restrictive environment principle.[40] For employment purposes, the principle of reasonable accommodation can determine employment eligibility, while in education the concept of reasonable accommodation is used to determine the least restrictive intrusion on the student's right to a free appropriate public education. A student with a severe reading disability would be qualified to take a test in a content area if a reasonable accommodation (e.g., reading the test to the student) allowed the student to demonstrate content ability, that is, perform the "essential function" of the test which is demonstrating content knowledge. However, a student with a severe developmental disability with limited language skills would not be qualified to take a test in a content area such as social studies or science if no accommodation would allow the student to demonstrate content ability. In this instance, the student might be otherwise qualified to perform the test task; that is, if the student were not developmentally disabled, the student might be able to demonstrate content ability.

Finally, if an individual is not qualified for a specific job, there is no employment mandate that another job be provided; in education if a student is not qualified for a certain educational environment, another environment (albeit more restrictive) must be provided. In terms of test accommodations, the concepts underlying *reasonable accommodation, qualification,* and *least restrictive environment* are extremely important in that a test should be modified or an accommodation made when "appropriate," but not all students will be qualified to take all tests.

Section 504 regulations also uses the term "modifications"[41] to describe "academic requirements as are necessary to ensure that such requirements do not discriminate or have the effect of discriminating, on the basis of the handicap, against a qualified handicapped person or student." Modifications include extending the time to complete degree requirements, substituting courses, "and adaptation of the manner in which specific courses are conducted." In addition, rules may not be imposed (e.g., not using a tape recorder) which limits participation in an education program or activity.

State guidelines. Individual states are generally more explicit concerning the meaning of test accommodations. The New York State Education Department describes test modifications as enabling "students with disabilities to participate in test programs on an equal basis with their nondisabled peers. They provide an opportunity for students with disabilities to demonstrate mastery of skills and attainment of knowledge without being limited or unfairly restricted due to the effects of a disability" (New York State, 1995, p. 6). The Wisconsin Department of Public Instruction (1996) directs that students with disabilities be provided "with any necessary modifications or accommodations to ensure their participation" in the Wisconsin Student Assessment System (providing the accommodations are "allowable"). Texas (1994) allows for the accommodation of students' test needs which "do not cause the result to be invalid." In Connecticut, modifications are used "in an effort to make tests more accessible to those students with certain disabilities" but "an appropriate or reasonable accommodation must not interfere with the interpretation of an individual's score" (p. 7).

For individual states, statewide guidelines often refer to accommodations specific to the state testing program, and are not necessarily guidelines for all educational and psychological testing conducted within the state. This, of course, depends on the statewide guidelines in question, and how the guidelines are interpreted by individual schools and districts. For lack of an appropriate benchmark or direction, a district might use statewide guidelines which refer to specific statewide tests for all standardized tests used by the district.

Accommodation and Participation

Friend and Bursuck (1996) reiterated IDEA regulations by stating that "most important in testing students with disabilities is making sure that the test results reflect their knowledge and skills, not their disabilities" (p. 373). These authors, using Section 504 terminology, described the need for reasonable accommodations for adapting instructional methods which are determined "by carefully analyzing students' learning needs and the specific demands of the classroom environment, teachers can reasonably accommodate most students with special needs in the classroom" (p. 21). They described test adaptations as comprising three categories: before the test (e.g., practice tests), during the test (e.g., extra time), and after the test (e.g., changing grading criteria).

Salvia and Ysseldyke (1995) defined accommodations as involving "adapting or modifying measures to enable students with disabilities to participate in assessment" (p. 180). These authors ask the following question which captures the essence of the test accommodation issue: "What legitimate modifications can be made in assessment materials and/or procedures that will allow valid assessment results to be obtained?" In other words, the task is not to haphazardly adapt and modify tests, but to make legitimate adaptations and modifications which will yield valid test results.

Thurlow, Ysseldyke, and Silverstein (1993, p. 1) suggested that the term *modifications* (e.g., using large print) is often associated with changes in test format, while *accommodations* (e.g., extending time limits) with changes in the testing environment. These authors noted that, overall, the terms "accommodation," "modification" and "adaptation" are often used interchangeably. Thurlow et al. described four major types of accommodations: (1) presentation format (e.g., Braille, large print), (2) response format (e.g., pointing, oral response), (3) setting of test (e.g., individual, small group), and (4) timing of test (e.g., extended time, test breaks).

On a similar basis, the Wisconsin Student Assessment System (Wisconsin Department of Public Instruction, 1996) describes four major categories of test accommodation: (1) time modifications (e.g., shorter sessions, more breaks, most beneficial time), (2) environment modifications (e.g., small group or individual testing, study carrel, use of comfortable part of room, allow special education teacher or aide to test), (3) format modifications (e.g., large print, braille, more practice tests items, assist student in tracking items) sign instructions), and (4) recording modifications (e.g., someone records responses, communication device, tape recorder).

The Council of Administrators of Special Education (1992) outline four categories of "classroom and facility accommodations" based on Section 504: (1) communication (e.g., scheduling parent/teacher meetings, providing parents with duplicate texts), (2) organization/management (e.g., adjust placement of student in the classroom, reduce external stimuli), (3) alternative teaching strategies (e.g., change test time, administer test orally, using computer technology, and (4) student precautions (e.g., air purifier, accommodate allergic reactions, classroom accessibility).

Hargrove and Poteet (1984) defined modified assessment techniques as "those diagnostic activities selected by the educational diagnostician in an attempt to determine why a student erred responding" (p. 54). This is similar to Sattler's (1974) reference to *testing of limits* to indicate that the standard administration procedures were not used in order to gain additional insights about the child being tested. He cautioned that testing-of-limits techniques should only be used after the standard administration of the test (p. 59). If a test is used diagnostically and standardization procedures are not followed, the problem of test validity are not an issue if normative scores are not used. For example, a standardized test is given to a student, and, following each item, the student is asked to explain his or her answer to better understand the student's problem-solving strategy. The information retrieved from this diagnostic application might be invaluable, but the resulting score should not be used to interpret the student's normative performance.

The Scholastic Assessment Test (SAT)[42] uses *special accommodation* to identify "special testing arrangements for students with disabilities to minimize the effects of disabilities on test performance" (College Board, 1994, p. 1). The American College Testing program (ACT) interprets "special testing" as all formats and administration accommodations which depart from "standard conditions at a national test center..." (ACT, 1995).

Salvia and Ysseldyke (1995) noted that the "practice of test accommodations runs the gamut from permitting no modifications and requiring that any students who are included in local, state, and national assessments take standard versions of tests being used to allowing extensive alternative assessment procedures" (p. 190). Overall, there is no single definition of test accommodations but the term is defined by legislative mandate (e.g., state regulations), philosophy, and use. Ysseldyke et al. (1994), stated that "it is particularly important for states to look at conflicting guidelines. For example, some states use accommodations that other states specifically prohibit such as reading items to a student, allowing extended time, and out-of-level testing" (p. 10).

For the purposes of this book a test accommodation is defined as an adaptation, modification, alternative test or a test exemption which eliminates, mitigates or minimizes the effect(s) of a disability on the factor being assessed, except where the skill is the factor that the test purports to measure.

A Continuum of Accommodations

In addition to the need to provide fair and nondiscriminatory testing, the basis for test accommodations under IDEA is very much related to the concept of least restrictive environment (LRE) so that

> to the maximum extent appropriate, children with disabilities, including children in public or private institutions or other care facilities, are educated with children who are not disabled, and that special classes, separate schooling, or other removal of children with disabilities from the regular educational environment occurs only when the nature or severity of the disability is such that education in regular classes with the use of supplementary aids and services cannot be achieved satisfactorily, and procedures to assure that testing and evaluation materials and procedures utilized for the purposes of evaluation and placement of children with disabilities will be selected and administered so as not to be racially or culturally discriminatory.[43]

One provision of LRE is the use of supplementary aids and services to promote participation in the regular education program,[44] where "modification" is interpreted to be a form of a supplementary aid or service.[45] The concept of least restrictive environment and a continuum of services can be applied to test accommodations as follows:

> 1. That to the maximum extent appropriate, disabled children are evaluated with children who are not disabled,

> 2. Testing exemptions and/or exclusions from testing occur only when the nature or severity of the disability is such that testing cannot be achieved satisfactorily,

> 3. A continuum of test accommodations be available to bypass or minimize the effects of a disability.

The concept of least restrictive environment does not mandate or imply that the only recourse for educational programming or services is the regular classroom. In the case of testing, there are many occasions when the least restrictive environment is not the regular classroom. For example, many tests used in special education are individually administered and a location other than the regular classroom is necessary. Likewise, certain test accommodations are often best implemented outside of the regular classroom. If a student requires extended testing time, depending on the test and the length of the time extension, testing outside of the regular classroom might be the least disruptive technique. If a student requires special equipment, a room containing such equipment might be the only practical solution.

With all special education programs and services, test accommodations should be thought of as a continuum of services which range from no accommodations (the least restrictive accommodation) to a complete exemption or exclusion (the most restrictive accommodation) from a test or all testing. The goal for every student is to participate in the regular school assessment program to the maximum extent possible. As a result, a continuum of test accommodations must be provided. Smith, Polloway, Patton and Dowdy (1995) noted that "accommodations should be designed to offer the *least* amount of alteration from regular programming and still allow the student to benefit from instruction" (p. 434).

In terms of a hierarchy of services, test accommodations are not as amenable to linear structuring as are a series of placements or services (e.g., instruction in regular classes, resource rooms, special classes, special schools, etc.). Within the range of "no accommodations" (the least restrictive possibility) and a complete "test exemption" (the most restrictive accommodation) are an array of test adaptations, test modifications and test alternatives. As with the concept of least restrictive environment, the least restrictive test accommodation is one which best approximates regular educational testing; the most restrictive test accommodation is the one that departs the most from regular educational testing.

For every test accommodation, there are two important inclusionary considerations: (1) the least restrictive environment, and (2) the least restrictive accommodation. The former concerns where the test is given, and the latter the extent an accommodation causes the test to depart from the normal test format or protocol. If a student with a disability "is so disruptive in a regular classroom that the education of other students is significantly impaired, the needs of the handicapped child cannot be met in that environment."[46] The reverse situation could also exist so that regular classroom distractions prevent a meaningful assessment of a student with a disability. If a student is able to take a test with minimal accommodations, and if these accommodations can be implemented in the regular classroom or during regular school testing, the student should be tested in this environment and not elsewhere simply because the student has a disability. There is no regulatory directive to offer special education and related services in the regular classroom, but there is an obligation to provide "to the maximum extent appropriate" the least restrictive environment.[47] As it is, there are many occasions when testing a student with a disability requires a location other than the regular classroom.

The second type of restriction concerns the test itself. The degree to which a test is restrictive depends on the extent to which the test departs from the regular assessment in terms of what is being measured. Using a large print version of a test will probably have minimal effect on test validity; but an alternative test might measure different concepts than the test it replaces, or might be less (or more) difficult. Not testing a student is the most restrictive test accommodation which can be made. In this extreme situation, no adaptation, modification or alternative test is deemed appropriate and the ability measured by the test cannot be measured (e.g., no test format can be developed) or is not measurable (e.g., the student does not possess the ability). Concerning the inability to develop a test format, this should be the result of psychometric rather than financial limitations. A student might not be tested because an appropriate format cannot be developed, and not because there are insufficient funds to develop such a format. This, of course, is the essence of FAPE and includes "an obligation to provide or to pay for services provided to a child with a disability."[48]

Test adaptations involve preparation, administration and interpretation; modifications entail actual test changes; and alternative testing necessitates selecting a different test entirely. All factors being equal, the relationship between the various accommodations (viz., adaptations, modifications, alternative testing and test exemptions) does represent a general hierarchy in that adapting test instructions will generally be less severe than modifying a test, and modifying a test is generally less severe than selecting a different test. However, this is not always so and selecting an alternative test might be less restrictive than modifying an existing test, and modifying an existing test might be a less severe accommodation than adapting the way in which a test is administered.

The situation is further complicated by the fact that test users simply do not have complete freedom to employ whatever accommodation is deemed necessary. If a test is not available in Braille, selecting a different test might be the only recourse. Or an IEP might state that a calculator can be used when testing for mathematics skills, but the standardized test being used disallows this modification. Finally, for standardized tests, the practitioner generally does not have the freedom to modify test items at will for reasons ranging from the time needed to make modifications to matters involving copyright.

Test Accommodation Hierarchy

The continuum of test accommodations shown in Table 1.2 portrays a linear albeit ideal relation between the general categories of test accommodations. The continuum of accommodations ranges from the least restrictive where *no accommodations* are specified to the most restrictive where the student is given a *test exemption*. In most situations, a minor adaptation to a test (e.g., having the student sit toward the front of the room) is less restrictive than a test modification (e.g., changing the test format). With respect to "least restrictive assessment," the "least restriction" is that which has the least affect on how a test is designed to be used and what the test purports to measure.

No Accommodations

The possibility that a student does not need a test accommodation should always be considered. Indeed, administering a test with minimal or no accommodations should always be the goal. A cavalier approach concerning test accommodations, such as when a long list of adaptations and accommodations is made with little consideration given to need or circumstance, might accomplish little more than trivializing the importance and effectiveness of test accommodations. Test accommodations should be based on need, have the intent of minimizing the effects of a disability on whatever is being assessed, and should be periodically evaluated to insure that they are both needed and effective.

Before making a test accommodation recommendation, the question must be asked as to whether the accommodation will help diminish the effects of a disability and thereby provide a fair evaluation of educational performance. Testing a student individually might be a good idea, but this is probably a good idea for all students. Providing extra time might be warranted for some students, but what if a student does not need extra time? Overall, test accommodations are not mandatory for all students having a disability, are not intended for all students with disabilities, and should be reserved for only students with disabilities needing the accommodation. If a test accommodation is not necessary, it should not be used. If it is not known whether an accommodation should be used or not, an attempt should be made to determine the actual need for the accommodation.

Table 1.2 Hierarchy of Testing Restrictions.

Restriction	Accommodation
Least Restrictive	None
↓	Adaptations
↓	Modifications
↓	Alternatives
Most Restrictive	Exemptions

One reason for giving a test with no accommodations is to provide a reference point for determining the need and scope of necessary accommodations. McLoughlin and Lewis (1990, p. 91) stated that "it is possible to modify administration procedures for standardized tests, although tests should be given under standard conditions before attempting any modification." This is really the concept of needs assessment in that the test administered with no accommodations becomes a frame of reference for understanding test performance when test accommodations have been made. The ultimate test is this: Does the test accommodation result in a better measure of ability without compromising the test's validity? Of course, administering a test with and then without accommodations has several drawbacks. First, the first administration might influence performance on the second administration if the time between the two administrations is not substantial.

Second, if the time between the two administrations is relatively small, the student's motivation to respond might be compromised.

There are several reasons why a test might be administered with no accommodations: (1) the sometimes overlooked possibility that no accommodation is necessary; (2) the exact need or nature of the test accommodation is not known; (3) the disability involves the skill being evaluated; (4) the student is given an opportunity to demonstrate his or her skill; or (5) the student and/or parent refuses the accommodation. Not every student classified as having a disability will need a test accommodation. One deaf student might need an interpreter, while a second deaf student is able to participate in all aspects of educational testing with no accommodations whatsoever. If the exact test accommodation needs of a student are not known, a test without accommodations might be given to "test" a student's ability to participate in regular educational testing, or as part of a diagnostic evaluation period to determine the scope and magnitude of needed accommodations. If the student's disability is what the test purports to measure, no accommodation is made. And, every student is entitled to an opportunity to participate in testing with or without test accommodations, even though evidence might suggest that the disability might impede an accurate assessment of ability.

Test Accommodations

Test accommodations consist of adaptations, modifications, alternatives and exemptions to standardized and nonstandardized tests and testing procedures that result in a more accurate assessment of an ability, knowledge or skill being measured rather than the student's disability. For the purpose of this book, a distinction is made between test adaptations and test modifications. A test adaptation is defined as an accommodation that results in no substantive change to the test being used; a test modification is defined as an accommodation that results in a change in test administration, the format of test items, or the mode of response.

Obviously, the type of test involved often dictates whether an accommodation is permissible and/or feasible. Most classroom tests can be adapted and modified as desired, providing the necessary resources to make the accommodation are available. The ability to adapt and modify standardized tests depends on the test and the test publisher. For standardized tests certain test adaptations are often available, providing the adaptations do not violate the procedures specified by the test publisher. If a test publisher explicitly prohibits extended time for testing, this ethically restricts the use of this accommodation for this test.

For the most part, schoolwide general achievement tests (e.g., Stanford Achievement Test, California Achievement Test, etc.) are generally agreeable to minor adaptations, but substantive test modifications are often not practical or even possible (e.g., changing the format of a complete standardized achievement test). Although there are relatively few test publishers who provide modified test formats (e.g., large print, Braille, recorded tests), state agencies are more inclined to meet the special test needs of students.

For students who are being evaluated for a possible disability or are already classified, there are myriad psychological tests, diagnostic tests and miscellaneous wide-range tests which can be adapted and modified to various degrees depending on the test, the skill or task being assessed and the test publisher. Because of the unique character of many of these psychological/diagnostic tests, adaptations are sometimes possible but more often than not these tests are selected to meet specific testing needs. For example, the Peabody Picture Vocabulary Test-Revised (Dunn & Dunn, 1981) might be selected for use with a student who is not able to provide an oral response, and the performance subtests of the Wechsler Intelligence Scale for Children-III (Wechsler, 1991) might be used with students having limited expressive language skills.

Test adaptations. A test adaptation entails preparing a student for a test, administering a test, or interpreting test results to best meet the student's needs without changing the format or substance of the test. For example, giving a student a practice test or a test simulation to acquaint the student with the task might facilitate test performance without changing either the administration guidelines or the format, or response mode of the actual test. Similarly, providing a special location for testing, repeating instructions, or analyzing test responses after the test has been given are test adaptations that might not be used with nondisabled students but that would result in a meaningful assessment of a disabled student's ability or performance.

Test modifications. A test modification is an actual change in the test administration or test format which alters the format of the test, the method for presenting questions, the use of aids when answering questions, or the manner in which responses are made. Test modifications can range from those which have minimal effect on the nature or difficulty of the test (e.g., using large print, allowing students to write multiple-choice answers in the test booklet) to those that radically affect what the test measures (e.g., changing the test difficulty). In some instances, the exact effect of changing the format of a test might be unknown such as when a test is translated in a different language. The non-English version of a test might be a close parallel to the English version, although this really depends on the language, the translator, and the degree to which the translation remains faithful to the content and difficulty of the original test. Determining the degree a test modification actually changes a test, if at all, is an exceedingly difficult task. Testing a student in a different location might eliminate distractions, but this might be a notable departure from how the test was standardized and an argument can be made that test has been "changed."

Again, more for the purposes of providing a schema for dealing with the vast number of test accommodations possible, modifications are used to designate substantive test changes, and adaptations are used to refer to accommodations that are made before, during, and after testing, and which do not change the test or test format.

Test alternatives. If a test fails to provide adequate assessment information, with or without accommodations, an alternative test might be used; that is, a test is selected to replace the normally used test. The following are several situations when an alternative test might be appropriate: (1) the test is too difficult and another test with a lower difficulty level is needed; (2) the test does not provide appropriate norms (e.g., norms for hearing impaired students); or (3) the test cannot be modified (e.g., transcribed into Braille).

If a student is scoring so low so as to prevent the meaningful use of standardized test norms, a wide range achievement test might be used which provides a broader normative base. For a student with a severe language disability, a nonverbal test or a test which assesses receptive language might be used. If a standardized test is not readily available in Braille or large print, a completely different standardized test which is available in one of these formats might be selected.

Out-of-level testing also represents a form of alternative testing. Rather than using a test designed for a student at the fifth grade level, a test designed for a lower age group from the same group is used.

For example, the Stanford Achievement Test Primary Level 2 (2.5-3.5 grade level) is used instead of the Intermediate level 2 (5.5-6.5 grade level is used. This is not simply an alternative test of the same test (e.g., using Form J instead of Form K), but using a different test entirely (although the test formats and standardization procedures are similar).

When standardized test difficulty is too high, out-of-level testing is a seemingly simple accommodation; that is, a different test form or level is used (e.g., a primary level is used for a 12-year-old). Although a 12-year-old might very well be achieving at a primary level, comparing this student to an eight-year-old normative group might be misleading with respect to the student's ability, and certainly misleading if norms from the primary group are used to interpret the student's score. The Kaufman Assessment Battery for Children allows a limited amount of out-of-level testing, but Kaufman and Kaufman (1983) cautioned (no doubt based on the many abuses traditionally associated with out-of-level testing) that "examiners may not use out-of-level testing procedures arbitrarily, based on whimsy, or because a child experiences difficulty with some subtests at the age-appropriate level" (p. 43).

There are very legitimate reasons for selecting an alternative test to meet the assessment needs of students, but the results are not interchangeable with those produced by the test that it replaces. If the achievement test used by a school relies on local norms for interpretation, and the alternative test relies on national norms, the matter of comparing normative scores will be very difficult. And with alternative tests, the number of items used, content sampled, and test format can result in major test differences.

In addition to using an alternative test to better meet individual testing needs, a completely different test model can be used to identify needs and evaluate progress. Rather than using normative tests, curriculum-based measures or a more inclusive portfolio assessment might be used. There is no question that curriculum-based and portfolio assessment techniques can be extremely useful when evaluating disabled students. If nondisabled students are using a nonstandardized assessment model, the same model should be used, with the appropriate test accommodations, with students classified as disabled. However, designating the use of such a model solely because of a disability, in place of existing normative testing, can deprive a disabled student of an opportunity to demonstrate proficiency with or without test accommodations. There is an essential need for nonstandardized and qualitative measures in both regular and special education, but this does not justify the elimination of normative tests because other assessment techniques are thought to provide more useful assessment information. Using alternative assessment information is important, is valued, and should be encouraged. But this must be tempered with the need to provide inclusive and nondiscriminatory assessment, as much as possible, using school-based tests.

One last point concerning curriculum-based and portfolio assessment should be made. These assessment models can provide extremely rich evaluation data, but the need for accommodations which apply to standardized forms of assessment also apply to content and performance-based evaluation models. A portfolio might contain a sample of work both with and without a specified test accommodation. The underlying point is that test accommodations are an integral part of all aspects of an individual evaluation and not simply a practice confined to standardized testing.

Test exemptions. There will be occasions when a test, or all standardized testing, is completely inappropriate because of either test format or difficulty. Exempting a student from a test can have very serious consequences in that the student will not be able to demonstrate competence. If an error is made as to the appropriateness of using a test, it is better to err on the side of giving a test which is too difficult rather than discriminating against a student by not giving the test at all. Of all the accommodations, a test exemption is the most restrictive and potentially the most discriminatory. Exempting a student from a test or testing program can make participation in the regular education program all but impossible, and thus curtail or preclude an appropriate education.

If a student has limited verbal skills and requires a curriculum which emphasizes communication and self-help skills, requiring this student to take a statewide reading test in order to measure reading proficiency might be pointless. There are occasions when a test exemption is the only sensible course of action, and there are occasions when a test exemption might be a restriction which prevents the attainment of an otherwise reachable goal such as taking certain courses, graduation or college admission.

A more insidious form of exception is a *de facto exemption* by which a test is modified so extensively that what the test originally purported to measure is no longer measured. This might be the result of a belief that helping a student select the correct answer is the purpose of remediation, or that reading can somehow be measured by not requiring reading. The motive for drastically changing what a test measures might be well-intentioned, but the fact remains that when this is done the student has been exempted from taking the test. If the student is clearly not able to perform the task without the aid, and if scores or norms are not used to suggest a level of ability involving the task in question, these tasks might have some educational and/or inclusionary value. However, if the test modification results in the student being "excluded from participation in, be denied the benefits of, or otherwise be subjected to discrimination under any program or activity"[49] the test modification is discriminatory. If a test incorrectly portrays a student's ability, this might preclude participation in what would otherwise be necessary remedial activities. If the student does have a measurable ability level, any modification which incorrectly portrays that ability level, or results in a needed service not being given, is discriminatory.

Developing a student's self-concept is certainly important for the well-being of all students. However, creating a fictitious portrait of a student's academic performance is neither the intent of the regulations nor an activity that will be in the student's best interests. An actual test can be practiced with a student beforehand so that the student eventually receives an extremely high score, legitimate test criteria can be ignored, and countless test accommodations that completely confound the interpretation of test performance can be used. But this is not fair to the student and will likely convey an incorrect picture of the student's ability and progress. The goal is not to give "easy or easier" tests, or to provide an evaluation that is "pleasant" albeit misleading, but to assess and interpret, as best as possible, the student's actual ability or performance level.

Fair Opportunity

When making test accommodations, care must be taken not to deprive an individual of an opportunity to demonstrate an ability or skill by using an accommodation which distorts the test or test results, or by excluding the individual from testing. The purpose of making a test accommodation is to provide a fair assessment of a student's ability. This does not mean that once a student is classified as disabled that traditional testing is no longer meaningful, but that assessment should attempt to accommodate a student's disability as much as possible. Depriving a student of an opportunity to demonstrate ability under the guise of "helping" the student is not the type of help that most students need. For example, assume that an eighth grade student is reading at the seventh grade level. This is somewhat below average, but the student would appear to have sufficient reading skills to take most tests. If the student is classified as emotionally disturbed, stipulating in the student's IEP that tests be read because of the student's classification and not because of an actual need to have tests read would deprive the student of an opportunity to demonstrate ability. One might argue that the test accommodation might benefit the student, but in actuality the accommodation might be discriminatory if it deprives the student from participating in or benefiting from an aid, benefit, or service.[50] Contrary to what some believe, the purpose of a test accommodation is not to benefit a student but to mitigate the effects of a disability. This distinction is extremely important: the goal is to mitigate a disability which might well benefit the student; the goal is not to benefit the student because the student has a disability.

This is the inherent problem when accommodations are made on a categorical basis; that is, all students with a disability are given a certain accommodation such as extended test time or are tested individually. Because of individual differences within categories, certain accommodations may not be necessary. One might conclude that all students classified as learning disabled would profit from having extended time on reading tests. This might be so. However, if some of these students do not have specific learning problems in reading (e.g., they were classified as learning disabled in math, writing, etc.), the accommodation would be unnecessary. And, for the most part, an unnecessary accommodation will likely be discriminatory because it deprives the student of "the opportunity to participate in or benefit from the aid, benefit, or service" and by not providing "an aid, benefit or service that is not as effective as that provided to others."[51]

The testing of students who are classified as having a disability is sometimes regarded as unavoidable and should be minimized as much as possible. An opposite viewpoint is that testing can provide an opportunity to reenter the normal assessment mainstream, and provide access to a multitude of educational and vocational opportunities.

If a qualified person with a disability (i.e., a person who has the ability or skill being assessed) can benefit from testing, belonging to a disability group alone should not disqualify the person from receiving the benefits of such tests.

IDEA Amendments of 1997[b]

The importance of making a concerted effort to include students with disabilities in statewide and districtwide assessments is emphasized in the IDEA amendments of 1997:

> Children with disabilities are included in general State and districtwide assessment programs, with appropriate accommodations, where necessary. As appropriate, the State or local educational agency (i) develops guidelines for the participation of children with disabilities in alternate assessments for those children who cannot participate in State and districtwide assessment programs; and (ii) develops and, beginning not later than July 1, 2000, conducts those alternate assessments.[52]

and

> if the IEP Team determines that the child will not participate in a particular State or districtwide assessment of student achievement (or part of such an assessment), a statement of (aa) why that assessment is not appropriate for the child; and (bb) how the child will be assessed;[53]

These amendments emphasize the following: (1) the need to include students with disabilities in statewide and districtwide assessment programs, (2) the need for a rationale explanation why a student cannot participate in such assessments, and (3) a statement explaining how the student will be assessed. The IDEA Amendments of 1997 also introduce the term "appropriate accommodation," which, one assumes, means an accommodation which does not render a test invalid, yet measures the student's ability rather than disability.

---

[b]Individuals with Disabilities Act Amendments of 1997, P.L. 105-17 (see H.R. 5 for the text version of P.L. 105-17 used in this book).

Issues of Fairness

The Code of Fair Testing Practices in Education (Joint Committee on Testing Practices, 1994) states that "test users should select tests that have been developed in ways that attempt to make them as fair as possible for test takers of different races, gender, ethnic backgrounds, or handicapping conditions" and when necessary to "use appropriately modified forms of tests or administration procedures for test takers with handicapping conditions. Interpret standard norms with care in the light of the modifications that were made." The need to be fair is apparent; the ability to be fair, in spite of a genuine effort to do so, is often easier said than done.

The National Center on Education Outcomes (Ysseldyke, Thurlow, McGrew & Shriner, 1994) stated the following as one of the assumptions underlying making accommodation decisions:

> Accommodations are used for equity, not advantage. Students who use accommodations during an assessment do so to be able to take an assessment on an equal playing board as other students who do not need accommodations. Accommodations are not provided to help the student with a disability do better than other students.

For some students, but not necessarily all, the evaluation process entails avoiding obstacles that prevent the fair assessment of an ability, skill, or trait. These obstacles can be a physical disability (e.g., expressive language), not having a prerequisite skill (e.g., English proficiency), or a less discernable factor (and less subject to remediation) such as a lack of motivation. Testing should reflect a student's ability, and for some students this ability is not readily accessible because of cultural factors, a sensory impairment, or a language, physical or learning disability.

The possibility exists that the ability in question might be quite low in comparison to others, or the ability might be average or even high. The goal of a test accommodation is not to artificially inflate a test score because a student has a disability, or to misrepresent actual ability, but to accurately measure what the test has been designed to measure and "to avoid unfair distortion of test results."[54]

Test accommodations do not guarantee a high or higher test score, and might have no impact on test performance whatsoever, but are intended to provide students with the opportunity to compete on a relatively even basis with nondisabled peers. Section 504 affirms this goal:

> For the purposes of this part, aids, benefits, and services, to be equally effective, are not required to produce the identical result or level of achievement for handicapped and nonhandicapped persons, but must afford handicapped persons equal opportunity to obtain the same result, to gain the same benefit, or to reach the same level of achievement, in the most integrated setting appropriate to the person's needs.[55]

Cases where standardized tests have been used unfairly have been the driving force for much of the legislation involving nondiscriminatory and valid testing. In *Larry P. v. Riles,*[56] the plaintiffs representing the class of black children in California who were classified as educable mentally retarded primarily on the basis of Standardized IQ tests contended "that the I.Q. tests in their present form are biased and that defendants have discriminated against black children by using those tests" (p. 931). The fact that the scores of black students were lower on verbal-type IQ tests is an artifact, a tautology which reflects the verbal (and no doubt socioeconomic status) of the primarily white standardization group. The injunctive relief in this case was that the defendants were "enjoined from utilizing, permitting the use of, or approving the use of any standardized intelligence tests...for the identification of black E.M.R. children, or their placement into E.M.R. classes, without securing prior approval from the court" (p. 989). Court approval for using IQ tests was predicated on the determination that these tests were not racially or culturally discriminatory, and had been validated for determining EMR[57] placements. In *Larry P. v. Riles,* the court, in effect, mandated some type of test accommodation by either validating the test, by modifying the test or how test scores were used so that there would not be a disproportionate number of blacks classified as EMR, or by not using IQ tests because the tests (as used to classify black students as EMR) are inappropriate and discriminatory.

For a test in which the stakes are quite high such as IQ tests and college admission tests, the need for fair and nondiscriminatory testing is subject to careful scrutiny. Even though a test might appear to be of the "low stake" variety (e.g., no major decisions are immediately based on the test results), this does not mean that the results are not important or do not have considerable (albeit not readily discernible) influence. For example, if a test results in a student not being admitted to a school or program, the immediate importance of the test score in the decision-making process seems far more clear than if a student received a low score on a test in a primary grade. However, the low score on the test in the primary grade might result in differential programming and/or expectations which, in the end, might have a tremendous impact on the student's eventual educational success or lack thereof.

When a test is associated with stated admission criteria, the question of discrimination becomes immediately obvious. If the consequences of a test are long term, the discriminatory effects of the test are less obvious but far more insidious. Thus, a test which measures a student's disability rather than ability leads to reduced expectations and de facto differential educational programming, which in turn eventually results in an "inability" which is associated with the "disability." In this situation, the disability exacerbates or even causes the "inability."

Undue Advantage

Fairness implies not only an attempt to give a student a fair opportunity to participate, but also an effort not to use test accommodations to give a student an undue advantage which results in an incorrect and unrealistic assessment of performance or ability. The primary research which has been done relating to undue advantage resulting form test accommodations involves the SAT and ACT college admission tests. The impetus for this research has been regulations which require tests be "validated for the specific purpose for which they are used"[58] and issues unique to college admission tests such as flagging where scores taken under special test conditions are so identified.

Unfortunately, the SAT and ACT are quite different than school level achievement and psychological tests, and the various statewide competency and mastery tests. Not only are there decided differences in administration procedures, test content, and allowable accommodations, but the sample of students taking the SAT and ACT is not comparable to the population of K-12 students. As a result, although the SAT and ACT provide a systematic approach for determining the validity of test accommodations, generalizing these data to all tests and to all students with disabilities must be done with caution.

With this sampling limitation in mind, there is some evidence that students receiving extended time or taking a special test format are sometimes given an advantage, depending on the disability and the test accommodation (see Ragosta and Wendler, 1992; Bennett, Rock & Jirele, 1986; Centra, 1986; Braun, Ragosta & Kaplan, 1988); ACT, 1995). For example, Ragosta & Wendler (1992, p. 15) found that for disabled students taking the standard administration of the SAT (N=397) and disabled students taking a special test administration that, with the exception of hearing-impaired students, the special administration scores were higher. For the standard administration group the mean verbal score was 385 and the mean mathematics score was 414. For the special administration group, the mean verbal score was 405 and the mean mathematics score was 438.

For the Spring 1995 ACT reading test the mean for school seniors (N=62,134) was 20.6 (SD=5.8), for learning disabled students (N=4,275) the mean was 18.3 (SD=59), and for ADD students (N=3,208) the mean was 22.3. In contrast to mean reading scores, the High School Grade Point Average was 3.00 (SD=.69) for high school seniors, 2.58 (SD=.64) for learning disabled students, and 2.56 (.70) for ADD students. Although the ADD students had the lowest HSGPA (Mean=2.56), this group also had relatively high reading scores (Mean=22.3). This suggests that the HSGPA did not reflect the students abilities when the disability had been mitigated, or that the ACT accommodation was too liberal. Of course, the possibility also exists that the ADD category was appropriate for all students, but that the test accommodations were simply excessive. This is not necessarily the fault of the student but of the inequity of the application of test accommodations based on the overall determination of a "disability" rather than individual need. Finally, although a cursory analysis seems to suggest an advantage for ADD students, the data might simply reflect sampling characteristics (e.g., the unique characteristics of those who elect to take the ACT), unique population characteristics of ADD students, or the fact that ADD students did not receive suitable accommodations in high school (thus accounting for the low HSGPA).

For the most part the existence of an unfair advantage resulting from a test accommodation is unintentional. Nonetheless, as the importance of a test increases, at least the perceived importance, there is an increased possibility (although probably small) that students and/or parents will seek an unfair advantage at any cost. For elementary age children the likelihood is probably small that a parent would seek test accommodations, either by formal classification or the development of a 504 Plan, simply to have an advantage on a school-based test. Of course, if graduation or a high school diploma depended on passing a test, the importance of the test and the need for a test accommodation might be viewed differently.

Accountability

Inclusion of test accommodations in a student's IEP requires a good faith effort to implement these accommodations. This does not mean that the accommodations will be effective or impact test performance, but that an honest attempt will be made "to assist the child in achieving the objectives and goals listed in the individual education program." The regulations state that "each public agency must provide special education and related services to a child with a disability in accordance with an individualized education program. However, Part B of the Act does not require that any agency, teacher, or other person be held accountable if a child does not achieve the growth projected in the annual goals and objectives."[59]

Although there is no way to ensure that an accommodation will be effective, the role of the classroom teacher, and not just the special educator, is becoming increasingly important. As more and more classified students participate in regular education environments, the classroom teacher shares the responsibility for implementing the IEP. If a teacher refuses to make a test accommodation specified in the student's IEP, the regular classroom teacher might be held accountable.

The case of *Doe v. Withers* (1993) provides an interesting account of an IEP accommodation went astray. The plaintiffs in the case were John and Jan Doe whose 16-year-old son, D.D., was identified as having a learning disability in the fourth grade and the resulting IEP specified oral testing by a learning disabilities teacher in a resource room.

When D.D. began high school his grade fell and his parents requested teachers follow the IEP oral test accommodation. All did...with the exception of D.D.'s history teacher. The end product of this noncompliance with the IEP was that D.D. failed history and was therefore not allowed to participate in extracurricular activities. As a result of a grievance concerning Withers to the State Board of Education, D.D. was retested. However, the time required to prepare for the retesting, and the subsequent embarrassment, resulted in lower grades in other classes. The complaint asserts that the principal and superintendent should have been aware that D.D. was not receiving a free appropriate public education.

The result of the ensuing grievance and litigation was that the principal and superintendent were not held responsible, but the history teacher did not abide by the IEP and that the school district was obligated to provide necessary instruction, the required oral testing, and the plaintiffs were awarded $15,000.

Does the *Doe V. Withers* case mean that if a teacher fails to follow an IEP regulation to the letter, the teacher is subject to compensatory and punitive damages? Not necessarily. The plaintiff's asserted that the defendant not only failed to comply with the IEP test accommodation, but "insulted and belittled" their son, and then failed to meet to discuss the problem.

In all likelihood the above litigation could have been avoided if the teacher made a good faith effort to comply with the IEP. The intent of the law is not to lower educational test standards or even disregard a student's disability when testing, but to make a reasonable effort to accommodate a student's test needs without substantially altering what a test measures.[60] Teachers are not expected to be special educators, to compromise the integrity of what is taught or what is tested, but simply to make a good faith effort to provide students with a fair opportunity to participate in regular educational assessment. If the teacher felt that the accommodation was inappropriate, this should have been discussed with the parents or during the development of the IEP. What the *Doe v. Wither* case indicates is that a student's IEP is an important document and that test accommodations should not be considered frivolous recommendations.

ENDNOTES

1. 34 C.F.R. §104.(b)(3)

2. 29 U.S.C. §794.

3. Approved Sept. 26, 1973 and amended by P.L. 102-569.

4. The term "disability" has replaced "handicap" in the IDEA and ADA regulations. Section 504 still uses the term "handicap" as of July 1, 1996 in the Code of Federal Regulations (34 C.F.R. §104 and published by the Office of the Federal Register, National Archives and Records Administration and available through the U.S. Government Printing Office, Washington, DC). Both terms, "disability" and "handicap," will be used in this work depending on the source and context.

5. 34 C.F.R. §§300.1 - 754 and Appendix C (in the process of revision for IDEA-1997).

6. IDEA is a reauthorization of P.L. 94-142 the Education for All Handicapped Children Act (EAHCA or EHA) of 1975.

7. P.L. 105-17 was signed into law by the President June 4, 1997. References to the text P.L. 105-17 which is the same as the Senate version or S.7. 717) will be referred to by the House of Representatives bill number or H.R. 5.

8. IDEA Amendments of 1997, H.R. 5, Section 612(a)(17)(A)

9. IDEA Amendments of 1997, H.R. 5, Section 614(d)(1)(A)(v)

10. Several internet sources are available for obtaining information relating to statutes, regulations and legal resources such as The House of Representatives Internet Law Library at http://law.house.gov/1.htm. See this source for additional internet links.

11. Read 29 U.S.C. §794 as Title 29 (Labor), United States Code, Part 794. 11.

12. Read 34 C.F.R. §300.1 as Title 34 (Education), Code of Federal Regulations, Part 300, Section 1.

13. 34 C.F.R. §300.550(a)(2)

14. 34 C.F.R. §300.532(c) states that tests reflect what "the test purports to measure, rather than reflecting the child's impaired...skills."

15. 34 C.F.R. §300.532(a)(2) which states that tests "have been validated for the specific purposes for which they are used."

16. 34 C.F.R. §300.532(1)(b)

17. 34 C.F.R. §300.532(c)

18. 34 C.F.R. §104.35(b)(3)

19. See rule 3301-35-032(B)(1)(c) regarding what is referred to as the "intervention-based multifactored evaluation (IBMFE).

20. 42 U.S.C. §12112(b)(7)

21. 34 C.F.R. §104.44(c)

22. 34 C.F.R. §300.532(c)

23. 34 C.F.R. §300.550(b)(1)

24. 42 U.S.C. §12112(b)(7)

25. 42 U.S.C. §12112(b)(6)

26. 34 C.F.R. §300.532(c)

27. The IDEA Amendments of 1997 (P.L. 105-17) are far more direct with respect to test accommodations in that "any modifications in the administration of State or districtwide assessments that are needed in order for the child to participate in the assessment," must be stated.

28. 34 C.F.R. §300.17(a)(1)

29. 34 C.F.R. §300, Appendix C (Question #48)

30. 34 C.F.R. §104.44(c)(d)

31. see 34 C.F.R. Subpart C - Services

32. 34 C.F.R. §300.7(a)(1)

33. 34 C.F.R. §104.33(b)

34. 34 C.F.R. §104.12(a) & (b)

35. 29 U.S.C. §794

36. see 34 C.F.R §104, Appendix A (#5)

37. 34 C.F.R. §104.3(k)(1)

38. 34 C.F.R. §104.3(k)(3)

39. 34 C.F.R. §104.35(b)(3)

40. 34 C.F.R. §300.550-556.

41. 34 C.F.R. §104.44

42. The Scholastic Assessment Test, previously called the Scholastic Aptitude Test, should not be confused with the Stanford Achievement Test which is referred to as the SAT or the Stanford 9 (for the 9th edition of the test).

43. 20 U.S.C. §1412(a)(5)(B)&(C) and in 34 C.F.R. ?300.550

44. 34 C.F.R. §300.550(b)(2)

45. 34 C.F.R. §300, Appendix C (Question #48)

46. 34 C.F.R. §104, Appendix (paragraph 24)

47. 34 C.F.R. §300.550(b)(1)

48. 34 C.F.R. §300.301(b)

49. 34 C.F.R. §104.4(a)

50. 34 C.F.R. §104.4(b)(i)

51. 34 C.F.R. §104.4

52. IDEA Amendments of 1997, H.R. 5, Section 612(a)(17)(A)

53. IDEA Amendments of 1997, H.R. 5, Section 614(d)(1)(A)(v)(II)

54. 34 C.F.R. §104(e)

55. 34 C.F.R. §104.4(b)(2)

56. Larry P. v. Riles, C-71-2270 RFP, United States District Court, N.D. California, 495 Federal Supplement, pp. 926-992.

57. Educable Mentally Retarded (EMR) which is used to refer to students with problems involving adaptive behavior and having IQ scores in the 50 to 75 range.

58. 34 C.F.R. §300.532(a)(2)

59. 34 C.F.R. §300.350

60. As described by Phillips (1993), an example of a substantial modification would be "altering the test content because a person was unable to learn the tested skills due to the disability" (p. xxvi).

Chapter 2

TEST ACCOMMODATION
RELIABILITY AND VALIDITY

Reliability and validity are important psychometric issues which must be considered before and after test accommodations are made. Reliability concerns the repeatability and consistency of tests, and validity addresses the issue of whether a test measures what it purports to measure.

Although reliability is necessary for validity, reliability does not imply validity. In other words, a test can be reliable but not valid. For example, a nonverbal test of visual discrimination might be statistically reliable but have limited validity for testing reading. Of course, if a test has limited reliability to begin with, there should be obvious concern for the test's underlying validity.

Traditional test theory (e.g, Guilford, 1954) states that every test score (X) is comprised of two components: a true score (X_∞) and an error component (X_e).

$$X = X_\infty + X_e$$

A student's true score is comprised of what common trait or ability the test measures and whatever is specific to the test. The error component of a student's score are those factors which are random and unrelated to what is being measured and cause a score to vary from one test to the next. The sources of error are many and are attributable to such factors as not understanding or following directions, examiner influence, guessing, poor health, lack of motivation or interest, test format, or the response required by the test.

For a student with a disability, a reading disorder, lack of motivation/attention, not understanding instructions, or the physical

37

response required by the test are all potential sources of test error. All factors which decrease the precision or accuracy of the test contribute to test error. If a student experiences a great deal of discomfort because of the desk being used or is distracted by other students being tested, test error can increase and test reliability decrease.

Paradoxically, although a test accommodation is designed to reduce the error of measuring a student's disability, the accommodation itself might introduce a new source of error into the equation or a new component which was not heretofore measured. For example, providing extra time might minimize one source of error (e.g., insufficient time to interpret items), but the extra time might affect interest and motivation thereby contributing to test error.

A far greater concern than reliability is the effect on what the test measures, that is, test accommodations which substantially alter a test's validity. If a test accommodation changes a test to the point where the test no longer measures what it purports to measure, the test might be reliable but obviously not valid. For example, if a test is read to a student rather than having the student read the test, the test accommodation might measure a skill not measured by the original test (e.g., oral understanding of content material), or the modified test might measure a unique skill specific to the modified test (e.g., oral short-term memory).

Although many test accommodations will have a minimal impact on reliability, an accommodation will not automatically cause an increase in test error. If extended or unlimited time is given, the result might be to increase the total test score variance and items attempted. If reliability were calculated for a group with greater test score variance, the reliability might be higher than for a group with lower test score variance. Bennett, Rock and Jirele (1986) found that for a sample of visual impaired students taking the Graduate Record Examination (GRE) with extended time that the reliability coefficient of the Analytical scale was somewhat higher. These authors surmised that "this higher value is likely due to the unusually large variation in Analytical scores found in this group" (p. 26). Obviously, a test accommodation will not necessarily result in higher reliability; but, by the same token, neither will a test accommodation automatically decrease reliability as might otherwise be suspected.

Because test accommodations can impact both reliability and validity, minimizing test accommodations is necessary in order to limit test error and to maintain test validity. Again, for reasons ranging from fair opportunity to reliability theory, the goal is to provide only those test accommodations which allow a student to participate in regular educational testing in a way which reflects the student's ability rather than disability.

For the most part, the reliability of tests (and especially standardized tests) is more than adequate. Low reliability more often becomes a concern with amorphous constructs (e.g., perceptual-motor performance), inadequate content sampling, and less rigorously constructed assessments rather than with the types of tasks found on major tests of intelligence and achievement tests. Even a cursory review of the vast number of tests in education and psychology will yield few measures which are not recommended for use because of inadequate reliability (especially by the respective test publishers). More often than not, a measure might be criticized for a lack of reliability data rather than evidence of low reliability.

For the most part the effect of a test accommodation on reliability is often minimal. Nonetheless, if a test has poor reliability to begin with, there is no reason to believe that a test accommodation will dramatically improve the test's reliability. An unreliable test will likely remain unreliable no matter what test accommodations are made.

The effect of a test accommodation on test validity, unlike reliability, is another matter. A reasonable argument can be made that small modifications will have minimal impact on a test's reliability, but even a small change in standardization procedures can alter what a test measures. The following portrays several psychometric constructs which should be addressed before and after a test accommodation has been made.

	Pre-accommodation	**Post-accommodation**
Reliability	Does the disability limit an adequate sampling of the ability or introduce random error?	Does the accommodation restrict the item sample or introduce random error?
Validity	Does the disability detract from what the test measures?	Does the accommodation alter what the test measures?

Before a test accommodation is made, a disability might limit test item administration, introduce error (e.g., inattention), or detract from what the test measures. Following a test accommodation, the affect of the accommodation on test length, random error (e.g., fatigue as a function of extended time) and what the test measures are primary concerns.   As discussed below, a major problem with many test accommodations is the addition of specific variance which is the measurement of a trait or ability specific to the accommodation.   This serves to detract from what the test measures (but does not necessarily decrease reliability) by measuring something different than what the original test was designed to measure.

Although psychometric information is usually available prior to making a test accommodation, data relating to reliability and validity is less forthcoming once an accommodation has been made.   More important, primarily because of sampling difficulties, there have been few empirical studies, aside from college admission test research, which have determined the effects of specific test accommodations on reliability and validity.   Part of this absence of research can be attributed to the need for samples of students with relatively homogeneous disabilities who receive relatively homogeneous test accommodations. Although state agencies generally have the resources to conduct this type of research, and are required to use tests which have been validated for the specific purpose for which they are used,[1] psychometric information concerning the effects of test accommodations is lacking. For the most part, state agencies and commercial test publishers of standardized tests used in schools have provided little in the way of either empirical-based guidelines or basic psychometric data relating to the use of test accommodations.

Reliability and validity focus. The focus of reliability and validity concerns both the standardization group and the group receiving the accommodation. The reliability and validity of the standardization group provides the frame of reference for determining the reliability and validity when an accommodation has been made. Most important, the reliability and validity of the standardization group is used to make decisions (e.g., as when using the standard error of measurement) if standardization group norms are used. In most instances, an assumption is made that a test accommodation does not change a test for the specific purpose for which it has been validated. Determining the effect of an accommodation on reliability and validity empirically by studying the accommodation with disabled and nondisabled sample is possible to a limited degree. For certain generic accommodations which require no special skill on the part of the testtaker (e.g, extended time, individual assessment, using large print), the relative effects of the accommodation could be examined. For accommodations such as Braille, signing instructions, or entailing augmentative communication tasks, there is no way to determine what effect these types of accommodations would have on the reliability and validity of the standardization group.

Determining the reliability and validity of a sample of students receiving an accommodation can provide invaluable information concerning the basic psychometric makeup of a test when used with a specific accommodation and specific sample of students. Indeed, this is exactly why the SAT and ACT data is so important even though the tests attract, for the most part, students with very good academic skills. The difficulty with doing such research concerns the need to (1) have a group of students who are receiving a specific type of accommodation, (2) have a group of students who have a relatively homogeneous disability, and (3) have reasonable sample sizes. This could be accomplished at the state level, but for schools and districts obtaining a sufficient sample size is often impossible.

Although reliability and validity data for specific accommodations and homogeneous groups of students with disabilities might not be readily forthcoming, there is still the need to consider the *possible* effects of an accommodation and how this might alter the test's reliability structure or validity.

Test Theory and Test Accommodations

The actual determination of both reliability and validity relies heavily on test score variance (σ^2).[a] Just as every score is comprised of a true and error component, total test score variance (σ^2_{total}) is comprised of true (σ^2_∞) and error variance (σ^2_e):

$$\sigma^2_{total} = \sigma^2_\infty + \sigma^2_e$$

The true score variance can be further subdivided into common-factor variance $(\sigma^2_{c1}, \sigma^2_{c2}, \text{etc})$ and specific test variance (σ^2_s). The common-factor variance is what a test has in common with other tests. The common-factor variance of a test might entail verbal ability, reading vocabulary, reading comprehension and content knowledge, all

---

[a]See Kerlinger (1973, pp. 469-473) and Guilford (1965, pp. 473-480) for a discussion of factor theory and the relation to reliability and validity.

factors which are shared with other tests. The sum of these variances is sometimes referred to as the communality of a test which is defined by Guilford (1965) as "the sum of the proportion of common-factor variances" (p. 475). The specific variance of a test are factors which are not measured by other tests and which are unique to the test. There is probably something unique about a test when the format is changed which makes it different from all other tests. This uniqueness might be minor, or quite substantial as when unlimited time is given or the test items are read or translated. These three sources of variance define true score variance and provide a model for understanding the effects of test accommodations on test scores.

$$\sigma^2_{total} = \sigma^2_{c1} + \sigma^2_{c2} \cdots \sigma^2_{cn} + \sigma^2_s + \sigma^2_e$$

When a test accommodation is made, the accommodation might add a new source of common-factor variance (e.g., auditory comprehension), specific test variance (e.g., a test format which is unique to the type of test being used), or alter the amount of test error. If a test accommodation adds a new source of common-factor or specific variance, what the test measures is changed. For example, the test format of a modified test might be unrelated to not only the regularly used version of the test, but to other tests which use this type of format. In other words, the test might be valid in terms of measuring a unique skill, but not valid with respect to what the regularly used test measures.

In terms of variance components, reliability is the sum of the common-factor variances and specific test variance, and validity is the sum of the common-factor variances or

$$\text{Reliability} = \frac{\sigma^2_{c1} + \sigma^2_{c2} \cdots \sigma^2_{cn} + \sigma^2_s}{\sigma^2_{total}}$$

and

$$\text{Validity} = \frac{\sigma^2_{c1} + \sigma^2_{c2} \cdots \sigma^2_{cn}}{\sigma^2_{total}}$$

Common-factor, specific and error variance are related in so far as an increase or reduction in one source of variance must have an effect on the remaining sources of variance. If the error variance of a test is increased from 20% to 30% as a result of a test accommodation, there must be a reduction in either the common-factor or specific test variance. In Table 2.1, several examples are presented to illustrate the relationship between the sources of variance. For a test which has a total variance of 100%, 60% is accounted for by common-factor variance, 20% by specific variance, and 20% by error variance. For test Accommodation #1, the specific variance is increased from 20% to 30% and common-factor variance decreases; for Test Accommodation #2 the error variance is increased from 20 to 30% and common-factor variance is reduced; and for Test Accommodation #3, because both specific and error variance have increased, the impact on common-factor variance is substantial. In contrast to the first three accommodations, Test Accommodation #4 illustrates a situation where validity is increased but where the accommodation validity is lowered. Although the common-factor variance measured has increased to 70%, what is being measured is different than the original test. The goal of an accommodation is not to make the test better (where "better" in this restricted sense is higher correlations) or to measure different abilities, but to measure what "the test purports to measure."[2] Thus, although the common-factor or specific variance of a test might increase as a result of an accommodation, which will either increase correlations with other tests or increase reliability coefficients, this is tantamount to creating a new test which requires validation and standardization.

Table 2.1 Relation Between Variance Sources.

Test	Variance			Total
	Common-factor	Specific	Error	
No Accommodation	60%	20%	20%	100%
Test Accommodation #1	50%	30%	20%	100%
Test Accommodation #2	50%	20%	30%	100%
Test Accommodation #3	40%	30%	30%	100%
Test Accommodation #4	70%	10%	20%	100%

Common-factor, specific and error variance components are not independent. As shown by the above examples, a change in one component must change one or more of the other components. If the error component of a test increases, either the common-factor or specific variance must be affected; if the test is changed so that it measures a very unique ability, there must be a corresponding decrease in the test's common-factor or error variance. In all likelihood, a test accommodation might result in very complex changes. For example, an accommodation might increase the test error and the specific variance of a test which would lower the test's common-factor variance substantially. Of the different testscore components, reliability is relatively simple to determine in comparison to validity where the sources of common-factor variance necessitate comparing and/or analyzing different tests.

Reliability

The essence of reliability concerns consistency and repeatability. A reliable test is one which provides consistent and repeatable results. The greater the consistency or repeatability, the smaller the error component. Reliability (r_{kk}) is defined as the ratio between true score variance and total test score variance. Because true score variance is not available, the ratio between error variance and observed score variance is determined and this value subtracted from 1.0 to yield a estimate of reliability:

$$r_{kk} = 1 - \frac{\sigma^2_e}{\sigma^2_{total}} = 1 - \frac{SE^2_{meas}}{SD^2}$$

The second formula above shows the relationship between the much used Standard Error of Measurement (SE_{meas}) and the total test variance or squared value of the test standard deviation (SD). The SE_{meas} is used extensively in the interpretation of test scores (e.g., establishing confidence intervals) and comparing test scores and is usually determined by

$$SE_{meas} = SD_x\sqrt{1 - r_{kk}}$$

There are three methods generally used to determine test reliability: (1) internal consistency, (2) alternative forms, and (3) test-retest.

Internal consistency. Internal consistency provides an essential method for determining a test's upper level of reliability. Nunnally (1967) referred to a domain-sampling model in which a test is considered "a random sample of items from a hypothetical domain of items" (p. 175). In the case of internal consistency or coefficient alpha, this represents the expected correlation between an actual test and a hypothetical alternative test (p. 197).

Estimates of internal consistency are based on the number of items and the average correlation between test items. A test with high internal consistency is one which provides a good sample from the larger domain of possible test items. If either of these factors is modified, there can be a corresponding effect on the test's internal consistency. As shown in the following Spearman-Brown formula, a test accommodation which decreases the number of test items or the item intercorrelation will decrease the test's internal consistency. If a test is comprised of 20 items and the average intercorrelation is .25, the reliability is .87; if 10 items are eliminated, the reliability decreases to .77; and if the average item intercorrelation is reduced .15, reliability is further reduced to .64.

$$r_{kk} = \frac{n\bar{r}_{ij}}{1 + (n - 1)\bar{r}_{ij}}$$

Nunnally (1967) considered coefficient alpha as "one of the most important deductions from the theory of measurement error" (p. 196). There are several methods for calculating coefficient alpha using average item-test correlations (Guilford, 1965), item variances (Cronbach, 1970), and analysis of variance approaches (see, Kerlinger, 1973 & Winer, 1971). The formula for coefficient alpha shown below illustrates the relation between item number (n) and the various test score variance components.[3]

$$\text{Coefficient Alpha} = r_{kk} = \left(\frac{n}{n-1}\right)\left(\frac{\sigma^2_{total} \cdot \Sigma\sigma^2_i}{\sigma^2_{total}}\right)$$

From a theoretical standpoint, a test accommodation which results in more items being answered might actually increase the reliability of the test. However, a test examiner cannot say that by using a test accommodation a test will be more reliable. The test would be more reliable if the entire normative group were given the test accommodation, and if norms were then determined using this accommodation. Although a test accommodation might theoretically result in higher reliability, the exact opposite can occur. If a test accommodation drastically reduces the item difficulty so that the test is extremely easy, the number of items attempted might increase but the overall variance would decrease. In the extreme case, if all students answered all items correctly, the reliability of the test would be 0. The essential question concerns the reliability of the available norms and not what the reliability "might be" if the test were renormed using the test accommodation. The need to minimize test accommodations is not only for inclusionary purposes, but to provide tests with accommodations which parallel, as much as possible, the regularly used test so that the impact on both reliability and validity is minimized.

Although the internal consistency of a test is reasonably robust with respect to item reduction, eliminating test items is generally an impractical test accommodation unless the entire test is renormed. Because of different item difficulties, the only situation when items could be deleted without radically affecting test validity is when items are randomly selected for deletion. Obviously, if only difficult items are deleted, even though these items might be worthy of deletion, the general test difficulty is reduced. In this situation, original normative test data could not be used as a frame of reference. For standardized tests containing a series of subtests which generate a total test score, eliminating subtests will tend to decrease test reliability. Again, this is probably not a major concern unless many subtests are deleted. For classroom tests, reducing the number of items can have a substantial effect on both reliability and validity depending on the length of the test, how many and what items are deleted.

A more important concern when specifying a test accommodation by reducing or eliminating test items concerns practical matters relating to fair opportunity, prorating scores, and interpreting the resulting scores based on the reduced item version of the test. For multiple-choice tests that have no penalty for guessing, reducing the number of items can deflate score performance. If a student knows anything that might even remotely result in a correct response, the student should be given the opportunity to respond. This is even more critical if test items are not arranged by item difficulty.

Determining the reliability of a test when used with a student receiving a specific test accommodation is difficult because of the unique characteristics of the accommodation and the student receiving the accommodation; that is, a vast number of different accommodations are used to varying degrees with very diverse groups of students. With definable special education samples (e.g., visually impaired students taking the SAT) the reliability of a test following an accommodation is probably relatively stable. However, the actual internal consistency of a test with any given test accommodation will not be known and is dependent on the degree to which the format, task, item difficulty and test length have been altered.

The need for reasonably high internal consistency, and therefore a degree of interrelationship between items, relates to the need to measure a defined underlying construct. Indeed, if the only concern is to produce a test which correlates with a criterion (e.g., predicting achievement from IQ scores), the best IQ test would not be one that was internally consistent but rather a test in which item intercorrelations were as small as possible. Although this would maximize the apparent predictive capacity of the test, the underlying construct sampled would be an undefinable hodgepodge of dissimilar and unrelated items.

There is not a wealth of data available concerning the internal consistency of tests when used with students receiving specific test accommodations (although there is considerable data relating to internal consistency of specific disability groups). The reason for this can be attributed to the fact that random sampling is often not possible, sample sizes are small, and the chronological age and mental age variability within these samples is often quite large. Examples of studies which have evaluated internal consistency based on large samples and relatively homogeneous test accommodations include Holt, Traxler and Allen (1992) who evaluated alpha coefficients for eight levels of deaf and hard of hearing students (Primary 1 to Advanced 2) who took the 8th Edition of the Stanford Achievement Test (N=6,932) and reported coefficients ranging from .54 to .89. These authors stated that "the values for Cronbach's alpha are excellent for the subtests that appear at all eight levels" (p. 12).

Bennett, Rock and Kaplan (1985) reported alpha coefficients ranging from .84 to .99 for five different disability groups taking the SAT (N=5,213 and N=4,236) using nine types or combinations (e.g., cassette and large print) of test accommodations (e.g., Braille, cassette, large print, regular type). Extended test time was an option for all special test administrations. With the exception of several LD samples, these alpha coefficients were in keeping with the nondisabled student reference reliabilities ranging from .91 to .92 (Table 8, p. 55). The two lowest alpha coefficients were .85 (LD-cassette) and .86 (LD-cassette/regular type) for the Verbal section and in keeping with the restricted score range of these groups (i.e., these groups had the lowest scaled score standard deviations).

Bennett, Rock and Jirle (1986) reported alpha coefficients ranging from .83 to .91 for relatively homogeneous groups of students (N=447) with disabilities taking the Graduate Record Examination (GRE). Overall, the SAT/GRE data suggest that given reasonable homogeneous disability samples, there is reason to expect adequate levels of internal consistency.

Alternate-forms reliability. The reliability of most standardized tests is based on the method of rational equivalence (Richardson & Kuder, 1939) where "the reliability coefficient is defined as the coefficient of correlation between one experimental form of a test and a hypothetically equivalent form" (p. 681). Although alternative forms estimates of reliability can provide useful information, Nunnally (1967) suggested that this technique is necessary "if the trait is suspected to vary considerably over relatively short periods of time, as would be true for measures of moods and some measures of attitudes" (p. 213). Overall, internal consistency will yield higher estimates of reliability than alternate-forms reliability because of changes over time, different scoring or different testing circumstances. The major drawback in the determination of alternate-forms reliability is that many tests do not have alternate forms and determining the time interval between alternate forms administration is far from standardized. Nunnally (1967, p. 211) suggested a two-week interval but there is no basis for using a one week, two week, or one month interval, and each of these intervals will impact reliability in different ways. In summary, although alternate-forms provides both a theoretical and historical basis for test reliability, most test publishers and users rely on internal consistency to estimate the upper level limits of test reliability.

The one occasion when alternate-forms reliability is necessary occurs when a test is highly speeded. In this situation the internal consistency of the test will be spuriously high because all items attempted are correct, and the only factor that differentiates among scores is the time allowed to complete the test. An inspection of split-half scores would reveal identical scores for each test taker so that the correlation between the odd and even scores would be perfect. This problem can be overcome by using alternate forms reliability,[b] or a split-half variation of alternative forms reliability. Split-half alternate forms reliability is accomplished by dividing the test into two parts,

---

[b]When speed is a factor, test-retest reliability can also be used, as was done by Dunn and Markwardt (1970, p.43), but practice, memory and the time interval between testing become important variables.

one part consisting of odd items and the other part comprised of even items, administering one form first, immediately followed by the second form. The correlation between the two forms is then found and then corrected using the following the Spearman-Brown formula when a test is comprised of two parts:

$$r_{kk} = \frac{2r_{xy}}{1 + r_{xy}}$$

Bennett, Rock and Jirele (1986) used sections within the General Test as "parallel forms of the same test" (p. 26) as one approach for determining the reliability of GRE scores for students with physical disabilities taking the national timed test, students with visual disabilities using large print and extended time, and students with visual disabilities taking the national timed test. The rationale for using GRE sections as the basis for reliability was that each section contained the same number, type and difficulty so that each section could be viewed as "parallel forms of the same test." After correlating these sections and applying the Spearman-Brown formula (because each form is half the length of the full test), parallel forms reliability coefficients ranged from .81 to .90. The coefficients were similar to the nondisabled students and only slightly lower than internal reliability coefficients which ranged from .83 to .91.

Test-retest reliability. Although test-retest reliability is often cited as how reliability is measured, this is the least acceptable method for determining test reliability. The major drawback of test-retest reliability is that as the interval between testing decreases, the possibility that taking the same test on a second occasion improves test performance. As Anastasi noted "the score on the two administrations of the test are not independently obtained and the correlation between them will be spuriously high" (p. 111). Also as the interval between testing increases (e.g., three or four months), instructional and developmental changes might result in low test-retest correlations.

Explaining why the test-retest method was used to determine the reliability of the PIAT (Dunn & Markwardt, 1970) stated that the "split-half methods were rejected as likely to result in spuriously high estimates of reliability for a test on which items have been carefully ordered in difficulty and on which the basal and ceiling procedure is utilized" (p. 43). The degree to which using basal and ceiling levels inflates internal estimates reliability is problematical, but for the most part, unless a test is unduly speeded, an estimate of internal consistency should provide the basis for determining a test's reliability.

Interpreting Reliability

Reliability is a requisite for test validity, but there are probably few occasions when a low reliability coefficient has dissuaded a practitioner from using a test. If reliability is low, the number of items, the item domain, and item content should be carefully examined. Mehrens and Lehman (1973, p. 122) recommended a reliability coefficient of at least .85. Nunnally (1967, p. 226) suggested a minimum reliability of .90 when "important decisions" are being made, and Anastasi (1982, p. 109) cited reliability coefficients of .8 to .9 as being in the "desirable" range for reliability coefficients.

Having a statistical guideline for determining adequate reliability is obviously useful, but even an acceptable reliability coefficient can mask sources of error specific to students with disabilities. In the Bennett, Rock and Jirele study (1986, p. 19), the reliability coefficients of students with and without disabilities were in the same range (.83 to .91) but the authors also found that for the students with disabilities taking the GRE without extended time, the test completion rates were lower than for the national sample. This is important because the test has no correction for guessing, and even randomly marking answers would benefit a student's score. There are many explanations why this might occur, but this does seem to be a new source of error caused by end-of-test strategies for students with disabilities or a disinclination to randomly mark answers (even when doing so would be beneficial). Even though the reliability coefficients are acceptable for the groups with lower items completion rates, this potential source of error is cause for concern and can lower a student's test score.

As discussed in Chapters 9 and 10, the reliability coefficient goes beyond providing a theoretical index of test error. Reliability coefficients are used to determine the standard error of measurement of scores which, in turn, is used to interpret individual scores, to estimate true scores, and to statistically compare scores from different tests. Reynolds' is correct in stating that the amount of error introduced is "inestimable" when a test is administered in a nonstandard fashion. However, because the effect of a test accommodation on reliability is often marginal (albeit often unknown), the primary risk involved with using a test accommodation is changing test validity.

Validity

Validity is a critical issue when considering the effects of a test accommodation. IDEA regulations state that "tests and other evaluation materials have been validated for the specific purpose for which they are used."[4] As with reliability, the impact of a test accommodation on validity can be considered theoretically but is difficult to determine empirically. Theoretically, if a test accommodation were used with the original normative sample, and the reliability was the same and the correlations with other tests remained the same, this would be evidence that the accommodation did not affect either reliability or validity.

However, a test accommodation might interject a new source of common-factor variance, specific-factor test variance, or error variance in which case the validity of the test might be affected. For example, tests which give unlimited time might be similar in a way than tests which do not give unlimited time are not. To make the theoretical interpretation of validity even more complex is the use of test accommodations which would never be used with the original normative sample. Thus, a test given in Braille might have something in common with other tests given in Braille, but this source of validity cannot be determined with respect to the original normative sample. The validity of the test can be determined by comparing test performance of Braille-formatted tests, but this does not address the impact of the Braille format when used with a test which was normed using a regular print version.

The following assumption must be must be made for all test accommodations: If the test accommodation were used with the original normative sample, there would be minimal impact on test validity. The problem is partially solved if the test accommodation is used with a norm group, new norms generated, and reliability and validity determined. For certain homogeneous groups (viz, visually impaired and hearing impaired) where an assumption can be made that the disability norm group is similar to the original norm group, with the exception of the unique test format, the content and content difficulty measured for both groups are similar. However, for many disability groups this assumption is not tenable. For example, a norm group comprised of students with severe developmental disabilities is decidedly different than a norm group drawn from the regular education population, and the content and content difficulty suitable for these two groups will not necessarily be similar.

Often the question of test validity arises when a test accommodation is deemed necessary in order to provide a fair opportunity to demonstrate ability. Depending on the test and circumstances, validity is sometimes considered secondary to proving a fair opportunity. In New York, the relation between validity and opportunity is regarded as follows:

> The use of test modifications during tests such as the California Achievement Tests (CATs), though contrary to directions of the publisher for standardized test administration, permits an equitable opportunity to demonstrate abilities and competencies. Although, from a statistical perspective, test modifications may invalidate results..." (New York State Education Department, 1995).

In Wisconsin (Wisconsin Department of Public Instruction, 1996), "the rules do not permit districts to read any of the reading passages or items to students as this does compromise the validity of the reading score." For the Texas Assessment of Academic Skills (Texas Education Agency, 1994) certain accommodations are thought to invalidate the test, and examinees are not allowed to receive any special reading assistance, to use a calculator, slide rule, English-language or foreign-language reference materials, or "other modifications that would make the test invalid." If a test is invalidated, statistically or otherwise, it probably will not provide a fair opportunity. The goal is to maintain validity and to provide a fair opportunity, but often test validity is affected or the test measures more of the student's disability than desired.

A test accommodations can change what a test measures and alter the fundamental validity of a test. The actual degree to which the validity of a test is changed because of an accommodation will vary from inconsequential (e.g., allowing a student to sit near the front of the room) to a major alteration of the test's validity (e.g., reading a reading test to a student). In the Seventeenth Annual Report to Congress (1995), the potential impact of test accommodations on test validity is acknowledged: "It is recognized that some modifications may affect measurement validity. These accommodations should still be used and the scores from them identified so that the impact of the modifications can be further analyzed" (p. 105). This philosophy addresses both the fact that a test accommodation can affect test validity, and that an accommodation may or may not be valid.

A very conservative interpretation would suggest that any change in the standardization procedures would preclude the use of normative data, while a more liberal interpretation would endorse a "best effort" attempt to use accommodations which have a minimal effect on test validity. The central question is this: *To what extent does a test accommodation alter what the test purports to measure?* The American Psychological Association Standards for Educational and Psychological Testing (1985) cautions that "when feasible, the validity and reliability of tests administered to people with various disabilities should be investigated and reported by the agency or publisher that made the modification." (p. 80). Even for large scale standardized tests this is no easy task, but for schools and districts where test accommodations are highly individualized and the number of students receiving accommodations is often small, the empirical determination of validity and reliability is virtually impossible.

The importance of validity cannot be overstated, but there is another dilemma for those intent on administering fair and valid tests. If tests must be "validated for the specific purpose for which they are used," how can a test be administered so as to best ensure that the ability rather than the disability is being measured? On the surface, the solution is readily apparent: Test accommodations should be validated before they are used. But this is often impossible because of the individualized nature of accommodations, the lack of homogeneous samples and sample sizes, and the unique characteristics of special education samples and populations. For example, learning disabilities is often operationally defined differently by school districts and samples of students classified as learning disabled are far from homogeneous. One district might regard a learning disability as a severe discrepancy between achievement and mental ability, another as an alternative to the stigma of a mental retardation label, and a third as a convenient bureaucratic contrivance for classifying students who do not fit other special education categories. For studies which have been able to use an adequate sample size (e.g., SAT and ACT programs), there is some data that for relatively homogeneous samples and specific test accommodations that the impact on validity is minimal. Willingham (1988) concluded that "the measurement characteristics of the SAT and GRE are much the same in nonstandard and standard form. Good reliability is obtained, and similar abilities are represented" (p. 182).

Willingham (1988) addressed the validity "problem" and stated that "in evaluating the validity of a test for a subgroup such as handicapped people, the primary concern is test fairness, and the measure of fairness is comparability" (p. 11). Transliterating a test from 10-point type to 18-point type should not drastically change the content being measured. If a large-print version requires more time than a regular-print format, extra time might be necessary in order to make the tests comparable. But the concept of comparability works both ways: If too much time is given and scores are thereby inflated, the resulting scores are no longer comparable to other normative scores.

To further confound the issue of validity and comparability are the effects of secondary accommodations which are the direct result of the primary accommodation. Braille, large print and cassette-test versions all require extended time because each of these tasks requires more time, and not necessarily to provide the student with extended problem-solving time. Likewise, testing a student orally or providing extended time might require an individualized administered test apart from the regular classroom. The goal is not to test outside of the regular classroom or to provide extra time, but the primary modification might require these secondary accommodations.

The Accommodation Dilemma

The regulations require that testing should be fair when assessing students prior to classification and placement,[5] and that "...a full and individual evaluation of the child's educational needs must be conducted..." and tests

1. are provided and administered in the child's native language or other mode of communication, unless it is clearly not feasible to do so;

2. have been validated for the specific purpose for which they are used; and

3. are administered by trained personnel in conformance with the instructions provided by their producer;[6]

The above emphasizes the importance of basic communication, test validation, and acceptable practice regarding test administration. Using a test in English for a non-English speaking student is unfair; using a traditional test with a student who relies on Braille is unfair; and administering a test over a period of days, rather than in a single day, when this type of accommodation is prohibited by the test publisher, is unfair.

Blatantly unfair assessment should be obvious, but there is a murky area between unfair and fair assessment which can pose a dilemma in the determination of a suitable test accommodation. If a test must be validated for the specific purpose for which it is used, the incorporation of many test accommodations would be in doubt. Although it might be necessary to evaluate a student's mastery of science as measured by a standardized test, poor reading ability might prevent a meaningful evaluation. The test can be read to the student because, ostensibly, the test is not designed to measure reading ability, but the test *does* measure reading ability to some extent, was standardized via a reading task, and was validated using a reading format. What is being measured by reading this test to a student is not entirely clear in spite of the fact that the accommodation is reasonable from an assessment point of view. Is this fair or, according to McLoughlin and Lewis (1990, p. 91), is this a case when "...norm-referenced scores become meaningless because the norms assume administration under standard conditions"?

The fairness of a test accommodation is further muddled when language or task and content are related. If the purpose of a test is to spell content words from dictation, then spelling and content are inextricably related in the assessment task. Although there might be certain instances where the task and content are not easily disentangled, a disinclination to test content ability apart from a task seems overly restrictive and possibly discriminatory. Reading comprehension ability is probably an important aspect of most content tests involving reading, but generally reading comprehension is incidental to the measurement of content knowledge. An example of a situation when a content test would not be read to a student would be a diagnostic test which was specifically designed to assess reading comprehension in the content area.

The dilemma of specifying fair test accommodations is the choice between providing what are perceived to be necessary and suitable test accommodations, but generating meaningless test information; or measuring a disability rather than ability, but generating misleading and unfair test information. The key to resolving this dilemma is seeking a *balance* between the accommodation and the integrity of the test *as much as possible.*

Flagging and Validity

Flagging is a way to show that a test has been administered in a nonstandard fashion and the validity of the test might be affected. Because of the differences between specific test accommodations, flagging does not indicate how or to what extent validity is affected. A large print version of a test might have minimal impact on validity, extended time moderate impact, and the combined test accommodation of large print with extended time a considerable impact on test validity.

For the SAT an asterisk is recorded next to the test date and the message NON STD ADMIN (Nonstandard Administration) is placed on the report for special administrations or national administrations with extended test time. For the ACT ARRANGED is recorded, and SPECIAL for special accommodations (e.g., Braille, large print, cassette, calculator, extended time). At the state level, a form of flagging comparable to SAT/ACT tests is sometimes used. For the Texas Assessment of Academic Skills, NS is used to indicate "nonstandard administration" and OA "oral administration."

The rationale for flagging given by the College Board (1994b) is that because "enormous variation exists in the extent and nature of disabilities among and within groups of students with hearing, learning, physical, and visual disabilities...the College Board is not able to provide meaningful interpretative data for scores earned in nonstandard administration" (p. 4). In spite of this caution, and the fact that tests administered in a nonstandard fashion are flagged, the College Board notes that scores are "comparable measures of the cognitive abilities of both test takers with disabilities and test takers without disabilities and that admission decisions were related to test scores and prior grades in much the same manner for applicants with disabilities and applicants without disabilities" (p. 4). Ysseldyke et al. (1994) in a report of a conference concerning statewide assessment programs and disabilities, acknowledged the tenuous relationship between test accommodations and test purpose and commented that "some modifications may raise questions about the validity of measures. These modifications should still be used, with the scores from them flagged so that they can be examined further" (p. 10).

Although tests are flagged to signify a nonstandard administration, this does not mean that the tests will be used differently in the admission process. There are usually substantial differences concerning the affects of an accommodation on a student's normative performance, yet all are identified as involving a nonstandard administration. Indeed, if a college uses a flag to deny admission this would almost certainly be a case of discrimination in that the flagging indicates a disability and does not suggest that the test accommodation is either valid or invalid. Both the ADA and Section 504[7] state that "a recipient may not make use of any employment test or other selection criterion that screen out or tends to screen out the disabled or any class of handicapped persons" unless the test is job-related or tests which do not screen out the disabled are not available. If a disabled student is given a test under the guise that this will lead to a demonstration of competency or meet some stated criterion, but the test is not used for this reason, the student is not being given an opportunity to demonstrate knowledge, skill or proficiency.

Ragosta and Wendler (1992) discussed the "flagging" dilemma and stated that "although the flags on test scores from special administrations originated because a standardized test was administered in a nonstandardized way, the flag has also been perceived as a precaution against the misuse of special testing accommodations" (p. 1).

The importance of flagging for any given test is related to the predictive validity of the test. If the predictive validity of a test were beyond reproach, then flagging a nonstandard administration of a test would be necessary. However, this is not the case with most tests which is the reason Section 504 prohibits the

> use of any test or criterion for admission that has a disproportionate, adverse effect on handicapped persons or any class of handicapped persons unless (i) the test or criterion, as used by the recipient, has been validated as a predictor of success in the education program or activity in question and (ii) alternate tests or criteria that have a less disproportionate, adverse effect are not shown by the Assistant Secretary to be available.[8]

Section 504 also addresses the need for periodic "validity studies:"

For the purposes of paragraph (b)(2) of this section, a recipient may base prediction equations on first year grades, but shall conduct periodic validity studies against the criterion of overall success in the education program or activity in question in order to monitor the general validity of the test scores.[9]

Braun, Ragosta and Kaplan (1988) provided one of the few research efforts which have attempted to determine the effect of test accommodations on the predictive ability of a test. The results of this study suggest that special test administrations can lead to overpredicting performance and that "overprediction arising from the practice of allowing unlimited time on standardized tests has the effect of reducing the validity of those test scores and decreasing the correlations between predicted and actual scores...by accommodating the needs of handicapped students in this way, we decrease the potential for obtaining special test administration data with validity as high as that for standard test administration" (p. 130).

The APA Standards for Educational and Psychological Testing (1985) states that "until test scores can be demonstrated to be comparable in some widely accepted sense, there is little hope of happily resolving from all perspectives the issue of reporting scores with or without special identification" (p. 78). The APA's solution is to use "professional and ethical considerations" to reach a solution. An interpretation of the APA guideline regarding flagging suggests that if a test accommodation has no significant effect on test validity, and the result will not mislead the test user, flagging is not warranted. However, if the validity of a test accommodation is subject to question or the result might mislead a test user without special identification, then flagging is necessary.

Accommodation Validity

The ultimate goal of every test accommodation is to eliminate the effects of the disability, while measuring what the test was originally designed to measure. The task is to remove the effects of the disability, but to maintain the test's underlying validity. When a test accommodation eliminates the effects of a disability but measures what the test was designed to measure, the test accommodation is valid; the validity of a test accommodation decreases as the effectiveness of the accommodation for eliminating the effects of the disability decreases and/or the test accommodation changes what the test measures.

A test accommodation which has no impact on better measuring the student's ability rather than disability, is not a valid accommodation. In this instance, an invalid test accommodation does not necessarily change the test's underlying validity. For example, if a student is tested individually for no other reason than because the student is classified as learning disabled, the validity of the test might be unchanged but the accommodation itself is superfluous and thus invalid. A primary concern when using an accommodation which has no impact on the student's disability, but does not affect validity, is the possibility that a valid accommodation might be overlooked because a gratuitous test accommodation (i.e., an accommodation which is not needed) has been provided, that the unnecessary accommodation might have an exclusionary effect, and that inappropriate decisions might be made as a result of the information generated by tests using unnecessary accommodations. Of course, a test accommodation which does mitigate a disability can detract from the test's validity. If extended test time distorts normative performance, or the difficulty of the test is either increased or decreased by a format modification, the effect of the disability might be mitigated (even when the test is made more difficult[c]), but the test would no longer be valid. As shown in Table 2.2, the only valid test accommodations are those which mitigate a disability and do not substantially alter what the test measures:

Table 2.2 Determining Valid Test Accommodations.

Changes Test Validity

		No	Yes
Mitigates Disability	Yes	VALID ACCOMMODATION mitigates disability and does not change what the test measures	Accommodation mitigates disability but substantially changes what the test measures
	No	Accommodation does not mitigate disability and does not change what the test measures	Accommodation does not mitigate disability and substantially changes what the test measures

---

[c]The test format might be changed because the student's disability precludes the use of the original format. Although the accommodation makes testing possible, the complexity and/or difficulty associated with the accommodation serves to increase overall test difficulty and thus decreases normative performance.

A test is valid when it measures what it purports to measure; an accommodation is valid when it eliminates the impact of a disability, but has little or no impact on test validity. A test accommodation which substantially alters what a test measures creates, in essence, is an entirely new test which must be subjected to validation. For the vast majority of test accommodations, an assumption is made that the accommodation addresses the disability, and has minimal impact on what the test measures.

Consider a situation in which the format of a test is modified (e.g., reading passages are highlighted and the test is right-justified) so as to accommodate the reading needs of a student. If the student received a higher score on the modified test than on the standard test (as determined by a random administration research design), one might conclude that the accommodation was effective but the impact on test validity would be unknown. If a similar study was conducted for nondisabled students, and the results revealed no difference between modified and standard test performance, one might further conclude that the accommodation mitigated the disability and did not change test validity. In other words, if accommodation X is used with students with and without disabilities, and only the scores of students with disabilities increase, this would provide some evidence that accommodation X moderated the disability rather than affecting test validity.

The degree to which a test accommodation affects a test or test score was discussed by Phillips (1993) who, in an analysis of case law, reported that tests need not be "substantially modified," (p. xxvi) and that "the closer the accommodation to the standard test administration conditions, the more valid the inference from the test score" (p. 82).

The purpose of a test accommodation is tied to the underlying purpose of the test and what the test result is intended to convey. Administering a test in which questions have been deleted, test content and difficulty changed, or using the test as a study guide might be useful for diagnostic purposes, to develop test taking skills, or for inclusionary reasons. However, these are not valid test accommodations if the purpose of the test is to interpret the student's ability in relation to the ability of other students. In this respect there is no difference between standardized tests and classroom tests. If the goal of a standardized test is to convey the student's level of performance in comparison to a normative population, practicing with the same questions used to measure this ability would be an invalid test accommodation.

Likewise, if the purpose of a classroom test is to indicate what classroom content a student has acquired, giving the student easier questions than other students or practicing the actual test questions with the student would also be invalid test accommodations. If the test adaptation is used for all students, the within-classroom equity issue is solved, but then the issue of school and districtwide standards is raised. The goal of a test accommodation is not to subvert existing educational standards, but to enable students with disabilities to demonstrate the ability to reach a given standard when reasonable test accommodations have been made.

Validity continuum. Based on the fact that as a test accommodation departs from what the test measures, or what the resulting test score means, test accommodations will range from those which are likely valid, to those which have a substantial but tolerable impact on validity, and to those which are clearly invalid. Whether a test accommodation is valid, invalid, or somewhere in between depends on the test, the accommodation, and how the accommodation is implemented. The method for implementing a test accommodation is instrumental in determining the validity of a test accommodation. Allowing a student to dictate a response to a test item designed to measure writing ability may not be valid if the transcriber provides spelling, punctuation and other editorial enhancements, because the test no longer measures writing ability. However, if a student uses a nontraditional method to write (e.g., single switch writing as discussed in Chapter 8), the writing sample might be a valid estimation of writing ability. If a transcriber records exactly what a student dictates, and the student is required to spell all words above a certain difficult level (or even all words), the result might be a valid assessment of writing ability.

Many test accommodations fall between those which are valid and those which are clearly invalid. Whether or not a test accommodation leans to validity or invalidity depends on the test, the purpose of the test, and how the test results are used. For some content tests, reading might be an integral part of what is being measured; extended time might dramatically inflate test scores, and an individual assessment might give a student a decided advantage.

The validity of a test accommodation cannot be determined apart from the specific test with which it is used. If a test is a power test, and the goal is to determine content knowledge, extended time is probably a reasonable accommodation. However, if the test has a substantial speed component, extended time accommodation might be invalid. On a similar basis, using a calculator for math might be appropriate as long as the test does not have answers which can be obtained directly from the calculator. The following describes various types of accommodations which occupy the accommodation continuum:

Table 2.3 A Continuum of Accommodations.

Valid	Possibly valid	Invalid
Develop test-taking skills	Extended time	Reading reading-test questions
Individual administration	Eliminating biased items	Eliminating difficult items
Enhanced instructions	Reading content questions	Changing test content
Physical accommodations	Examiner aid	Practicing with exact test
Large print	Calculator for math problems	Calculator for math facts
Braille	Using a scribe	Nonauthored test responses

Content Validity

For identifying, implementing and evaluating the effectiveness of test accommodations, a consideration of test content is essential. When faced with the prospect of using a test which is not valid because of a student's disability, consideration must be given as to how the test can be adapted or modified to provide a valid estimate of ability. If a test accommodation is made, the impact on test content must be minimized. If the accommodations are so radical, the test content so compromised, then the accommodation is not appropriate.

Anastasi (1982) defined content validity "as the systematic examination of te content to determine whether it covers a representative sample of the behavior domain to be measured" (p. 131). Content validity requires careful examination and consideration of what is being measured, what the purpose of the assessment is, and provides the mainstay of test validation when a test accommodation has been made.

Kerlinger (1973) stated that "content validation, then, is basically judgmental" (p. 459). This requires a reflective and critical approach concerning what a test does and does not measure, and to what extent a test accommodations somehow changes what a test measures. To this end, the process of determining the content validity of a test is enhanced by seeking input from a variety of sources. Parents, teachers, aids, school psychologists, special education teachers, and other professionals providing related services (e.g., remedial reading, speech and language specialist, etc) and the student might have essential information concerning appropriateness of test content, how test accommodations change test content, and the effectiveness of test accommodations.

A test is a series of items designed to measure a greater population of items which comprise a distinct content domain. Selecting or eliminating certain items based on a criterion thought to be important can radically alter the content makeup of a test. Likewise, changing the difficulty of a test by modifying items (e.g., the language of items) or how items are presented (e.g., signing rather than requiring items to be read) can change the content validity of a test. For standardized tests, changing the content generally precludes the use of norms (at least in any meaningful way); while for nonstandardized tests, changing the test content should be done in order to better understand individual performance rather than for comparative purposes.

There are occasions when content validity is changed as a result of the accommodation which is used to bypass the disability. An example of this is signing items to a student rather than having the student read items. Not only is signing an entirely different mode of input, but the exact extent to which content is changed depends on the signs used, the amount of fingerspelling, and the student's ability to read signs and fingerspelling. Nonetheless, if changing the content is the only way to assess an ability or skill, such an accommodation might be the only recourse to a test exemption. Changing test content might be unavoidable, but an attempt to minimize these changes is essential.

Many test adaptations will have negligible impact on a test's content validity. Allowing a student to sit near the front of the room, administering a test individually rather than in a group, or permitting the student to record answers in the test booklet should have little ostensible effect on the content being measured. On the other hand, format modifications can have substantial impact on the content being measured. Transcribing a test from one language to another, signing items, or reading items might substantially affect the content and the content difficulty.

If the content of a test is inappropriate prior to a test accommodation, an accommodation will not improve the test or the content. The purpose of a test accommodation is not to rectify a test's deficiencies, change a test's validity, or to improve a demonstrably bad test. If a group paper/pencil IQ test is used to determine a student's IQ score, no accommodation will rectify the inherent weaknesses of the test. Of course, a major accommodation might make the test a better test, but to do this would require changes in either the format and/or content. The "modified" test might be a much better measure of ability than the original measure, but it would also measure something quite different than the original measure. This can lead to a rather unusual situation in which a test accommodation results in a better test of the skill or knowledge being assessed, but a version which might not "have been validated for the specific purpose" which it is being used, and a test which is "not administered...in conformance with the instructions provided by"[10] the test producer.

If a test accommodation substantially changes content so that standardization data is virtually useless, a new test has been created. The modified test might be a welcome replacement of the original version, but this results in the use of an "alternative" test rather than the test in question. And although it might seem that an "alternative" test is a reasonable solution, the test itself might have no information relating to reliability or have available data for interpreting scores. Kerlinger (1973) stated that "the items of a test must be studied, each item being weighed for its presumed representativeness of the universe. This means that each item must be judged for its presumed relevance to the property being measured, which is no easy task" (p. 459). Maybe the most obvious example of this attention to test item composition is the restandardization of the Stanford Achievement Test-Form J (see Bradley-Johnson, 1994, p. 156). Because certain items were eliminated when transcribed into Braille by the American Printing House for the Blind, the test was renormed using the original normative data but eliminating the biased items.

Evaluating test content. The following are several factors which should be considered when evaluating the content of a test before and after test accommodations have been made. (1) Item content: Do the test items measure what the test purports to measure? (2) Item sample: Do the test items provide a reasonable sampling of the domain? (3) Item number: Are there a sufficient number of items? Too many items might result in fatigue, while too few items (e.g., using one or two primary facts to provide an estimate of all primary fact knowledge) might be insufficient to adequately sample the domain. (4) Item difficulty: Are the items at an appropriate difficulty level? If test items are not within the ability range of the student, the test will not provide an assessment of the student's content ability. If the test is comprised of reading comprehension questions for use with an eighth grade student, but the student is reading at the second grade level, the test might provide a valid estimate of reading "at the eighth grade level" but not a valid estimate of general reading comprehension. (5) Item format: Does item format hinder test performance? The format of a test itself can detract from a test's content validity. (6) Response time: Is there sufficient time to complete the items? (7) Item response: Does the required test response hinder test performance?

Construct Validity

The Standards for Educational and Psychological Testing (American Psychological Association, 1985) states that "the evidence classed in the construct-related category focuses primarily on the test score as a measure of the psychological characteristic of interest" (p. 9). Construct validity is embedded in theoretical framework and is established in by sound principles of test development and both quantitative (e.g., correlational analysis) and qualitative (e.g., content analysis) test techniques. The key to reliability is not simply sampling items, but sampling items which comprise a domain of items which represent an educational or theoretical construct. Establishing construct validity begins with reliability and uses a variety of qualitative and quantitative techniques to determine the uniqueness of the construct in question.

Qualitative constructs. Validity has the unfortunate connotation of implying or necessitating statistical evidence (e.g., correlation coefficients). Construct validity is essential for both qualitative (e.g., curriculum-based measures, portfolio assessment) and quantitative assessments. For example, a curriculum-based measure should not only reflect the domain of the curriculum being evaluated, but it should provide an adequate sampling of the curriculum-content. If a curriculum-based measure uses reading cloze to assess reading, and the task was never used in the curriculum, the validity of this assessment would be suspect. This is not a question of statistics or elaborate correlational analyses, but a reflection of a very basic tenet: a test should measure what it purports to measure.

For many tests which are adapted or modified for students with disabilities, elaborate statistical analyses may not be available or even feasible. However, the original test construct and the impact of the test accommodation on the test construct should be considered. A paper/pencil writing test signifies a construct that is different than a writing test using Braille or a writing test using single-switch technology. All three no doubt share a common construct, but each focuses on a specific task. The Standards for Educational and Psychological testing cautions that "the construct measured by speeded tests may change when test format is changed, for example, from paper and pencil to computer" (p. 15).

Guilford (1954) discussed the concept of "validity by assumption" and argued that a measure such as an achievement test is assumed to measure achievement. He stated that to justify this "we must be clear as to the objectives to be achieved during learning and as to the kinds of items it takes to indicate the realization of those objectives" (p. 399). An assumption of validity is based on a critical analysis of the test objectives and the ability of test items to measure these objectives. No statistical analysis will overshadow the importance of considering test objectives and the ability of test items to measure these objectives when a test accommodation has been made. In so far as statistical data is often unavailable for modified tests, this is frequently the only method for determining the validity of a modified test.

Quantitative constructs. There are many statistical techniques which can be used to define educational and psychological constructs including factor analysis and related multivariate analytic techniques, but the mainstay of statistical construct validation is often the correlation coefficient. Campbell and Fiske (1959) discussed two types of construct validity: convergent and discriminant validity. Simple constructs as measured by tests should correlate higher than dissimilar constructs or tests. Consider the hypothetical example in Table 2.4 which shows the correlation matrix between three mathematics tests (Math A, Math B & Math C) and three Reading tests (Read A, Read B & Read C). If the mathematics-related tests measure computational skills, number concept and math word problems, and the reading-related tests measure reading vocabulary, reading comprehension and language (e.g., mechanics), one hypothesis would be that the math tests correlate more with one another than with the reading tests, and vice versa for the reading tests. As shown by the multitrait-multi-method matrix in Table 2.4, correlations between different tests using different methods (the correlations in the rectangles) are higher than correlations between different traits and different methods).

Table 2.4 Hypothetical Multitrait-multimethod Correlation Matrix.

	Math A	Math B	Math C	Read A	Read B	Read C
Math A						
Math B	.85					
Math C	.80	.80				
Read A	.65	.70	.75			
Read B	.65	.70	.75	.90		
Read C	.65	.70	.75	.80	.80	

There have been relatively few attempts to use multitrait-multi-method correlation matrix. Holt, Traxler and Allen (1992) did use this approach to study the pattern of correlations across levels of the Stanford Achievement Test (8th edition) of the deaf and hard of hearing students in a large normative sample. The results revealed that "the pattern of correlations...provides evidence supporting construct validity of the Stanford for the three age groups of deaf and hard of hearing students" (p. 14). In this case, the normative sample was sufficiently large and homogeneous to make the results meaningful.

As is often the case, small sample sizes, unique samples, and selection criteria can make correlations drawn from samples of students with disabilities extremely difficult to interpret. Depending on the disability, the sample may or may not represent a random sampling of the general population. For an area such as learning disabilities, the problem is further complicated by the existence of distinct populations of students with learning disabilities (e.g., students with reading disabilities, mathematics disabilities, etc.). In most instances, random sampling is not possible and the size of the samples are often quite small. If students are selected using a certain criterion (e.g., verbal behavior) there will likely be a restriction in sample variances and the ensuing correlations. Even for the SAT and ACT data, where samples are relatively large, the samples are not representative of students with disabilities but students with specific disabilities who have requested to take the SAT. Finally, although a correlation will provide a linear rep-

take the SAT. Finally, although a correlation will provide a linear representation of the relationship between two variables regardless of the underlying distributions, using only a linear model might ignore other nonlinear relationships. These methodological problems should not diminish efforts to determine the statistical characteristics of tests when used with students with disabilities, but should highlight the need to evaluate such statistics with caution.

ENDNOTES

1. 34 C.F.R. §300.532(a)(2)
2. 34 C.F.R. §300.552(c)
3. The simplest version of this formula (see page 49) entails correlating two halves of a test (e.g., odd versus even items) and then correcting the resulting correlation using $(2r_{o\text{-}e})/(1+r_{o\text{-}e})$.
4. 34 C.F.R. §300.532(a)(2)
5. 34 C.F.R §300.531
6. 34 C.F.R. §300.532(a)
7. 34 C.F.R. §104.13(a)
8. 34 C.F.R. §104.42(a)(2)
9. 34 C.F.R. §104.42(d)
10. 34 C.F.R. §300.532(a)(2)&(3)

Chapter 3

TEST ACCOMMODATION PLANNING

Because test accommodations tend to be highly individualized, developing a single strategy to meet the test accommodation needs of all students is not an easy task. Test accommodations can range from a common sense test strategy as repeating instructions to a formalized statement which explicitly indicates what test accommodations are required to best meet a student's testing needs.

Individual states are required by IDEA to develop procedures relating to the identification, location, and evaluation of children with disabilities,[1] Individualized Education Program (IEP) requirements,[2] protection in evaluation procedures,[3] and annual evaluation.[4] A State Educational Agency (SEA) might develop procedures for providing test accommodations, guidelines for using test accommodations with specific SEA competency/mastery tests, or a general consideration to measure ability rather than a student's disability.[5] State procedures provide a framework for providing special education and related services, but individual states and school districts must articulate a workable test accommodation plan which meets the specific tests and diverse needs of the students being evaluated.

The emphasis on the need for thorough and integrated planning is emphasized in the IDEA Amendments of 1997 which has a provision for a State Improvement Plan (SIP) which encourages partnerships between state and local agencies, collaborate efforts between agencies and between states.[6] In addition, the IDEA Amendments encourage planning at the schoollevel through School-based Improvement Plans[7], which can impact the quality and effectiveness of test accommodation services, to reform and improve

69

their systems for providing educational, early intervention, and transitional services, including their systems for professional development, technical assistance, and dissemination of knowledge about best practices, to improve results for children with disabilities.[8]

Much of the confusion regarding test accommodations could be eliminated by some consensus among states concerning the use and implementation of accommodations, and providing in-service and pre-service training relating to test accommodations.

There is no agreed upon plan as to how test accommodations should be made, what tests accommodations are most appropriate, or the best vehicle for implementing test accommodations. There is a lack of consistency among individual school districts concerning the designation and implementation of test accommodations; there are major differences among state agencies as to what test accommodations are allowed; and test publishers run the gamut from saying virtually nothing about test accommodations to college admission testing programs which have extensive and detailed plans for identifying students needing accommodations.

The lack of agreement concerning a generally accepted test accommodation plan can be attributed to three factors: First, the concept of fair opportunity can be interpreted to mean every student is entitled to take every test in which case no or minimal accommodations are used; or fair opportunity can also be used to minimize all possible effects of a disability in which case an extensive array of test accommodations might be available. The range of test accommodations used by schools is predicated on the interpretation of fair opportunity, and vary from minimal to excessively detailed accommodations.

Second, the needs of students within each disability grouping are quite varied. Although three students might be classified as blind and have the same level of visual acuity, one might use Braille, a second large print, and a third might require a reader. In short, there is no simple protocol for matching a student's disability with a corresponding test accommodation.

Finally, determining when an accommodation mitigates the effects of a disability without compromising the test's validity is subject to considerable interpretation. One test prohibits the use of extended time, a second suggests that extended time might affect validity, and a third allows extended testing time as a modification. Some tests can be read, others cannot; one math test might prohibit the use of a calculator, while another test might allow a calculator for use with certain types of problems. The interpretation of validity, and the perceived importance of validity, determines the scope and tenor of a test accommodation plan.

Integrated Test Accommodations

Test accommodations are often relegated to a small section of an IEP,[9] but test accommodations should play an important role in all the primary components of the IEP process. The range of test accommodations to consider are extant accommodations which are in effect prior to the referral for services, test accommodations conducted as part of the individual evaluation to determine the need for special education and related services, IEP test accommodations in the form of goals, services, or "appropriate evaluation procedures,"[10] a Section 504 plan (which can be an IEP-type document), or specific test accommodations which are provided pursuant to Section 504.

Table 3.1 illustrates the various phases before, during and after the multidisciplinary team evaluation when test accommodations must be considered. As shown in Table 3.1 test accommodations can be classified as existing or extant accommodations, accommodations used during the evaluation phase, and IDEA and Section 504 test accommodations.

Table 3.1 Types of test Accommodations.

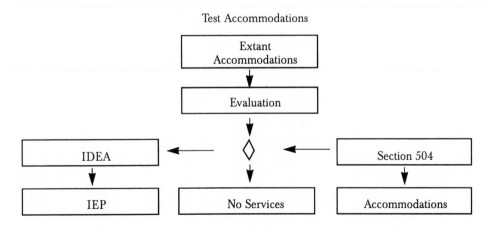

Extant accommodations.   Extant accommodations are those which are in use prior to referral for services and a multidisciplinary team evaluation. One teacher might allow extra time for a student to complete a test even though there is no formal disability that has been identified. A social studies teacher might realize that a student has made an attempt to understand the material but that a test which requires reading is not an adequate gauge of achievement. As part of the referral process, information should be gathered concerning these extant accommodations, what accommodations have been considered, and what accommodations are being recommended by parents and teachers.

Extant accommodations are important, but this cannot be the basis for a thorough test accommodation plan for a student. When an informal test accommodation is made by a teacher, test examiner or other professional apart from a formal plan, there is no assurance that this accommodation will be used in similar test situations; and there is no apparatus to evaluate either the need or effectiveness of the accommodation. A social studies teacher might allow the use of a reader, but other teachers are not required to implement this type of accommodation. Although informal accommodations might be necessary for meeting the test needs of a student for a specific test, or might only be needed for a specific test, these accommodations might result in an inconsistent plan for meeting a student's overall test needs.

Individual evaluation accommodations.   Prior to the development of the IEP, present levels of educational performance must be evaluated. To this end, tests must be valid, are administered by trained personnel, and are designed to "assess specific areas of educational need."[11] If a test measures the student's disability rather than ability or skill, an attempt must be made during the evaluation phase to assess present levels of performance by moderating the effects of the student's disability. Assume a student is given a diagnostic test during the individual evaluation phase but the test format precludes a meaningful evaluation of the student's actual ability. In order to report present levels of performance, the test examiner must either modify the format, use a different test or format, or interpret test performance so that the effects of the disability are taken into account (e.g., by using special norms).

IDEA and Section 504 accommodations.   If a student requires special education and related services, an IEP must be developed prior to providing services. As discussed in Chapter 4, test accommodations can be indicated when describing present levels of education performance, describing goals, delineating services, and planning appropriate evaluation procedures. If a student is not eligible for special education, the student might be eligible for services or a test accommodation under Section 504. There is no substantive difference between test accommodations under IDEA or Section 504, and the difference primarily concerns eligibility requirements for IDEA and Section 504 and not substantive differences between the types of accommodations used under either plan.

General Eligibility Requirements

Referring to the accommodation of extra testing time, Ragosta and Wendler (1992) noted that "most test takers would like to have the extra testing time allowed for people with disabilities" (p. 1). Unfortunately, allowing students to self-select accommodations such as extended testing time because of a perceived need on the part of the student (and even though the basis for the need might be quite valid) would compromise the integrity of most standardized tests and seriously confound the interpretation of nonstandardized tests.

A student's IEP provides a local educational agency the opportunity to identify necessary test accommodations, and for showing that a good faith effort has been made to test what each test purports to measure rather than reflecting the student's disability. Although a student's IEP can provide a general guideline for accommodations, and test accommodation eligibility, there are other circumstances which require test accommodations, such as when a student is not disabled under IDEA but has an impairment, a record of an impairment, or is regarded as having an impairment.[12] The following sections describe different circumstances when, either with or without an IEP, test accommodations are required or a student is eligibility for a test accommodation.

Current IEP

As shown in Table 3.2 there are approximately 4.9 million students between the ages 6 through 21 served under IDEA in 1994-95. Each of these students should have an IEP, and every student with a current IEP might require test adaptations, modifications, alternatives or exemptions for classroom, school, and statewide tests. The current IEP is used throughout the student's educational career to provide a plan for fair and nondiscriminatory testing, and encompasses every form of educational and psychological assessment, including postsecondary assessment (e.g., the IEP is used as one means to determine SAT and ACT eligibility).

The focal point of IDEA/IEP test accommodations centers about students with disabilities and

> means those children evaluated in accordance with §§300.530-300-534[a] as having mental retardation, hearing impairments including deafness, speech or language impairments including blindness, serious emotional disturbance, orthopedic impairments, autism, traumatic brain injury, other health impairments, specific learning disabilities, deaf-blindness, multiple disabilities, and who because of those impairments need special education and related services.[13]

To receive a test accommodation under IDEA, a student must meet two conditions: (1) have one of the disabilities specified by IDEA, and (2) need special education. If a student does not have one of the disabilities defined by IDEA, or does not need special education, the student is not entitled to a test accommodation under IDEA. A student who needs a reader to read tests but does not have a disability under IDEA (e.g., the student does not have a specific learning disability) or does not need "specifically designed instruction" would not be entitled to reader services under IDEA (although the student might be eligible for this service under Section 504).

---

[a]These sections deal with protection in evaluation and placement.

Table 3.2 Students 6 to 21 Served Under IDEA.[14]

Category[15]	1990-91		1994-95		Change	
	N	%	N	%	N	%
Specific learning disability	2,144,017	49.2	2,513,977	51.1	369,960	17.3
Speech or language impairments	987,778	22.7	1,023,665	20.8	35,887	3.6
Mental retardation	551,457	12.6	570,855	11.6	19,398	3.5
Serious emotional disturbance	390,764	9.0	428,168	8.7	37,404	9.6
Multiple disabilities	97,629	2.2	89,646	1.8	-7,983	-8.2
Hearing impairments	59,211	1.4	65,568	1.3	6,357	10.7
Orthopedic impairments	49,340	1.1	60,604	1.2	11,264	2.8
Other health impairments	56,349	1.3	106,509	2.2	50,160	89.0
Visual impairments	23,682	0.5	24,877	.51	1,195	5.0
Autism	NA	--	22,780	.46	22,780	--
Traumatic brain injury	NA	--	7,188	.15	7,188	--
Deaf-blindness	1,524	<.1	1,331	<.1	-193	-12.7
All disabilities	4,361,751	100.0	4,915,168	100.0	553,417	12.7

The number of low-incidence students (e.g., disabilities resulting from visual impairments, traumatic injury, etc.) requiring consideration for services is far less than high-incidence categories (viz., learning disabilities, mental retardation and emotional disturbance). For example, as shown in Table 3.2, 1.3 percent of students with disabilities have hearing impairments, and only .51 percent visual impairments in 1994-95. Although Braille is routinely listed as a test accommodation on many IEP's, very few students will actually use this accommodation. Wright and Wendler (1994) reported that of the 103 students with visual disabilities who took SAT, 2 percent used the Braille test. This is consistent with a survey by Wendler and Wright (1994) of the most frequently reported accommodations cited by 1,001 students with disabilities surveyed in the development of the new SAT: extra time (57%), separate room (23%), reader (20%), different test (8%), special equipment (7%), cassette test (5%), recorder/scribe (4%), large-type test (4%), and Braille (<1%). As shown in Table 3.2, of particular concern for planning test accommodations is the increase in the Specific Learning Disabilities (17.3) and Other Health Impaired (89%) categories.

Section 504 Plan/Accommodation

Section 504 provides an avenue for test accommodations for students who do not meet IDEA criteria but have an impairment or are treated as having an impairment:

> Handicapped person means any person who (i) has a physical or mental impairment which substantially limits one or more major life activity, (ii) has a record of such an impairment, or (iii) is regarded as having such an impairment."[16]

Of special interest is the phrase "is regarded as having such an impairment." This is further defined as meaning:

> (a) ...a physical or mental impairment that does not substantially limit major life activities but that is treated by a recipient as constituting such a limitation; (b) has a physical or mental impairment that substantially limits major life activities only as a result of the attitudes of others toward such impairment; or (c) has none of the impairments defined...but is treated by recipient as having such an impairment.[17]

Although the IDEA regulations relating to the development of an IEP are fairly specific,[18] the implementation of Section 504 is less rigorous in that the primary requirement is to meet the individual educational needs of students with disabilities[19] and that a "plan" such as an IEP, developed in accordance with regulations governing IEPs, is one way to meet this standard.[20] Thus, when a student is entitled to a test accommodation under Section 504, such an accommodation is often referred to as "Section 504," "Section 504 Accommodation," "Section 504 Plan," "504 Plan," "504 Accommodation," "Student Accommodation Plan,"[21] or "Section 504 Individual Accommodation Plan."[22,23] In this book a test accommodation resulting from Section 504 will be referred to as simply Section 504 Accommodations.

Because the definition of disabilities is much broader in Section 504, a test accommodation must be developed for students who cannot receive services under IDEA but who have an impairment, a record of an impairment, or is regarded as having an impairment. Examples of situations in which Section 504 rather than IDEA apply include individuals who had an impairment but the condition no longer exists, persons who have been misclassified or who have a history of a disability (e.g., mental illness, cancer), or individuals who are regarded or treated as disabled but might not be classified under IDEA.[24] Although the concept of a disability is far broader under Section 504, there is a stipulation that the disability "substantially limits one or more major life activities."

The increase in the number of students identified as having ADD or ADHD (attention-deficit/hyperactive disorder) illustrates the tenuous relationship between a disability category and test accommodations, as well as the difference between the application of IDEA and Section 504. In the 18th Annual Report to Congress (1995), the disability of Other Health Impairments increased from 56,349 (1990-91) to 106,509 (1994-95) or a 89 percent change. The report states that "the increase in the number of students with other health impairments appears to be the result of growth in the service population" (p. 8). Specifically, the number of students with attention deficit disorder reported by states appears to be increasing. An attention deficit disorder appear to come under the auspices of *specific learning disability* in that this "term includes such conditions as perceptual disabilities, brain injury, minimal brain dysfunction, dyslexia, and developmental aphasia."[25] Apparently, one reason why ADD advocates[26] are disinclined toward the specific learning disability classification is the belief that ADD is not a learning problem (although this is not always the primary issue in defining a specific learning disability).

In a memorandum (United States Department of Education, 1991) written to clarify services for students identified as having ADD, the possibility was noted that some students with ADD would be covered by IDEA under Other Health Impairment "in instances where the ADD is a chronic or acute health problem that results in limited alertness," while other students with ADD would not be covered by IDEA but by Section 504:

> The list of chronic or acute health problems included within the definition of "other health impaired" in the Part B regulations is not exhaustive. The term "other health impaired" includes chronic or acute impairments that result in limited alertness which adversely affects educational performance. Thus, children with ADD should be classified as eligible for services under the "other health impaired" category in instances where the ADD is a chronic or acute health problem that results in limited alertness, which adversely affects educa-

tional performance. In other words, children with ADD, where the ADD is a chronic or acute health problem resulting in limited alertness, may be considered disabled under Part B solely on the basis of this disorder within the "other health impaired" category in situations where special education and related services are needed because of the ADD.

Students with ADD are also eligible for Part B services Under Other Disability if Children with ADD are also eligible for services under Part B:

> if the children satisfy the criteria applicable to other disability categories. For example, children with ADD are also eligible for services under the "specific learning disability" category of Part B if they meet the criteria stated in ''300.5(b)(9) and 300.541 or under the "seriously emotionally disturbed" category of Part B if they meet the criteria stated in '300.5(b)(8).

If ADD results in "limited alertness" (which is certainly not a factor cited in most definitions of ADD), the disability is covered by IDEA under Other Health Impairments, or if students with ADD meet requirements for specific learning disability or seriously emotionally disturbed then IDEA special education and related services can be provided. If the ADD is not covered by IDEA under the very specific limitations of the Other Health Impairment category or as a learning or emotional impairment, then it might be covered by Section 504 if the disability "substantially limits one or more major life activities."[27] Although a limited number of ADD students might be covered by the Other Health Impairment IDEA category in cases where the disorder is manifested by "limited vitality, strength or alertness," this seems contrary to many definitions of ADD which stress attention and behavioral problems, impulsivity, and hyperactivity. For example, Friend and Bursuck (1996) stated that "students with ADHD have a medical problem often characterized by an inability to attend to complex tasks for long periods of time, excessive motor activity, and impulsivity" (p. 19-20). These characteristics are consistent with the Diagnostic and Statistical Manual of Mental Disorders (American Psychiatric Association, 1994) diagnostic criteria of Attention-deficit/Hyperactivity Disorder (e.g., careless mistakes, difficulty organizing tasks, easily distracted, fidgets, often "on the go," blurts out answers, interrupts).

The point of all this is that there is definitely some confusion as to what ADD is, how it should be defined, and even whether it is a disability. This is not to say that ADD is not a legitimate disability, but that a construct with such definitional vagueness does not lend itself to readily discernible test accommodations. In the case of ADD, based on the prospect of either including an ADD student as either having a specific learning disability (as manifested by poor attention, impulsivity, etc.) or "limited vitality" (and thus being eligible under IDEA by the Other Health Impairment category), two students with ADD might require completely different and diametrically opposed test accommodations.

The ADD clarification memorandum, while explaining when IDEA applies to ADD, also stresses the importance of educational agencies to coordinate regular classroom and special education services for students who might have attention deficit disorders or other disorders which do not readily fit one of the existing IDEA disability categories. Activities cited in the memorandum as relevant to test accommodations which can be undertaken in the regular classroom include repeating and simplifying instructions, supplementing verbal instructions with visual instructions, adjusting class schedules, modifying test delivery, using tape recorders, computer-aided instruction use of one-on-one tutorials, classroom aides and notetakers, involvement of a services coordinator to oversee implementation of special programs and services. The point of this reference to the coordination of special and regular education is that before a test accommodation is used, it need not be in an IEP or Section 504 plan and that many accommodations can be provided as part of normal regular educational activities.

Consolidated Plans

Before a student receives special education services under IDEA, the student must be evaluated as having a disability, and must have an individualized education program before services are provided. IDEA offers guidelines for evaluation by a multidisciplinary team, and the IEP represents the primary vehicle for providing IDEA services, but this is not the case with Section 504. With respect to evaluation and planning, Section 504 regulations do require the establishment of "standards and procedures for the evaluation and placement of persons who, because of handicap, need or are believed to need special education or related services,"[28] and that the "implementation of an individualized education program developed in accordance with the Education of the Handicapped Act is one means of meeting"[29] this standard. Overall, IDEA regulations are amenable to the consolidation of different plans:

> In instances where a child with a disability must have both an IEP and an individualized service plan under another federal program, it may be possible to develop a single, consolidated document only if: (1) it contains all of the information required in an IEP, and (2) all of the necessary parties participate in its development.
>
> Examples of individualized service plans which might be consolidated with the IEP are: (1) The Individualized Care Plan (Title XIX of the Social Security Act (Medicaid)), (2) the Individualized Program Plan (Title XX of the Social Security Act (Social Services)), (3) the Individualized Service Plan (Title XVI of the Social Security Act (Supplemental Security Income)), and (4) the Individualized Written Rehabilitation Plan (Rehabilitation Act of 1973).[30]

If IDEA regulations do not apply, but a student is covered by Section 504, some type of written program/plan is necessary "to meet the educational needs of"[31] students with disabilities. The Council of Administrators of Special Education (1992) have suggested the use of a Student Accommodation Plan which is comprised of a statement of the concern, the basis for determining the existence of a disability, how the disability "affects a major life activity," and a listing of the necessary "reasonable accommodations" (p. 22).

Section 504 administration. Under Section 504 students with disabilities must be located[32] and be provided with "regular or special education and related services that...are designed to meet individual educational needs."[33] In accordance with this task, an educational agency must conduct an evaluation[34] and "that the placement decision is made by a group of persons, including persons knowledgeable about the child, the meaning of the evaluation data, and the placement options."[35,36] From a practical standpoint, the IEP multidisciplinary team is the most likely group to conduct a Section 504 evaluation, and the IEP meeting the most likely place to develop, review and revise, test accommodations pursuant to Section 504. Needless to say, circumstance, test needs, and educational setting might dictate some other format for evaluating students covered by Section 504 and for providing "special education or related services."[37]

Section 504 and services. In addition to how a disability is defined under IDEA and Section 504, there is another important distinction between IDEA and Section 504 and that is to receive a related service under IDEA a student must need special education. "If a child does not need special education, there can be no related services"[38] so that if a student does not need special education under IDEA there can be no IDEA-based test accommodations. Under Section 504 the existence of a disability is not predicated on the need for special education, and therefore special education is not a prerequisite for related services. Because of this, Section 504 often meets the needs of those requiring "related services" or other accommodations which do not necessitate special education. The ability of Section 504 to offer services apart from special education, and thus to offer test accommodations without special education, is the primary reason why Section 504 is often associated with test accommodations.

In Massachusetts (Massachusetts Department of Education, 1995), "if a student is found *not* eligible for special education but needs a related service, e.g., speech articulation services, this need should be considered a prereferral strategy or Section 504 service." Likewise, "where a student *is fluent* in ASL and providing ASL is an accommodation that enables the student to participate in regular education, the student might not need special education services but would require an accommodation, e.g., sign language interpreter, under Section 504 of the Rehabilitation Act." Although Section 504 can be used to provide the complete range of special education and related services, it is often used to meet a specific test need or to provide a specific test strategy.

Rothstein (1990) noted that "the student with an orthopedic impairment who requires neither special education or related services is probably one of the most frequent cases where the student would fall under Section 504, but perhaps not" IDEA coverage (p. 62). In the case of a student with an orthopedic impairment, a student who is deaf, or auditorily impaired student, no special education programming or services might be needed other than relatively minor classroom adjustment (e.g., preferential seating).

No Current IEP

If a student has been declassified, but requires accommodations as indicated by the initial IEP (and therefore "has a record of such an impairment"), these accommodations are provided for the remainder of the student's education unless otherwise changed. As discussed above, an individual with a record of a disability is covered under the Section 504 definition of a disability.[39] Declassification is an often neglected goal of special education, but once a student had been declassified there might still be a need for test accommodations.

No IEP or Section 504 Plan

There are four situations when a student with no IEP or Section 504 Plan might receive test accommodations. First, many teachers will automatically make what might be called formative test accommodations. If a student does not understand test instructions, one would hope that a written mandate is not necessary before a teacher will repeat the instructions. As a result, even though a student might not have an IEP or Section 504 plan, there might be extant test accommodations in use either on a test-by-test basis or as a general service. Long before the emergence of the IEP, the test needs of students with many types of disabilities have been accommodated as a result of the perspicacity and individual efforts of teachers and other school personnel.

Second, "before any action is taken with respect to the initial placement of a child with a disability in programs providing special education and related services, a full and individual evaluation of the child's educational needs must be conducted".[40] Test accommodations might be necessary in order to accurately determine present levels of performance and/or to determine what test accommodations are necessary in the way of goals and services.

Third, if a student is disabled shortly before a test is to be administered, or if a student has a disability but no record of such a disability, test accommodations are generally possible but usually some type of documentation is required. For example, the SAT requires an IEP or two-signed documents (e.g., physician, psychologist, LD specialist), but the IEP has priority over the two-signed document stipulation. At the statewide level, if a student has a disability but no IEP or Section

504 Plan, the school principal or the Multidisciplinary Team might have authority to make such modifications, depending on the state, and nature of the disability. In any case, if an individual is regarded or treated as having a disability, the individual is covered by Section 504.

Finally, even if a student does not have an IEP or a written Section 504 Plan, the student is nonetheless covered under Section 504 and is entitled to necessary and appropriate test accommodations. In this case, a student is entitled to at least those accommodations used during the normal course of instruction. If a student has no current IEP, and no formal Section 504 accommodation plan, and classroom test and other directions are signed to the student, standardized test directions under more formal test conditions should also be signed.

Based on IDEA and Section 504, both classified and nonclassified students are entitled to test accommodations. Accommodations for nonclassified students might be required because of a temporary need (e.g., resulting from an injury), non-English speaking or ESL students, a disabling condition which has not resulted in classification, or in an attempt to meet the needs of a student who has been declassified. For non-English speaking, ESL students or minority students, the necessary accommodation might involve providing a test which is not "racially or culturally discriminatory." If a student has limited English or has learned English as a second language, an individually administered test of intelligence which is standardized on students whose first language is English would not be appropriate.

Range of Test Accommodations

The number of possible test accommodations and various combinations of test accommodations (e.g., a reader plus the regular print test) is extremely large. In the development of a general test accommodation plan the following areas should be considered: (1) possible test accommodations, (2) the permissibility of using test accommodations, (3) test-related accommodations, and (4) disability-related accommodations. These four dimensions are not independent from one another and can act in concert or be diametrically opposed to one another. As a result, the test accommodation plan must consider not only possible accommodations, but the specific tests which require these accommodations, and the permissibility of using these accommodations with different tests and different disabilities.

Table 3.3 provides a general idea of the type and scope of accommodations which are available. Of course, a number of the modifications listed have several variations. For example, examiner training might include specific test training or developing diagnostic testing techniques, and augmentative communication can range from a relatively simple yes/no language board to sophisticated single-switch matrix alphabet scanning.

Table 3.3 Range of Test Accommodations.

Pretest Adaptations

Examiner rapport
Testing practice
Reading instructions
Signing instructions
Simplifying instructions
Individualized testing
Special testing location
Special seating

Format Accommodations	Using Aids	Response Modifications
Extended time	Magnification devices	Response simplification
Managed time	Auditory amplification	Nonverbal responses
Signing items	Computational aids	Oral responses
Reading items	Problem-solving aids	Recorded responses
Braille format	Computer aids	Multiple choice modifications
Recorded tests	Examiner aid	Augmentative communication
Large print format	Reading aids	Braille
Item layout	Writing aids	Amanuensis[11]

Posttest Accommodations

Alternative scores
Predicted scores
Using local norms
Using special norms
Content interpretation
Revised scoring
Response analysis
Modified grading

Permissibility of Accommodations

A test accommodations cannot be made without considering the permissibility of using the accommodation. There are several sources which can prevent an accommodation from being used such as the student, parents, the multidisciplinary evaluation team, the IEP development team, state guidelines, or test publisher guidelines.

A state agency, test publisher or school/district can all restrict the use of test accommodations. Because test accommodations are not uniform across different tests and different accommodations, the following examples illustrate the types of potential conflicts which can occur between various tests and test accommodation guidelines:

- A district might allow extended time, but a test publisher might prohibit this accommodation;
- A state agency might require that a competency test be given in one day, but a student's IEP states that tests can be given over a period of days;
- Tests are to be given in Braille, but the standardized test used by a school does not have a Braille format;
- An IEP allows reading tests to be read to a student, but this is prohibited by state and federal guidelines;
- A student with a physical disability is provided a scribe to record answers, but a writing test prohibits this accommodation;
- Content tests are to be read to a student, but a teacher feels that this type of accommodation is inappropriate;
- An IEP states that a test should be given by someone familiar with the student, but this might not be allowed by an agency or publisher.

Not all test accommodations can be used with all tests. For some tests an accommodation might not be permitted or even possible. If a test accommodation is disallowed by an agency, publisher or state, this does not mean that the accommodation is not important or should not be included in the student's IEP. For example, the use of a calculator might be disallowed for a certain mathematics test, but this does not necessarily mean that the accommodation is disallowed for all mathematics tests. School districts frequently use test accommodations designed for specific state competency tests as a guide or general plan for providing test accommodations for all tests, even though the state guidelines might be intended for use with a specific test. A competency test might prohibit the use of a calculator for fact-type problems, but allow this accommodation when the ability being measured involves problem-solving rather than fact recall. Likewise, state guidelines might prohibit the use of extended time for specific state tests, but this would not apply to all tests nor, in all likelihood, would the intent of this prohibition be to preclude the use of extended time for all tests.

There are no hard and fast rules concerning precedence between different individuals, agencies and test publishers when the permissibility of an accommodation is in question. For the most part, the following will prevail: (1) teachers are expected to make a good faith effort to implement IEP mandated test accommodations, and (2) IEP-designated test accommodations should be secondary to specific prohibitions against using these types of accommodations.

The permissibility of a test accommodation is not always known. Standardized achievement tests generally do not articulate every possible accommodation which is allowed or disallowed, but usually offer a provision which states that departing from the standardization procedures will detract from the test validity and meaningfulness of the test norms. If a test publisher explicitly prohibits the use of an accommodation, this guideline should be followed. However, the legal/bureaucratic consequences associated with following or not following test publisher guidelines is not the same for all tests. If a standardized achievement test states that "time limits for tests should be strictly adhered to," a need might exist whereby this guideline is not followed in order to test a student's ability rather than disability. In this case, the test publisher is offering a disclaimer that a certain type of test accommodation (viz., extending time limits) might adversely affect test validity. If a state agency prohibits a certain accommodation, or a teacher decides not to use a mandated accommodation, the legal if not bureaucratic repercussions can be severe.

For the most part, classroom tests provide the greatest flexibility in terms of permissible test accommodations. Commercial tests generally have sparse guidelines, little research concerning test validity when used with students having disabilities, and limited special test formats. Statewide competency test programs tend to be very idiosyncratic with respect to allowed and disallowed test accommodations. The result of all this is often a relatively incoherent overall test accommodation plan when viewed in toto.

Test-related Accommodations

Often when developing a test accommodation plan, the suitability of a test accommodation for specific tests is not considered. An accommodation which is available for a statewide test might not be available for a school achievement test; extended time might be possible with one test but prohibited by the publisher of a standardized test; providing large print or a Braille format might be possible with some tests, not possible with others, and require "related services" (e.g., the technology and personnel resources to transcribe tests). Table 3.4 describes several categories of tests which might require adaptation or modification, or which provide test adaptations or modifications.

Each category of tests has its own set of restraints as to what accommodations are and are not possible. The accommodation plan should be at least aware of what accommodations are possible for each type of test, which are prohibited, and which are not possible. If the test accommodation requires a translator to sign directions, provisions must be made to insure that such a format is available. If for some reason the test cannot be given in this format, this should be considered during the specification of the accommodation. Likewise, reading content test items might be necessary, but this accommodation would be inappropriate if prohibited by the state or test publisher.

Disability-Related Accommodations

There is a relationship with the type of test accommodation recommended for a student and specific disability categories. A student classified as learning disabled with a severe reading problem might require a scripted or recorded test; a visually impaired student might require either large print or Braille; and an orthopedically impaired student might require a modified response mode. For several categories the relationship between the disability and accommodation is quite close. Braille is obviously associated with visual impairments, sign language with hearing impairments, and augmentative communication with physical disabilities (e.g., orthopedic impairments). Nonetheless, these three categories account for only 3.01 percent (see Table 3.2) of all students receiving services. The vast majority of accommodations are not necessarily bound to a specific disability category. For example, extended time might be appropriate for some stu-

Table 3.4 Tests Which Might Require Test Accommodations.

Category	Example
Classroom Tests	Quizzes Basal-series Tests Essay Tests End-of-term Tests
Achievement Tests	Stanford Achievement Test Metropolitan Achievement Test Iowa Test of Basic Skills California Achievement Test
Wide-Range Tests	Keymath–Revised Peabody Individual Achievement Test–Revised (PIAT-R) Wide Range Achievement Test–Revised (WRAT-R) Woodcock Reading Mastery Tests–R (WRMT-R)
Psychological Tests	Wechsler Intelligence Scale for Children–III (WISC-III) Stanford-Binet Intelligence Scale–Revised (SB-R) Peabody Picture Vocabulary Test–Revised (PPVT) Kaufman Assessment Battery for Children (K-ABC)
Statewide Tests	Connecticut Mastery Test (CMT) New York Regents Competency test (RCT) Wisconsin Student Assessment System (WSAS) Texas Assessment of Academic Skills (TAAS)
Admission Tests	SAT (Scholastic Aptitude Test) ACT (American College Testing Program)
Certification Tests	General Education Development (GED)

dents in all category groups or completely inappropriate for some students in all category groups.

Although disability categories are intended to represent a homogeneous group of students with respect to a specific impairment, the educational needs of students within any given category is extremely heterogeneous so that there are students who are deaf who cannot use sign language and legally blind students who cannot read Braille. This diverseness is a function of wide-ranging ability levels, the confounding affects of secondary disabilities, and varying if not diametrically opposed instructional methodologies (e.g., sign language versus oral communication in deaf education). For a school achievement test, one orthopedically impaired student might be able to use a single switch device; a second student might have the cognitive ability to use such a device but a lack of instruction might preclude its use; and a third student might not only have a severe expressive motor problem but an underlying cognitive deficit as well.

Categories of disabilities do have an element of commonality with the exception of specific learning disabilities. A specific learning disability is a category created more by exclusion rather than by an identifiable disability. If a student has a problem (i.e., "...understanding or in using language, spoken or written..." etc.), a student can be classified as having a learning disability if the student's problem is not "primarily the result of visual, hearing, or motor, of mental retardation, of emotional disturbance, or of environmental, cultural, or economic disadvantage."[42] Table 3.5 describes IDEA disability categories and corresponding test accommodations which are sometimes appropriate.

Table 3.5 Test Accommodations by Disability.

Category	Possible Accommodation
Specific learning disability	Reader, separate room, extended time, large print, reading aids, writing aids, computational aids
Speech or language impairments	Nonverbal tests, augmentative communication, measures of receptive language
Mental retardation	Enhanced instructions, reader, extended time, individualized testing, special seating
Serious emotional disturbance	Extended time, individualized testing, separate location, periodized testing, managed testing time
Multiple disabilities	Individualized testing, augmentative communication, special location, special facilities
Hearing impairments	Interpreter, extended time, separate location, special seating
Other health impairments	Extended time, breaks, special location, accessible location, individualized testing, accessible location
Orthopedic impairments	Special facilities, augmentative communication, separate location, extended time
Visual impairments	Magnification devices, Braille, large print, scribe, recorded tests, extended time, special seating
Autism	Augmentative communication, individualized testing, nonverbal assessment, separate location
Brain injury	Augmentative communication, special facilities, separate location, individualized testing
Deaf-blindness	Magnification devices, auditory aids, nonverbal assessment, augmentative communication, interpreter

Test accommodations cannot be made without consideration of prior educational experiences. A student with a hearing impairment may or may not be able to use sign language. Indeed, using an inappropriate mode of communication might have a deleterious effect on test performance (in addition to precipitating the wrath of the student's parents or guardian).

Test accommodations and the regular classroom. Students in regular classes, either on a full-time or part-time basis, will probably be evaluated using tests specific to the regular classroom environment as opposed to students in separate classes or schools. Thus, 78.9% of the students with specific learning disabilities, and 94.6% of the students with speech or language impairments receive services in either regular classes or resource rooms. However, 47.1% of students with multiple disabilities receive services in separate classes, 35.9% of students with autism receive services in separate schools, and only 28.6% of deaf-blind students receive services in residential facilities (16th Annual Report to Congress, 1994, p. 14).

Generic accommodations. If identifying accommodations on an individual basis has resulted in a lack of agreement, the use of generic test accommodations is even more problematic in terms of meeting explicit test accommodation needs. Grise, Beattie and Algozzine (1982) modified the Florida State Student Assessment test for use with 344 fifth grade learning disabled students. The modifications included arranging items in terms of difficulty, using a vertical format for multiple-choice items, and using unjustified reading passage format, using boxes to highlight reading passage items, and sample items. Although the intent of these modifications was to facilitate the performance of LD students, developing tests which are easy-to-follow, hierarchical in nature, and have ample sample items will probably benefit students who are not classified as having disabilities but need remediation, and also benefit all students whether or not they have a disability. For the most part, generic test accommodations are appropriate when the accommodations are used with all students, but these types of accommodations should not be used based solely on categorization rather than specific test needs.

Accommodation Plans

With respect to the concept of a "plan," test accommodations have been dealt with as part of an overall assessment plan, as part of an IEP or IEP-type document, and in relation to Section 504 accommodation plans. McLoughlin and Lewis (1990) described the need for an Individual Assessment Plan (IAP) which is a systematic approach for evaluating students with disabilities (p. 33). The essence of the IAP is the development of a series of precise questions which lead to a focused and efficient assessment of a student's needs. On a similar basis, selecting test accommodations should be the result of a systematic effort involving all aspects of referral, evaluation, determining goals and providing special education and related services.

State Accommodation Guidelines

State test accommodation guidelines vary from general plans which are intended to apply to classroom, local, state and national examination programs to those which are intended for specific state tests. The New York State test accommodation manual (New State Education Department, 1995) provides "policies and information regarding test access and modification which will assist school staff, parents, students, and others involved in designing educational programs and setting academic and career goals for students with disabilities" (p. vi). In Connecticut (Connecticut State Department of Education, 1996), guidelines are provided for "school district personnel when making decisions about testing students on the Connecticut Mastery Test and/or Connecticut Academic Performance Test" (p. 1). Test accommodations allowed by a state relating to specific tests produced by the state is straightforward enough, but when a highly questionable test accommodation such as reading reading-test questions to a student, a conflict can arise when the state guidelines are used as general guidelines for all testing.

Thurlow, Ysseldyke and Silverstein (1993) evaluated the written guidelines for 21 states and noted the "tremendous variance in the number and types of accommodations" (p. 18). Several accommodations were "directly prohibited in a written document" by several states (p. 18) such as interpreting directions (Georgia), extended time (Delaware & Tennessee), and more test breaks (Maryland). The ten accommodations cited most frequently by the 21 states were reported as follows (where the number in parentheses indicates the number of states): Braille (16), large print (14), individual testing (13), small group testing (12), computer/typewriter response (11), more breaks (9), oral reading/signing directions (9), more time (8), response assistance/interpretation (8), special education class testing (7). Thurlow et al. (p. 19) reported that the basis of accommodations by states included allowing those which are used in the classroom (3), accommodations determined by a committee (4), and accommodations specified by the IEP committee (11).

College Admission Test Accommodation Plans

The College Entrance Examination Board (the Scholastic Assessment Test or SAT) and The American College Testing (ACT) assessment program have very thorough test accommodation plans. For both the SAT and ACT, a variety of test accommodations are allowed if the accommodations are stated in the student's IEP or if other documentation is available (signed documents). The accommodations for these tests fall into four general categories as shown in Table 3.6: (1) aids (e.g., calculator, recorder), (2) format (e.g., Braille, large print), (3) location, and (4) extended time. Both the SAT and ACT require documentation before an accommodation is allowed, and the IEP, although not the only means for obtaining a test accommodation, is central to this task. Ragosta and Wendler (1992, p. 11) indicated that the likelihood of an accommodation being made is almost certain if the student has a current IEP. This possibility falls into the "likely" category for high school students who have acquired the disability shortly before or after completing high school. A student who had an IEP in elementary school but not in high school is a "possible" candidate for an accommodation. And students who have no IEP and no history of needing an accommodation are in the "doubtful" category as to qualifying for a test accommodation. The following table provides a brief summary of SAT and ACT requirements for documentation, possible accommodations, and position on flagging (which is discussed in detail in Chapter 2).

Table 3.6 SAT and ACT Test Accommodation Plans.

Category	SAT	ACT
Documentation	1. IEP or two-signed documents (e.g., physician, psychologist, LD specialist). The IEP has priority over the two-signed document stipulation 2. Currently receiving accommodation for tests as those requested for SAT	IEP within the last three years. "Only students with current, documented disabilities who have been professionally diagnosed as having physical, psychological, or learning disabilities, and cannot test under standard conditions are eligible for special testing" (p. 1).
Aids	Reader Recorder Sign-language (instructions only) Magnifying devices Typewriter Calculator Large block answer sheets	Sign language for instructions Recorder Calculator
Format	Regular type Large type Braille Cassette (used with above) Script (for reader)	Regular type Large type Braille Cassette with regular type Cassette with large type Cassette with raised line/braille Reader's script with regular type Reader's script with large type Reader's script with raised Line/braille
Location	Separate room	"Mutually convenient"
Extended Time	4.5 hours allowed (1.5 to 2 hours)	Based on ACT guidelines
Flagging	"Nonstandard Administration"	"SPECIAL" under type of testing on reports (reasons for the testing accommodations are not stated in the students reports)

GRE accommodations. The Graduate Record Examination provides several alternative formats including Braille (1972 Nemeth Code), 18-point large print, and Cassette with large print or Braille figure supplement. The subject tests are available in 14-point large print. Other accommodations available include additional testing time, separate testing room, recorded answers, test reader, and interpreter. In order to receive a test accommodation, the GRE requires a letter stating accommodations needs and a letter of certification indicating the need and use of the accommodation being requested at the student's college or university. If a letter of certification is not available, a letter from a certified professional indicating the disability and needed accommodations, and a letter from the college or university indicating that similar accommodations are currently being used.

The GRE also provides several accommodations for students with disabilities for the general GRE test given through the computer-based testing program. These accommodations include additional time and breaks, adjustable colors, Kensington Trackball Mouse, HeadMaster Mouse, and Zoomtext.

Miller Analogies Test. The Miller Analogies Test (MAT) is licensed by the Psychological Corporation to Controlled Testing Centers and is used by some colleges and universities as one criterion for graduate school admission. The MAT is comprised of 100 multiple-choice partial analogies which are administered in 50 minutes. If a candidate can provide current documentation from a professional (e.g., physician, social worker, optometrist) that a disability requires an accommodation in order to take a standardized multiple-choice test, a nonstandard administration will be given. Test accommodations for the MAT include extra time, Braille and large print editions, a reader, or scribe.

GED accommodations. The General Educational Development (GED) testing program provides three special test editions: audio-cassette, Braille, and large print. In 1990, the General Educational Development Testing Service administered 391 cassette, 14 Braille, and 999 large print versions of the GED.

Developing a Test Accommodation Plan

Although a state educational agency might have information relating to test accommodations or test exemptions, the local educational agency is ultimately responsible for identifying individual needs and providing services. As discussed in Chapter 4, a major criticism of the IEP is that it is primarily used to demonstrate compliance rather than to meet individual student needs. As is the case with IEPs in general, an effective test accommodation plan does not center about a list of allowable test accommodations, but an overall commitment to consider the many variables which determine what test accommodations are appropriate, for what tests, and for what students.

The purpose of a test accommodation plan is not to generate another document, but rather to consider factors which will facilitate the process of providing individualized and effective test accommodations. The following are several areas which should be considered when developing an overall test accommodation plan:

Review regulations. A test accommodation plan should begin with a thorough review of both federal and state laws, regulations and/or guidelines which are available concerning test adaptations, modifications and exemptions.

Review tests. All test accommodations might not be possible with all tests, and there might be certain tests which will have no accommodations. Test accommodations must be viewed in relation to the types of accommodations allowed and tests used. The IEP team must be aware that not all test accommodations are permitted or even feasible for state, schoolwide and classroom tests.

Consider disabilities. Available statistics concerning disabilities provides a general idea as to the type and number of disabilities which might be expected within a school district. A consideration of the needs of students with different disabilities will provide a practical frame of reference for identifying effective accommodations and potential problems.

For certain students and disabilities, the necessary test accommodations are fairly obvious. For a student who uses Braille, tests should be in Braille. However, these types of obvious accommodations will actually be relatively few in number. The majority of accommodations will involve students with learning, behavioral and intellectual disabilities. As a result, serious attention must be given to test accommodations required by students with these types of disabilities, and problems and questions which occur regarding these disabilities. Whatever the test accommodation needs of a school or district, an attempt should be made to evaluate the validity and effectiveness of frequently used test accommodations.

Examine services. The amount of services to be provided must be stated in the IEP, so that the level of the agency's commitment of resources will be clear to parents and other IEP team members. The amount of time to be committed to each of the various services to be provided must be appropriate to that specific service, and stated in the IEP in a manner that is clear to all who are involved in both the development and implementation of the IEP.

Review documentation. Examine the appropriateness of IEP forms and Section 504 documentation with respect to test accommodations. The goal should not be to simply show compliance (e.g., by providing a long list of every conceivable test accommodations) but to develop a plan which provides test accommodations that results in the assessment of ability rather than disability. Often a modest degree of reflection concerning the suitability of test accommodation documentation is all that is needed in this regard.

Provide inservice training. Inservice training is essential for developing an effective test accommodation plan. A workshop might be held to consider test accommodation services, techniques (e.g., orally reading tests), or general topics relating to test accommodations. What is most essential is the need to recognize that a valid and effective test accommodation entails more than checking a box on an IEP form. Workshops and inservice training should be used to provide a foundation for the implementation of test accommodations. A general workshop regarding the IEP process and test accommodations will help clarify misconceptions relating to accommodations, and responsibilities concerning the implementation of accommodations. For personnel involved in providing services, special inservice workshops might involve assistive technology, oral reading or individualized testing.

ENDNOTES

1. 34 C.F.R. §300.128
2. 34 C.F.R. §300.130
3. 34 C.F.R. §300.133
4. 34 C.F.R. §300.146
5. 34 C.F.R. §300.532
6. IDEA Amendments Act of 1997, H.R. 5, Section 653(c)(3)
7. IDEA Amendments Act of 1997, H.R. 5, Section 613(g)
8. IDEA Amendments Act of 1997, H.R. 5, Section 651(b)
9. Although test accommodations are often associated with IEPs or Section 504 needs, other plans might necessitate assessment adaptations, alternative assessments, and modifications. For infants and toddlers an Individualized Family Service Plan (IFSP) is required which entails "a multidisciplinary assessment of the unique strengths needs" and which includes "a statement of the infants's or toddler's present

levels of physical development, cognitive development, communication development, social or emotional development, and adaptive development, based on acceptable objective criteria" (20 U.S.C. §1477). The types of assessment accommodations associated with an IFSP will obviously place emphasis on the factors cited above rather than school-based skills, but whenever an assessment is made "based on acceptable objective criteria" factors which can impinge on the assessment's reliability and validity should be considered. Just as for school-age students, infants, toddlers and preschool children are entitled to assessments and evaluations which "have been validated for the specific purpose for which they are used,

"are administered by trained personnel," and are administered so that the student's ability rather than disability is being measured (34 C.F.R. §300.532).

10. 34 C.F.R. §300.346(a)(2), (3) & (5)

11. 34 C.F.R. §300.532(b)

12. see 34 C.F.R. §300.104.3(j)

13. 34 C.F.R. §300.7

14. Source: 18th Annual Report to Congress on the Implementation of the Individuals with Disabilities Education Act (1996), Washington, D.C. (ED 400 673).As per P.L. 99-457, disability data by category is only collected for age groups 6-11, 12-17, and 18-21 (20 U.S.C. §1418(b)).

15. The IDEA Amendments of 1997 are less emphatic with respect to categorization and classification (but certainly not oblivious to special education categories in that "Nothing in this Act requires that children be classified by their disability so long as each child who has a disability listed in Section 602 and who, by reason of that disability, needs special education and related services and is regarded as a child with a disability under this part (Section 612(a)(3)(B)).

16. 34. C.F.R. §104.3(j)(1)

17. 34 C.F.R. §104.3(j)(2)(iv)

18. 34 C.F.R. §§300.340-.350

19. 34 C.F.R. §104.33(b)(1)(i)

20. 34 C.F.R. §104.33(b)(2)

21.See the Massachusetts Department of Education question and answer guide on the new special education IEP, 1995.

22. Depart of Public Instruction Guidelines for nondiscriminatory testing, Wisconsin Department of Public Instruction, 1996.

23. The term "plan" should be used to mean a program, schedule or agenda for achieving stated accommodation goals, and does not mean a written individualized education "plan." In Section 504 the only reference to a plan is a "transition plan" (34 C.F.R. §104.22(2)) involving a plan to be completed within a six month period to make a facility accessible.

24. See 34 C.F.R. §104, Appendix A 3., 4. and 5. for a discussion of "handicap" under section 504.

25. 34 C.F.R. §300.7(b)(10)

26. Children and Adults with Attention Deficit Disorders (CHADD)

27. 34 C.F.R. §104.3(j)(i)

28. 34 C.F.R. §104.35(b)

29.   34 C.F.R. §104. 33(b)(2)
30.   34 C.F.R. §300, Appendix C (Question #57)
31.   34 C.F.R. §104.33(b)(1)(i)
32.   34 C.F.R. §104.32(a)
33.   34 C.F.R. §104.33(b)
34.   34 C.F.R. §104.35(b)
35.   34 C.F.R. §104.35(c)(3)
36.   34 C.F.R. §104.35(c)(2) also requires the documentation of information used in the interpretation of data and making placement decisions.
37.   34 C.F.R. §104.35(b) requires the evaluation and placement of persons who need special education or related services.
38.   34 C.F.R. §300.17 (Note 1)
39.   34 C.F.R. §104.3(j)
40.   34 C.F.R. §300.531
41.   Amanuensis refers to an individual who copies from dictation. For example, a student might require an aid to record responses for essay-type tests where the task is content-based rather than an exercise to evaluate writing skills.
42.   34 C.F.R. §300.7(b)(10)

Chapter 4

IEP TEST ACCOMMODATIONS

The IEP Process

An IEP is "a written statement for a child with a disability that is developed and implemented in accordance with"[1] IDEA regulations. In addition, state agencies are responsible for ensuring that both public and private schools have IEP programs.[2] The IEP is not a "guarantee" that a student will achieve the stated IEP goals,[3] but that special education and related services will be provided in accordance with an IEP.

Each state agency is required to develop an annual program which ensures "that all children with disabilities, regardless of the severity of their disability, and who are in need of special education and related services are identified, located, and evaluated."[4] The process of identifying a student with a disability usually begins with a referral to an administrator, professional in special education or the chairperson of the multidisciplinary team. The multidisciplinary team plays a fundamental role in identifying and specifying needed test accommodations. The multidisciplinary team includes "at least one teacher or other specialist with knowledge in the area of suspected disability."[5] If the student is thought to have a learning disability, the team also includes a classroom teacher and a "person qualified to conduct individual diagnostic evaluations."[6]

After a referral has been made, the multidisciplinary team gathers information so that a decision concerning services can be made. If a decision is made that a student requires special education and related services, an IEP is developed and implemented. The participants[7] at the IEP meeting include a representative of the public school, the child's teacher, one or both parents, a member of the evaluation team, and other individuals at the discretion of the parents or agency. As previously noted, to be covered under IDEA, and thus to need an IEP, the student must have a disability as defined in the regulations[8] and must "need" special education.

The essential elements of the IEP process include the IEP meeting and the IEP document itself. In addition the IEP process has several distinct purposes and functions:[9]

> a. The IEP meeting serves as a communication vehicle between parents and school personnel, and enables them, as equal participants, to jointly decide what the child's needs are, what services will be provided to meet those needs, and what the anticipated outcomes may be.

> b. The IEP process provides an opportunity for resolving any differences between the parents and the agency concerning the special education needs of a child with a disability.

> c. The IEP sets forth in writing a commitment of resources necessary to enable a child with a disability to receive needed special education and related services.

> d. The IEP is a management tool that is used to ensure that each child with a disability is provided special education and related services appropriate to the child's special learning needs.

> e. The IEP is a compliance/monitoring document which may be used by authorized monitoring personnel from each governmental level to determine whether a child with a disability is actually receiving the free appropriate public education agreed to by the parents and the school.

> f. The IEP serves as an evaluation device for use in determining the extent of the child's progress toward meeting the projected outcomes.

In terms of test accommodations, the IEP can be used to (1) ensure that parents, teachers, and school personnel are aware of all necessary test accommodations, (2) determine and resolve the need for test accommodations, (3) specify resources (e.g., aids, interpreters, readers) necessary to provide the test accommodation services, (4) oversee the provision of test accommodation services, (5) demonstrate compliance with regulations relating to test accommodations, and 6) to determine the ability to participate in a regular education testing program.

As discussed below, the purpose and function of an IEP is sometimes secondary to showing compliance rather than developing a viable and effective plan for providing special education and related services. If a student needs a particular service (e.g., test accommodation), to be in compliance the service must not only be included in the IEP but the service must be provided. Depending on student test needs, test accommodations can be included in one or more parts of an IEP. For example, test accommodations can be used in the individual evaluation to determine present levels of educational performance, as one of the annual goals (e.g., to participate in group testing), or as a service or aid to benefit from special or regular education. During the individual evaluation phase, a test accommodation might be used to better evaluate ability and to determine general educational test needs. If necessary, a test accommodation can be part of a goal to demonstrate a level of performance as a result of the accommodation (e.g., passing a content area test when given orally), or a goal to reduce the restrictiveness of an accommodation (e.g., passing a classroom test without a previously used accommodation).

In addition to allowing a student to benefit from all manner of tests, one of the primary functions of a test accommodation is to maximize performance in the regular education program:

> If modifications (supplementary aids and services) to the regular education program are necessary to ensure the child's participation in that program, those modifications must be described in the child's IEP (e.g., for a hearing impaired child, special seating arrangements or the provision of assignments in writing). This applies to any regular education program in which the student may participate, including physical education, art, music, and vocational education.[10]

This does not mean that if a student is not able to participate in the regular education program, test accommodations are not necessary. First and foremost, tests should not be discriminatory. No matter what type of test is used, where the testing takes place, or whether the test is standardized or not, a test should not "deny a qualified handicapped person an opportunity to participate in or benefit from the aid, benefit, or service."[11]

The range of services which must be provided in an IEP, including test accommodations, is based on need and not on the availability or cost of such services:

> Each public agency must provide FAPE to all children with disabilities under its jurisdiction. Therefore, the IEP for a child with a disability must

include all of the specific special education and related services needed by the child – as determined by the child's current evaluation. This means that the services must be listed in the IEP even if they are not directly available from the local agency, and must be provided by the agency through contract or other arrangements.[12]

The IDEA Amendments of 1997 are more explicit with respect to the need for identifying test modifications in that "a statement of any individual modifications in the administration of state or districtwide assessments of student achievement that are needed in order for the child to participate in such assessment."[13]

IEP Criticisms

The IEP is the primary vehicle for designating and providing special education services. Unfortunately, the IEP concept has been used for purposes other than developing viable individual education programs. Smith (1990) offered a bleak evaluation of the status of the IEP by concluding that "...researchers have scrutinized the document for procedural compliance and quality indicators. Literature resulting from these analyses has clearly implicated the IEP process and document as ineffective, incomplete and faulty" (p. 85).

One of the basic criticisms of IEPs is that the document is used primarily to show compliance rather than to develop meaningful educational programs. What Lauer and Smith (1994) consider an "egregious example of this failure" to address real educational needs is the failure to link identified needs with goals and objectives. In other words, the IEP has become a legalistic device to show the school is in compliance with the regulations rather than actually providing meaningful and effective individualized educational programs and services (Smith, 1990; Smith, et al, 1995, p. 52). The need to comply rather than consider individual student needs is never more obvious than when examining the test accommodation component of many IEPs. With virtually no guidelines concerning either students, tests or disabilities, a usual practice is to list a series of high-profile accommodations (e.g., Braille, large print, extended time, etc.). The intent seems more to show that test accommodations have been considered rather than to develop a realistic accommodation plan for each student which takes into account the many factors which might influence the student's test performance, and to formulate a plan which will provide a valid assessment of ability.

Integrated IEP Components

IEP's are sometimes written so that the section or statement regarding test accommodations is seemingly unrelated to the other IEP components. As with all services specified in a student's IEP, test accommodations should be based on demonstrated need, should be designed to achieve a specific purpose, and should be evaluated whenever the IEP is reevaluated.

A student's IEP must include the following six elements:

1. Present levels of educational performance;

2. Annual goals and individual objectives;

3. Special education, related services, and regular education participation;

4. Dates for duration and termination of services;

5. At least an annual evaluation of instructional objectives;

6. Transition services no later than age 16 (or younger if appropriate).[14]

The relationship between the basic IEP components and the designation and implementation of test accommodations is shown below. The degree to which test accommodations are integrated into an IEP depends on the need and magnitude of the accommodation. For one student, a simple statement indicating no accommodations are needed might be sufficient; for a second student, one specific test accommodation might be cited (e.g., special seating); and for a third student, references to test accommodations might be made in all elements of the IEP.

Each of the six primary IEP elements can affect the use or interpretation of test accommodations: (1) Present levels: tests and data which misrepresent performance because of a lack of test accommodations should be cited, as well as the use of tests with appropriate accommodations. (2) Statement of goals: specific test goals should be specified with and/or without test accommodations. (3) Statement of services: test accommodations and corresponding services should be indicated. (4) Dates for services: if different from other services, dates for the initiation of test accommodations should be stated. (5) Evaluation: an annual evaluation of the effectiveness of the test accommodation goals should be included. (6) Transition services: the regulations[15] have been modified to include a section specifying transition services no later than age 16 (or sooner if appropriate). Regarding test accommodations, this section should include accommodations which are needed for postsecondary schooling or for certification purposes.

Developing useful and meaningful IEP test accommodations requires consideration of all IEP components. An IEP might require no test accommodations or only a single aid or service which is easily implemented; but there are circumstances when an IEP must delineate levels of performance with and without accommodations, test accommodation goals, a detailed list of services and aids involving accommodations, specific time period when a test accommodation will be used, or how test accommodations will be evaluated.

Present Levels of Performance

One component of an IEP, indeed, the foundation of an IEP, is the need for "a statement of the child's present levels of educational performance."[16] Part of this "statement should accurately describe the effect of the child's disability on the child's performance in any area of education that is affected."[17] In order to evaluate ability when a disability is a factor the possible effects on test performance of the disability if test accommodations have or have not been used must be examined.

If test accommodations have not been used to determine present levels of educational performance, extant test data (e.g., achievement test scores) and data collected as part of the individual evaluation might misrepresent the student's ability. If a student is significantly below average on a content-area achievement test, factors such as reading, attention, test format might have had a negative effect on test performance. Anecdotal reports by the student's teacher might suggest that the student does have considerable ability in the content area, or at least more than what is reflected by the test. If this is the case, if information exists which suggests that the student's ability is not being assessed, this might indicate that some type of test accommodation might be necessary.

Existing data and information may or may not have been collected with appropriate test accommodations. This possibility should be taken into account when evaluating present levels of performance. For most students referred for special education or related services, a considerable amount of test information is available. The fairness, and usefulness of this information must be evaluated in light of test accommodations that may or may not have been used.

A test accommodation might be necessary in order to evaluate present levels of performance, but if this is the initial IEP for a student, there will be no guidelines for determining what accommodations are necessary. If a student requires abbreviated testing sessions because of a health impairment, this accommodation should be incorporated, at least to some extent, in the collection of assessment information that will be used in the construction of the IEP. In this regard, the classroom teacher is often an excellent source for determining test accommodations that might have been used during testing (e.g., enhanced instructions, seating location, etc.), and as an important source for determining the need for additional test accommodations. In any case, great care must be taken to ensure that data collected in the determination of present levels of performance accurately reflects, as best as possible, ability so that specifically-designed instruction is not indicated when all that is necessary is a test accommodation.

During the assessment of a student's present level of educational performance, the multidisciplinary team must also determine what test accommodations will be included in a student's IEP. The multidisciplinary team should indicate the test-taking needs of a student and what test accommodations should be included in the IEP to best meet these needs. For a student who is highly distractible, individualized testing might be appropriate; for a student with a severe reading disability, reading test questions to the student might be required; or for a student whose response mode is slow because of the test format or the preferred rate of response of the student, extended test time might be needed.

Statement of Goals and Objectives

Every IEP is required to have "a statement of annual goals, including short-term instructional objectives."[18] Goals and objectives in relation to test accommodations are useful for reducing the need for a test accommodation, or for identifying a higher level of performance which can be attained as a result of a test accommodation. Providing access to previously exempted or excluded tests, providing tests in a least restrictive environment (e.g., in the regular classroom rather than a special education classroom), or eliminating a test accommodation either on a temporary or permanent basis are all aimed at minimizing the need for test accommodations. Concerning the identification of a higher level of performance, passing a statewide test when given an accommodation might be a very worthwhile and attainable goal.

According to the regulations an IEP annual goal is a statement which indicates what a student can accomplish in a 12-month period while IEP objectives are "benchmarks for determining progress toward meeting the annual goals."[19] A possible test accommodation goal might be to participate in the regular education test program, or to take a classroom test without an accommodation. If the student has been taking tests outside of the regular classroom, an inclusionary goal might be for the student to take a certain test in the regular classroom. If a student has been exempted from taking standardized tests, taking a test, with or without accommodations, might be an important goal for present and future educational progress.

For all tests, a goal can involve either increased participation or a higher level of performance. An annual goal might be for the student to participate in a test from which the student had heretofore been exempted, to participate in testing with no or reduced test accommodations, or to achieve a specified level of performance when tested. Whenever a student is exempted from a test or test program, the possibility that the student has developed sufficient skills to make test participation a possibility should always be considered. Although certain test accommodations will be necessary on an ongoing basis, other test accommodations might be reconsidered as a result of successful remediation. For example, if a student is provided a reader for content tests, a goal might be to take one or more tests using the regular test format or to take the test using both formats.

If a student has not been able to pass a statewide test, identifying a goal which requires a student to pass the test might be both useful and attainable. If the student has always participated in the testing program, this is simply a useful testing goal; if the student has no or limited participation in the testing program, this is a useful test accommodation goal.

Being able to pass classroom tests, either in the regular classroom or in the special education setting, is obviously important for all students to receive a "full educational opportunity."[20] As a result, goals are used to mitigate the effects of a previous accommodation (e.g., a test exemption or exclusion), or to suggest a level of performance when a test accommodation has been made. Although "passing" implies a specific level of test performance, using goals to identify levels of test gain is a far more difficult task. Stating that a student will gain 1.0 years in social studies when the test is read to the student probably stretches the meaningfulness of the underlying scale. A gain from a grade level of 1.0 to 2.0 can mean many things, all of which depend on the test content, the relation between test and curriculum content, item difficulty, the number of items, and a variety of other psychometric factors.

There is not always a need to identify a specific test accommodation goal. If test accommodations are permanently in place (e.g., the use of Braille, an interpreter, large print) and have been shown to be valid and effective, this service might be all that is necessary in the way of test accommodations.

The intent of IEP objectives is to link IEP goals with present levels of educational performance. Consider a goal which stipulates that a student will pass a statewide competency test at the end of the year. There obviously should be a plan which will result in this overall goal being achieved. For example, a series of instructional objectives relating to the statewide curriculum might be developed. If a student has been excluded from regular classroom testing, an initial objective might be to take a regular classroom test in the special education setting, then to take a test in the regular classroom, and eventually to participate fully in the regular education classroom testing activities.

Although IEP objectives can link IEP goals with present levels of educational performance, one criticism of IEP development is the time required to document objectives at the expense of more meaningful annual goals. The IDEA Amendments of 1997 (P.L. 105-17) have consolidated objectives in the form of "measurable annual goals, including benchmarks or short-term objectives."[21] A primary purpose of these annual measurable goals is to focus on regular education participation, and those services and modifications necessary to attain the annual objectives. The statement of measurable annual objectives is "related to meeting the child's needs that result from the child's disability to enable the child to be involved in and progress in the general curriculum; and meeting each of the child's other educational needs that result from the child's disability."[22]

Services

This section includes specific special education and related services, and the degree to which the student will participate in the regular school programs.[23] Related services "means transportation and such developmental, corrective, and other supportive services as are required to assist a child with a disability to benefit from special education."[24]

Related services are not just for a student in a special education class but for all students who are identified as needing special education. All students identified as needing special education are entitled to "psychological services"[25] (viz., administering and interpreting psychological and educational tests), "speech pathology,"[26] and related services which will assist the student "to perform tasks for independent functioning"[27] (e.g., using an augmentative communication device).

Supplementary aids and services are modifications to the regular education program "necessary to ensure the child's participation in that program."[28] A student might require enlarged print, special seating arrangements or extended time for a school or statewide achievement test.

The distinction between related and supplementary aids and services concerns focus rather than substance, but a distinction sometimes is made based on the extent of the service. For example, special seating arrangements, providing a large print test version, or ensuring that a student is able to understand test instructions might be classified as supplementary services; while using a reader to read tests, or having other professionals administer tests might be classified as related services. For the most part related services emphasize benefiting from special education, and supplementary services focus on the regular education curriculum. Obviously, a student might need large print, extended time, or special seating arrangements regardless of whether the testing involves special or regular education. Likewise, a student with transportation needs or communication needs might require a service to benefit from special education and to participate in regular education. Finally, there is not always a clearcut distinction between related and supplementary services based on the magnitude of the service. Using an aide or reader to administer tests is an extensive accommodations, while giving a student preferential seating, repeating instructions, or allowing extra time to complete a test is a minimal expenditure of time or money. However, if a student must be administered tests individually because of time restraints, or if a test version must be developed (e.g., transcribed), the magnitude of the accommodations can be changed considerably.

The inclusion of test accommodations can be integrated into the services section of an IEP but there are several reasons why this IEP section might be subdivided to highlight test accommodations. First, not all program services and test accommodations might be applicable to all tests. A student might have a translator in the regular classroom, be allowed to use a calculator, or have a reader read test questions, but certain tests or testing programs might disallow these accommodations. Second, tests and testing programs are subject to more stringent guidelines with respect to validity and administration than specifically designed instruction. A teacher has considerable freedom to tailor instruction to meet the needs of a student, but although tests are "tailored to assess specific areas of educational need," they are also administered "in conformance with the instructions provided by the producer."[29] Third, testing can be very important in determining whether a student will participate in regular education. If a student is excluded from school or statewide testing, this can exclude the student from receiving an appropriate education and from benefiting from a regular education. For this reason every attempt should be made to provide school and statewide tests individually, in a special education setting or in a regular education testing environment. The services section of an IEP must include a statement concerning participation in regular education programs, but when applied to testing, determining participation often requires how a test can be accommodated to allow participation rather than were that participation will take place. Because of the importance of testing, and the variety of tests used, a separate IEP test accommodation section will often clarify the rationale, use and implementation of accommodations.

Although IDEA seems to group the specification of test accommodations with special education, related services and regular education participation, individual states have used various approaches for incor-

---

[a]Testing might be a necessary part of special education and/or regular education in which case-related services might be necessary for the student to benefit from special education testing or to participate, via supplementary aids and services, in regular education testing programs.

porating test accommodations in IEPs. Some states follow IDEA guidelines which implicitly address the need for test accommodations,[a] while other states specifically identify the need for test accommodations in the IEP. Florida IEP guidelines[30] closely parallel IDEA IEP guidelines, while in California the IEP format is similar to IDEA but a distinction is made between "the specific special educational instruction and related services required by the pupil" and "the extent to which the pupil will be able to participate in regular educational programs."[31] In addition, California requires a statement of "any alternative means and modes necessary for the pupil to complete the district's prescribed course of study and to meet or exceed proficiency standards for graduation" for students in grades 7 to 12.[32]

New York requires a section dealing with services and regular participation, but also specifies an additional section detailing "those testing modifications to be used consistently by the pupil in the recommended educational program."[33] In Ohio services, related services, regular education participation and test accommodations are included in the following IEP components:

> (v) A statement of the specific special education and related services to be provided to the learner, which indicates the amount of time to be committed to each service, the projected date for initiation, and the anticipated duration of each service;
>
> (vi) A statement of the extent to which the learner is to be removed from the regular education environment, and justification for the removal;
>
> (vii) A description of the modifications and adaptations that are necessary for a learner with a disability to participate in a regular education program, including education, art, music, and vocational education;
>
> (viii) A statement of what modifications and adaptations, if any, are needed to enable a learner to participate in all tests and evaluations used for instruction, including proficiency tests. If a learner has been exempted from the proficiency tests, this must be documented in the IEP;[34]

And to the north of IDEA in Canada, IEPs in British Columbia (1994) must outline "all the required adaptations to educational materials, and instructional and assessment methods" and "all the support services to be provided."

Although the IEP elements[35] described in the IDEA Amendments of 1997 make a distinction between "a statement of the special education and related services and supplementary aids and services" and "a statement of any individual modifications in the administration of state or districtwide assessments of student achievement that are needed in order for the child to participate in such assessment,"[36] both are designed to maximize regular education participation.

As important as the goal of regular educational participation is, this should not overshadow the need to test a student's ability rather than disability regardless of where the student is educated or the extent the student participates in regular or special educational settings. For a student with no academic skills, a language board or augmentative communication device might be necessary to assess progress although there might be no appropriate state or districtwide test which could be used with this student. The accommodations needed to assess this student's ability are just as important as accommodations needed to assess another student's academic skills, the only difference being that the former might be referred to as "assessment accommodations" and the latter as "test accommodations." Both are necessary to measure ability and progress, and both should be included in the IEP or Section 504 document if necessary.

Refusing services. An assumption cannot be made that when a recommendation for a test accommodation is made, that the accommodation will be accepted by all interested parties. A teacher might feel that an accommodation gives a student an unfair advantage; an accommodation might be contrary to school policy or regulations; or a student (or parent) might want to be tested exactly as other students.

As best as possible, the student should be allowed to participate in test accommodation decisions and should be told what accommodations are being made and why. Requiring a student to take a test under conditions which the student finds disagreeable might not result in a refusal to be tested, but can result in a disinclination or motivation to fully participate in the testing. Coercing a student to take a test under conditions which are contrary to the student's wishes might yield results which are less informative than administering the test without the accommodation.

If there is a problem on the part of a student with an accommodation, especially if this affects the student's performance, the accommodation and the student's objections should be given serious consideration. More importantly, if a student refuses an accommodation, this refusal should be documented. The purpose of this documentation is to reevaluate the need of the accommodation, and to address the specific objection on the part of the student. If a student will not cooperate, an attempt should be made to determine the basis of the objection as soon as possible and to determine from the student what would be an acceptable form of accommodation. This does not mean that whatever the student wants in terms of receiving or not receiving an accommodation is given, but rather the student is an obviously important source of information for making or not making a test accommodation.

If a parent refuses the use of a test accommodation, this refusal must be given very serious consideration. A parent is a primary source of information concerning the use and effectiveness of special education and related services, and the parent's input is very important. If there is a disagreement concerning the use of a test accommodation, a mediation process might be needed to resolve the disagreement.[37]

As evidenced by the *Doe v. Withers* case discussed in Chapter 1, including a test accommodation in a student's IEP does not mean that the accommodation can be implemented without the cooperation of the teacher. There are administrative remedies for dealing with a reluctance to implement mandated test accommodations, but unless a legally contentious environment is sought, cooperation concerning the use and implementation of test accommodations is essential.

Duration

The length of time the test accommodations will be in effect should be stated, especially if it differs from the time frame for other programs and services. If not otherwise specified, the duration of an accommodation is 12 months. If content tests are read to a student, the need for this accommodation should be examined on an annual basis. If a student has been excluded from a test program (e.g., for behavioral reasons), the need for this restriction should be examined on an annual basis or even more frequently.

The duration of service can be less than a year if needed. For example, an accommodation might be used for a three- or six-month period and then the need or effectiveness of the accommodation reevaluated. There might be absolutely no way of knowing whether or not a certain accommodation will be effective or whether it might even be detrimental. Testing a student individually might seem a simple solution for a student, but if this accommodation has no impact on test performance, a different accommodation strategy might be necessary. Most test accommodations will be used for a period of 12 months before evaluation, but if there is doubt about the need or effectiveness of an accommodation, or that an accommodation is not needed for the entire year, then the duration should be stated in the IEP.

The duration of certain accommodations will sometimes be permanent. If a student requires an augmentative communication device or uses braille or large print, the duration of the accommodation will be ongoing although it still must be reviewed on an annual basis.[38]

Evaluation

The regulations require that an evaluation "is conducted every three years or more frequently if conditions warrant or if the child's parent or teacher requests an evaluation."[39] The fact is that the first IEP developed for a student is sometimes written in stone, and serious reconsideration of the IEP, much less test accommodations, is often minimal. At the very least, the general topic of test accommodations should be evaluated annually, while certain test accommodations will require careful examination. If oral testing is specified for content tests for a student who is also receiving services to improve reading performance, improved performance in reading might result in the need to change the test accommodation for some or all of the content tests.

Regardless of the form used to evaluate accommodations, or whether the evaluation is formal or informal, every review of an IEP should consider the need, fairness and effectiveness of the accommodations.

Transition Services

No later than age 16,[40] a student's IEP should include a statement of needed transition services which entail:

> A coordinated set of activities for a student, designed within an outcome-oriented process, that promotes movement from school to post-school activities, including post-secondary education, vocational training, integrated employment (including supported employment), continuing and adult education, adult services, independent living, or community participation.[41]

With respect to test accommodations, transition services should include the development of a post-school assessment plan (e.g., GED assessment), services for successful postsecondary assessment (e.g., college entrance examination preparation), and guidance as to the availability of test accommodations.

IEP Needs Assessment

In order to determine what skills or strategies are affecting test performance, with or without test accommodations, diagnostic information is necessary. Although the need for certain test accommodations is obvious, the use of accommodations might require a careful examination of test performance or test accommodation format. Diagnostic information can be obtained by several methods: (1) considering student performance before and after test accommodations have been made; (2) evaluating knowledge, skills and strategies with and without test accommodations; (3) examining the quality and quantity of errors before and after the accommodation has been used; and (4) using diagnostic tests to determine skill proficiency (e.g., the ability to finger-spell, to use Braille).

Diagnostic testing will provide insight as to the need and potential effectiveness of a test accommodation, but as shown in Table 4.1 there are a variety of other important information sources which can be considered when evaluating test accommodation needs.

Table 4.1 Sources for Determining Test Accommodation Needs.

Observational/Anecdotal Sources	Assessments
Regular classroom teacher	Group achievement tests
Special education teacher	Psychological tests
School psychologist	Specialized tests
Specialists (e.g, reading, speech)	Statewide competency tests
Occupational therapist	Inventories
Physical therapist	Diagnostic inventories
Guidance counselor	Wide-range assessments
Administrator(s)	Diagnostic tests
Aides	Classroom tests
Parents	Curriculum-based assessments
The Student	Portfolio assessments

The regulation that "a statement of the specific education and related services to be provided to the child"[42] has special meaning when considering test accommodations. A student might require a test accommodation which requires special expertise. If a student is visually impaired and uses Braille, there are several options available as to what test accommodations will best meet the student's needs. For a student who is visually impaired, a test accommodation might include oral responses, keyboarding answers, using a slate and stylus, taperecording responses, having an aide record responses, Braille-n-Speak, typing answers, or special answer sheets.

When determining test accommodations for students requiring specialized programs and services, the expertise from specialists must be sought. A student who is classified as orthopedically impaired might require a variety of related services, and the input from the providers of these services should be sought when necessary. In some cases, personnel providing services who would not ordinarily attend the IEP meeting might be invited to participate.

Input from the student regarding test accommodations is always important. For example, when using large print, information from the student regarding the readability of the font and point size should be routinely asked: Did you feel prepared to take the test? Did you understand the test instructions? Were you able to understand the test questions when they were read? If not, why? Did anything distract you or bother you during testing?

In some cases, especially when the student has important input regarding a test accommodation, the student "with a disability should attend the IEP meeting whenever the parent decides that it is appropriate" and "the parents and agency should encourage older children with disabilities (particularly those at the secondary school level) to participate in their IEP meetings."[43] Input from parents is imperative from a regulatory standpoint,[44] and not doing so ignores a potentially rich source of information.

The format for collecting information relating to test accommodation needs can vary from a general question to the consideration of many different categories that might be relevant for identifying potential accommodations. As shown below, a simple form can be used to consolidate information relating to test accommodations, especially from those involved with the actual assessment of the student (viz., classroom teacher, special education teacher, and school psychologist). This might be a simple request for information, or a routine memo to those even tangentially involved in testing. A valid test accommodation is the result of demonstrated need and reflection, and not an afterthought that is given a few scant moments at the conclusion of an IEP meeting. Table 4.2 illustrates a simple format for requesting information relating to test accommodation needs:

Table 4.2 Test Accommodations Needs.

1. Are test accommodations necessary: ❑ YES   ❑ NO
2. Please indicate any test accommodations which have been used with this student.
3. Briefly evaluate the effectiveness of these accommodations.
4. What other test accommodations might be appropriate for this student?

If there is some question as to what might necessitate a test accommodation, identifying factors which might influence a student's test performance as shown in Table 4.3 might be useful:

Table 4.3 General Test Accommodation Questions.

Category	Description
1. Accessibility	Is the location for testing easily accessible?
2. Facilities	Are the facilities (e.g., chair, table) adequate?
3. Acoustics	Are oral instructions easily heard in the room?
4. Lighting	Is the lighting conducive for testing?
5. Seating	Is the student able to see and hear the examiner?
6. Independence	Is the student able to function independently?
7. Motivation	Does this student seem motivated during testing?
8. Perseverance	Is the student able to cope with frustration?
9. Attention	Does the student attend to the instructions and task?
10. Instructions	Does the student understand the instructions?
11. Energy	Does the student maintain a reasonable level of energy?
12. Format	Is the test format clear and easy to follow?
13. Task	Is the task required by the test clear and easy to follow?
14. Difficulty	Is the difficulty level of the test appropriate?
15. Aids	Is the student able to answer items without the use of aids?
16. Language	Is the language mode (e.g., reading) suitable?
17. Reflection	Does the student consider the entire item and all choices?
18. Latency	Are responses given immediately after each item is presented?
19. Response	Is the student able to perform the response required by the test?
20. Time	Is there sufficient time to attempt all items?
21. Norms	Can the test norms be used with this student?

Observing Test Performance

Observing a student's test performance can provide invaluable information concerning the need, use and effectiveness of test accommodations. If a student is thought to need special education or related services, or if the student is currently receiving services, the teacher or test examiner should be aware of the student's general comfort and demeanor during testing (e.g., Does the student appear agitated?), time management skills (e.g., Is too much time spent on certain items), attention (e.g., Is the student attending to the test task?), rate of work, and latency (i.e., the length or time before a response is made). The examiner should note whether the student's rate of work is relatively consistent across test items (taking into account increasing item difficulty), or whether the rate of work drops drastically during the course of the test. Assuming that the problem is simply not due to increasing item difficulty, this might indicate that a brief within-test break might be appropriate or using a test with fewer test items.

As with rate of work, response latency can yield valuable information with respect to the usefulness of a test accommodation or the need for additional accommodations. The length of time required to respond after an item is first presented should be determined. A lengthy response latency might be the result of poor reading skill, item difficulty, or decision-making (e.g., the student has difficulty selecting an alternative on a multiple-choice task). A very short response latency might indicate that the student is not motivated or not attending to the task, the ability to attend to the task has decreased during the course of the test, or a lack of reflection on the part of the student. There is certainly no way to know what might cause a student to not consider all salient aspects of a test, but the examiner should be aware of a student who is not attending or is having difficulty responding. In either case, an individual assessment, alternative test, or strategies to maintain on-task behavior during testing might be necessary accommodations.

Diagnostic Testing

If there is a question as to the necessity of a test accommodation, or what that accommodation should be, a diagnostic test should be used to make this determination. If at all possible, and if normative data is required, standardized tests should be administered as per instructions before being used diagnostically. Diagnostic testing generally precludes the use of norms and focuses entirely on gaining insights into the student's performance and what the student is capable of achieving. For three students who incorrectly answer 46-27, one student does not consider all the alternatives, a second student is able to solve all problems of this type after the test task has been explained, and a third student did not attempt the problem. All three students provide incorrect answers, but only a diagnostic evaluation reveals what each is capable of achieving and, therefore, what the accommodation needs of this student are.

Instead of initially using a standardized test to gather diagnostic information, this can be accomplished by developing a test comprised of sample items, items similar to the actual test items, using an old test if available, or developing a practice test designed especially to evaluate test performance either with or without test accommodations. Practice tests provide an ideal opportunity to determine why a student is having test difficulty and to determine what accommodations might be useful for testing the student's ability.

Diagnostic testing involves techniques which require the examiner to probe and question in order to gain insights which might explain the student's test behavior. Vygotsky (Cole, John-Steiner, Scribner & Souberman, 1978) described a zone of proximal development which is defined as "...the distance between the actual development level as determined by independent problem-solving and the level of potential development as determined through problem-solving under adult guidance or in collaboration with more capable peers" (p. 86). Vygotsky's zone of proximal development is similar to the concept underlying the use of diagnostic probes which is described by McLoughlin and Lewis (1990) as discovering "whether changing some aspect of a classroom task will have positive effect upon student performance" (p. 177). For example, does increasing the amount of time to answer question influence performance?

With respect to test accommodations, diagnostic testing involves comparing and interpreting a student's performance first without and then with the test accommodation. When the need for a test accommodation is being determined, using different test formats, providing help, analyzing responses, task clarification, experimenting with time limits, demonstrations, or problem-solving strategies are all techniques which might be used. The following table describes several diagnostic strategies which can be used with most tests to determine or evaluate the need for test accommodations:

Table 4.4 Diagnostic Testing Techniques.

Technique	Example
Format	Use different items formats to determine the most appropriate
Cues	Provide initial sound of a word, or context cues
Time	Experiment with different time limits using small sets of items
Demonstration	Go through the problem step-by-step; ask what should be done at each step
Incorrectness	Explain why a response is not correct
Correctness	Explain why a response is correct
Strategy	Have student explain/show exactly how the problem was solved
Intervention	Correct faulty problem solving strategy
Test	Give the student a similar problem to solve
Difficulty	Give an easier problem(s) to solve
Redo	Slightly modify items incorrectly answered to determine learning
Retest	Repeat the test the following day

IEP Documentation

Written Documentation

As previously discussed, a test accommodation can be included in various sections of the IEP. However, if modifications (or supplementary aids and services) are necessary, they must be included in the IEP document.[45] An IEP need not include a specific test accommodation section, but written documentation must be provided for all modifications which are necessary for a student to participate in a regular education program.

If a test accommodation is specified in an IEP, the extent this accommodation is used in regular educational activities must be provided. In the case of reading, if a student is not able to read content material, but is able to conceptually understand the material, some provision must be made to provide appropriate instructional aids (e.g., a reader, tape-recorded text) during everyday instructional activities. In other words, there should be a high degree of consistency between instructional accommodations and test accommodations.

Although instructional accommodations are a part of daily educational activities, this should not preclude necessary remedial services.

If a student has a content test read orally because of a reading deficiency, the student must be given an opportunity to learn the content. If the student's ability to read is such that the content cannot be learned via reading, some provision must be made to impart this content (e.g., by using a reader). By the same token, remedial efforts in reading most often should not be abandoned otherwise the student will never develop independent reading skills. For a student with a reading disability there are really a number of educational goals: (1) learning content material, (2) being able to read content material, (3) developing independent reading skill, (4) demonstrating content ability with necessary test accommodations, and (5) eventually demonstrating content ability without test accommodations.

IEP Format

The content required in an IEP is well specified[46] but there is considerable flexibility as to how each category is conceptualized, and the content and detail within each category. Because of the emphasis on compliance, the layout of the IEP form has received a great deal of interest from school districts. Although compliance is not an altogether meaningless goal, the effectiveness of an IEP probably has less to do with the document form than a commitment to provide meaningful services.

Statement of Services

Test accommodations can be integrated in all of the primary sections of an IEP, but the statement of services[47] is the basis for providing IEP-designated accommodations. There are three primary elements of the statement of services: special education, related services and regular education participation. Test accommodations occur with both special education and related services, but are especially prominent in the section relating to regular education participation. For special education and related services a test accommodation might be necessary to determine the type or effectiveness of specifically designed instruction. For regular education, test accommodations are not only necessary to evaluate the type and effectiveness of instruction (e.g., classroom tests), but to denote competency, program eligibility and overall performance.

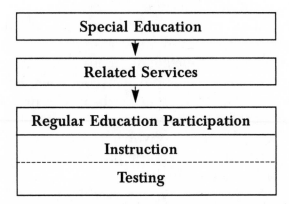

Because of the importance of testing in the regular education program, many IEPs include a separate section devoted entirely to test accommodations.

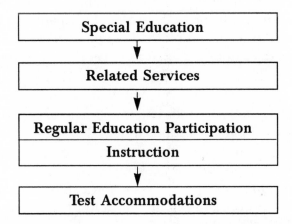

Special education. "Special education means specially designed instruction...to meet the unique needs of a child with a disability."[48] Implicit in the need for specially designed instruction is the need for specially designed tests which measure this instruction. When a student receives special education from a qualified special education professional, an assumption is made that testing will parallel the specially designed instruction. Unless there is some specific reason why the testing format and instructional formats should differ, there is generally no need to specify test accommodations as part of the identification of special education services.

Related services. Related services are those which allow a student to benefit from special education. If a related service entails augmentative communication which might be provided by a combination of special education, speech and physical therapy services, the augmentative device used might dictate the scope of assessment. If a student can only respond via a single-switch computer device, tests would need to be selected or modified which use this response mode. Likewise, a student might be able to function very effectively in a classroom with related service involving accommodations for visual impairments, speech disorders, or physical disabilities to guide test development and interpretation.

Although related services are reserved for students needing special education,[49] special education, and therefore related services, are not restricted to special education classes. The specially designed instruction and corresponding tests necessary to evaluate this instruction will occur in whatever least restrictive environment is most appropriate.

Regular education participation. Participation in the regular education program is achieved by the "use of supplementary aids and services."[50] This does not mean that test accommodations are only necessary in the regular classroom, but are used to enhance participation in the regular school program no matter how limited or restricted that participation might be. If a student is in a self-contained classroom, and regular classroom participation is minimal, if the student is able to participate in the regular education testing program with or without test accommodations, the student is entitled to such participation.

Because certain tests are necessary for a student to receive the benefits of a free appropriate public education (e.g., demonstrating competence, being allowed to participate in school programs, receiving a high school diploma), providing students with every opportunity to participate in the regular education testing program is critical. Whereas supplementary aids and services are modifications to the regular education program which allow the student to participate in that program, these same type of modifications are those which allow the student to participate in the regular education test program. Certain of these supplementary aids and modifications will be the same for regular education instruction and testing such as allowing a student with a hearing or visual impairment to sit near the front of the room, repeating directions, ensuring that students understand the directions, providing readable test (e.g., large print), allowing a student to use a place marker when reading, extended time, using a scribe to record responses, or reading content material and tests to the student.

However, there might also be supplementary aids and services which are unique to testing. The most notable difference between instructional and testing modifications concerns individualized testing. If a student requires extended time, or requires the use of a reader, reads in Braille, or requires a special receptive and/or expressive format, testing the student in a group situation might be distracting to the students and to other students in the class.

Test Accommodation Section

The primary reason for highlighting a specific test accommodation subsection is that although test accommodations must be specified in order to indicate the extent of participation in the regular education program,[51] test accommodations can also be offered as a related service to benefit from special education, to ensure nondiscriminatory testing in all educational environments, and to meet the specific instructional and test needs. A student who requires an itinerant teacher for Braille, might use tests which are not in Braille (e.g., test which are read, large print); while a student using an augmentative communication device might require that device for all instructional and assessment activities. Although related service generally suggest the scope of test accommodations, there are often specific accommodations or accommodations for specific tests which are not indicated by related services.

As with all attempts to show compliance, there is sometimes a tendency to attempt to anticipate every possible test accommodation contingency. The result can be an IEP mired in detail and not applicable to most students. There are many formats which can be used to designate IEP test accommodations, the only real criterion being that the format effectively addresses each student's test accommodation needs. A relatively simple open-ended test accommodation format might seem to lack the strength of a more detailed IEP test accommodation component, but this might result in greater reflection in that accommodations are not artificially limited to a list of items.

Table 4.5 IEP Test Accommodations.

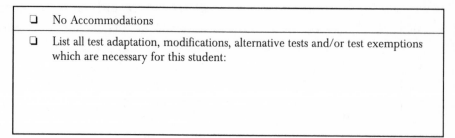

❏   No Accommodations
❏   List all test adaptation, modifications, alternative tests and/or test exemptions which are necessary for this student:

Depending on the use and importance of test exemptions, a three-part test accommodation section might be appropriate. As shown in Table 4.6, a specific test exemption component has been added which requires the following: (1) the name of the test, (2) the reason for the exemption, and (3) the method for assessing the student. Test exemptions can range from a general to a very specific exemption, but whatever the specificity an exemption is an extremely important decision and deserving of considerable reflection and documentation.

Table 4.6 IEP Test Accommodations.

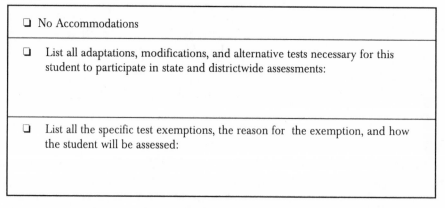

❏   No Accommodations
❏   List all adaptations, modifications, and alternative tests necessary for this student to participate in state and districtwide assessments:
❏   List all the specific test exemptions, the reason for the exemption, and how the student will be assessed:

Accommodation hierarchy. Assuming there is agreement as to what each component represents, a hierarchy of test accommodation categories can be used to structure an IEP: no accommodations, adaptations, modifications, alternative tests, and exemptions. To ensure that a student has a fair and least restrictive assessment, test exemptions should be stated in the student's IEP.

Table 4.7 Hierarchy of Accommodations

❏	No Accommodations
❏	Testing Adaptations (task readiness, instructions, setting, etc.)
❏	Testing Modifications (extended time, reader, Braille, signing, etc.)
❏	Alternative Testing
❏	Test Exemption(s)

Accommodation matrix. A matrix of possible accommodations consisting of different types of school accommodations can be used to correlate different tests with specific accommodations. As shown in Table 4.8 a distinction is made between classroom, school (e.g., Stanford Achievement Test) and statewide tests. A student might be able to participate in all classroom tests when read, but might be exempted from a certain statewide test which disallowed this modification. Or a diagnostic test might prohibit extra time, but this accommodation might be appropriate for most other tests.

Table 4.8 Test Accommodation Matrix.

Test	Accommodation		
	No	Yes	Explain
Classroom			
School			
State			
Other			

Accommodation lists. An IEP often contains a section that specifies a list of possible test accommodations. This is appealing from a compliance standpoint but can misleadingly suggest a finite number of possible test accommodations, or give the connotation that the accommodations listed are the only accommodations available. None the less, based on experience, such a list might be adequate, if the always nebulous "other" category is available. Lists of possible accommodations frequently follow the accommodations allowed by the state agency which are often intended for statewide test. If the statewide guide of test accommodations is not for all tests, the use of the guide with all tests must be carefully examined. The statewide guideline might prohibit multiday testing, but this might be permissible when using a school achievement test. A statewide test might allow extended time, but this might be prohibited by the publisher of a educational assessment. Or the statewide guideline might allow reading a reading test, but this might be anathema to the publisher of a commercially- produced reading test.

Table 4.9 List of Possible Test Accommodations

Indicate by an X those test accommodations which will best minimize the effect of the disability.	
No Modifications	
Braille	
Large Print	
Reading Test Items	
Signing Test Items	
Enhancing Directions	
Signing Directions	
Individualized Testing	
Using a Calculator	
Adaptive Responses	
Extended Time	
Reducing Testing Time	
Special Testing Location	
Test Exemption	
Other	

A list of test accommodations can provide direction for making an informed decision, but can also result in meeting what is thought to be a bureaucratic requirement. In keeping with the IEP criticisms discussed at the beginning of this chapter, the primary purpose of a list is often to show compliance with state guidelines and not to develop a thoughtful plan for best meeting the individual test needs of students. One school district has a list of over 35 possible test modifications in the IEP form of which the following are included: increasing spacing between items, reducing number of items per page and arranging answer choices in a vertical format. Using these test accommodations with all tests is virtually impossible. A long list of miscellaneous test accommodations might meet the testing needs of some students, but there is virtually no direction as to when these modifications might be appropriate, for what students, or under what circumstances. If increased spacing between items is deemed necessary for a student, guidelines for when to use this accommodation should be available. More importantly, who will make this accommodation and with what tests should be carefully examined.

Detailing a list of accommodations which are impractical and never used can weaken the effectiveness of any and all accommodations. The specification of test accommodations should not result in the cavalier use of the items listed, and each accommodation should be included to meet a specific and demonstrated need. The accommodation section shown below provides an expanded list of specific accommodations.

Table 4.10 Extended List of Possible Test Accommodations.

Test Accommodations	
❏ No Test Accommodations necessary	
❏ Braille	❏ Signing instructions
❏ Large print	❏ Signing items
❏ Practice testing	❏ Foreign language
❏ Enhanced instructions	❏ Extended time
❏ More sample items	❏ Extended breaks
❏ Reading instructions	❏ Multi-day testing
❏ Extra sample items	❏ Morning/afternoon testing
❏ Simplifying instructions	❏ Reduced testing time
❏ Reading non-reading items	❏ Special seating
❏ Modified response	❏ Individual testing
❏ Using a scribe	❏ Special location
❏ Assistive communication	❏ Special norms
❏ Using a calculator	❏ Test exemption
❏ Using a computer	❏ Other

There are numerous ways in which a list of test accommodations can be included in an IEP. The following test accommodation component combines a checklist format with several open-ended accommodations:

Table 4.11 Open-ended Test Accommodations

Test Accommodations
_____ Time limit waived.
_____ Minutes per test session.
_____ Minutes between sessions
_____ Special testing location: _____.
_____ Individualized testing.
_____ Special seating: _____.
_____ Modified instructions: _____.
_____ Student may use calculator for problem-solving mathematics.
_____ Alternative tests: _____
_____
_____
If the student has a severe reading disability
_____ questions for non-reading tests may be read to student.
_____ questions for non-reading tests may be signed to student.
_____ Braille.
_____ Large print.
_____ Oral responses may be given for non-writing tests.
_____ Signed responses may be used for non-writing tests.

A review of IEPs suggests that when a list of accommodations is provided the items comprising the list can be arranged with no particular order in mind, by the perceived importance of the accommodations, by frequency of use or even arranged in alphabetical order. If an IEP form is being reviewed for possible revision, this is an ideal time to collect information relating to the types of accommodations which have been used and to modify the list of accommodations based on actual use. However, because an accommodation has not been used does not mean that the accommodation should not be included in a list. A particular school might never have had a student who needed testing in Braille, but including Braille as an accommodation might be helpful to define the possible range and nature of test accommodations.

Monitoring Test Accommodations

Identifying an individual to assume responsibility for the implementation of an accommodation plan is suggested in Section 504,[52] but if test accommodations are an integral part of a student's IEP under IDEA, identifying personnel to ensure that test accommodations and related services are provided might be just as essential for the successful implementation of a test accommodation. Moreover, a test accommodation should not be made in the abstract and there should be a realistic determination of who will make and implement all necessary accommodations. If a test accommodation is required, there should be a statement as to who is expected to implement the accommodations. This will not only clarify test accommodation responsibilities, but will also necessitate that the time and ability to make the accommodations be considered. If there is an objection as to test accommodations responsibilities, the IEP meeting is the time when the problem is addressed rather than immediately before a student is tested. For many students requiring test accommodations, the ultimate responsibility will fall to the special education teacher. If an accommodation involves several teachers, the nature and scope of the accommodations should be discussed with the teachers. Problems involving teachers implementing test accommodations are usually the result of poor communication rather than a disinclination to implement appropriate test adaptations and modifications.

In some instances, regular classroom teachers will not be able to make the specified accommodation because of very real time restraints or technical know-how. If a student requires individualized testing at a different location, additional personnel (e.g., an aide) might be necessary; or if a test must be signed to a student, this might require the services of a professional with expertise in signing.

Specifying who will be responsible for test accommodations will also help focus on identifying accommodations. If increased line spacing of all tests is cited as an accommodation, a thought or two about for whom this accommodation is necessary, who will do these changes, and with what tests might give cause to reflect on the need for the accommodation.

Designating a coordinator or case manager to ensure that test accommodations are meeting a student's needs is not required but the regulations do suggest that some agencies have found it helpful to have a special educator or some other school staff member (e.g., a social worker, counselor, or psychologist) serve as coordinator or case manager of the IEP process for an individual child or for all handicapped children served by the agency. Examples of the kinds of activities which case managers might carry out are (1) coordinating the multidisciplinary evaluation; (2) collecting and synthesizing the evaluation reports and other relevant information about a child that might be needed at the IEP meeting; (3) communicating with the parents; and (4) participating in, or conducting, the IEP meeting itself.[53]

Flexibility

A flexible and common sense approach relating to test accommodations can sometimes suffer as the need to show compliance increases. An IEP should not be a rigid and uncompromising instrument which prevents reaching the very goals which it aspires to reach. For a visually impaired student the accommodations might involve oral testing for one class, but Braille testing for a second class if the task is not conducive to oral assessment (e.g., the task consists of column matching). For a physically disabled student a recorder might be used to record responses for classroom testing, but a single-switch device is used for statewide examinations. The test needs of students are quite varied, and often these needs require an IEP to provide some degree of flexibility.

Although one would like to think that IEP flexibility would be the product of a careful scrutiny of a student's test needs, from the standpoint of regulatory compliance a detailed IEP test accommodation component provides, at least on the surface, some insurance that the accommodation needs of students are considered. However, in order to ensure that every conceivable need of a student is being considered, the IEP could contain minuscule detail as to the type and implementation of test accommodations. If this were done, more time might be spent showing compliance rather than providing effective test accommodations.

The wording of a test accommodation can often guide the degree of flexibility which can be used when implementing the accommodation. If, for some reason, an accommodation might not be used (or has not been used), the wording should be such that there is no doubt that the accommodation *must* be used (e.g., Classroom tests *must* be read to the student; Classroom tests *must* be given in Braille; Test instructions *must* be signed to the student).

The regulations do provide some a degree of flexibility in relation to services in that "as long as there is no change in the overall amount, some adjustments in scheduling the services should be possible (based on the professional judgement of the service provider) without holding another IEP meeting."[54] There are occasions when an accommodation might not be used (e.g., when determining the need for the accommodation), but if there is a major change in the use of an accommodation, the IEP must be changed.

Minimizing Accommodations

The IEP should specify test accommodations which, as best as possible, minimally affect what the test purports to measure. Minimally affects what a purports to measure is best accomplished by minimally changing the test; that is, the test accommodation should mitigate the disability, *as best as possible*, and minimally affect the test's validity *as best as possible*. Although there are many test accommodations available, a special education classification does not dictate that test accommodations must be included in the student's IEP. A large print test format might be a good accommodation for a student, or for all students for that matter but if the disability does not warrant large print, this would not be an appropriate accommodation. Or, if actual testing reveals that a student completes all tests within the specified time limits, and time is empirically not a factor, specifying extra time would be an unnecessary accommodation.

Test accommodations should be specified that are thought to be influential in minimizing the effects of a disability. Specifying unnecessary accommodations, based on nothing but a vague hope that this will "help" a student, is contrary to the rationale for making test accommodations and can detract from making and implementing meaningful accommodations.

ENDNOTES

1. 34 C.F.R. §300.340(a)
2. 34 C.F.R. §300.341
3. 34 C.F.R. §300.350
4. 34 C.F.R. §300.128(a)(1)
5. 34 C.F.R. §300.532(e)
6. 34 C.F.R. §300.540(3)
7. 34 C.F.R. §300.344
8. 34 C.F.R. §300.7(a)
9. 34 C.F.R. §300, Appendix C(I)
10. see 34 C.F.R. §300, Appendix C (Question #48)
11. 34 C.F.R. §104.4(a)(i)
12. 34 C.F.R. §300, Appendix C (Question #44)
13. IDEA Amendments of 1997, H.R. 5, Section 614(d)(A)(v)(I)
14. 34 C.F.R. §300.346
15. 34 C.F.R §300.346(b)
16. 34 C.F.R §300.346(a)(1)
17. 34 C.F.R. §300, Appendix C (Question #36[a])
18. 34 C.F.R. §300.346(a)(2)
19. 34 C.F.R. §300, Appendix C (Question #39)
20. 34 C.F.R. §300.123
21. IDEA Amendments of 1997, H.R. 5, Section 614(d)(1)(A)(ii)
22. IDEA Amendments of 1997, H.R. 5, Section 614(d)(1)(A)(ii)
23. 34 C.F.R. §300.346 Content of individualized education program
24. 34 C.F.R. §300.16(a)
25. 34 C.F.R. §300.16(b)(8)
26. 34 C.F.R. §300.16(b)(13)
27. 34 C.F.R. §300.16(b)(5)(ii)
28. 34 C.F.R. §300, Appendix C (Question #48)
29. 34 C.F.R. §300.532(a)(3)
30. Florida State Board of Education Rules, 6A-6.03028
31. California Education Code, Section 56345(a)(3)&(4)
32. California Education Code, Section 56345(b)(3)
33. New York State Education Department, Regulations of the Commissioner of Education Part 200.4(c)(2)(vii)
34. Ohio Department of Education, Standards for Ohio Schools (Draft), 1996, p. 55
35. IDEA Amendments Act of 1997, H.R. 5 Sections 612(a)(4), INDIVIDUAL-IZED EDUCATION PROGRAM, and Section 614(d), which includes a description of required IEP elements, take effect on July 1, 1998 (Title II, Miscellaneous Provisions).
36. IDEA Amendments of 1997, H.R. 5, Section 614(d)(1)(A)(ii) and Section 614(d)(1)(A)(v)(I)

37. 34 C.F.R. §300.506
38. see 34 C.F.R. §300, Appendix C (Question #53)
39. 34 C.F.R. §300.534
40. 34 C.F.R. §300.346(b)(1)
41. 34 C.F.R §300.18(a)
42. 34 C.F.R. §300.346(a)(3)
43. 34 C.F.R. §300, Appendix C (Question #21)
44. 34 C.F.R. §300.345 Parent participation
45. 34 C.F.R. §300, Appendix C (Question #48)
46. 34 C.F.R. §300.346 which includes present levels of performance, special education/related services and regular education participation, initiation and duration of services, objectives and evaluation schedules, and transition services.
47. 34 C.F.R. §300.346(a)(3)
48. 34 C.F.R. §300.17(a)(1)
49. 34 C.F.R. §300.17 (Note 1)
50. 34 C.F.R. §300.550(b)(2)
51. 34 C.F.R. §300.346(a)(3)
52. 34 C.F.R.§104.22(e)(4) which requires the identification of "the person responsible for the implementation of the plan in relation to program accessibility.
53. 34 C.F.R. §300, Appendix C (Question #24)
54. 34 C.F.R. §300, Appendix C (Question #51)

Chapter 5

TEST ADAPTATIONS

A test adaptation is an accommodation which does not alter the test, the test format, the test content, the difficulty of the test, test response mode, or the normative interpretation. If a student's interest or behavior precludes the use of a statewide proficiency test, testing the student individually might result in a meaningful test score. In this case, the same test and test protocol is used for the student as for all students in the school population, the only difference being that the test is administered individually rather than in a group setting. For another student, clarifying instructions or providing extra sample items might moderate the affects of a disability without substantive alterations to the test being used. And a third student, practice using a certain test format might prepare the student for the actual test. In all three cases, the goal for each test is to measure exactly what each test was designed to measure, without modifying the test format, content, or response mode.

One might argue that any change from the normal administration procedure is a modification. Reynolds (1984) stated that "if a standardized test is not given explicitly according to the instructions provided, inestimable amounts of error are introduced and norm-referenced scores are no longer interpretable" (p. 470). This is certainly a possibility although changing what a test measures rather than increasing test error is a more important concern. The regulations do require that tests be "administered by trained personnel in conformance with the instructions provided by their producer,[1] but also that tests measure ability rather than disability.[2] Of course, administering a test under the exact same conditions which were used to standardize the test is generally not possible. There is no way to equate for such variables as examiner experience, different testing locations, interest generated prior to testing, and the emphasis placed on standardization prior to testing. The general test accommodation task is to determine whether validity changes and error caused by using an accommodation is greater than the validity changes and error caused by measuring a student's disability rather than ability.[a] For test adaptations, the error introduced by the test accommodation should be minimal.

As shown in Table 5.1 test adaptations can occur before, during and after testing. Pretest adaptations include all activities relating to test preparation, examiner training and test instructions. Test adaptations during testing include individual testing, developing rapport to maximize student performance, providing a comfortable test environment, or extending break between subtests. Posttest adaptations entail the use of score transformations, indices of learning test score comparisons and the diagnostic interpretation of test performance (e.g., inspecting multiple-choice responses of a student such as the number omitted, types of responses made, etc). Posttest adaptations are discussed extensively in Chapters 9 and 10. For adaptations made before, during and after testing, the test administration or format is not changed. For example, if test instructions are enhanced (e.g., providing more sample items), this is a substantive change to the test. This does not mean that this accommodation is not valid, but that it is a modification rather than a test adaptation. An example of a test adaptation involving instructions would be ensuring that students were attending to the instructions (e.g., making eye contact before giving an instruction). Likewise, extending the time to complete a test from that allocated by the test producer is a modification, while providing an extra 10 minutes between subtests of a standardized test battery might be well within the test instruction parameters.

Table 5.1 Test Adaptations.

Test Adaptations		
Pretest	During test	Posttest
Practice tests	Individual testing	Score transformations
Developing test strategies	Test environment	Predicted scores
Examiner training	Developing rapport	Learning indices
Test location	Magnification aids	Diagnostic interpretation
Presenting instructions	Amplification aids	Response analysis
Student interview	Test breaks	Norm use

---

[a]As discussed in Chapter 2, a test accommodation can change a test's common-factor variance, specific variance and/or error variance component. Changing one of these components will cause a change in one or both of the remaining components. Increasing a test's specific variance component can decrease the common-factor variance and/or error variance. As the result of an accommodation which increases specific test variance, either reliability or validity will be affected.

Test Instructions

Tests should be "administered by trained personnel in conformance with the instructions provided by their producer,"[3] and if the test producer explicitly prohibits an adaptation or modification, then this "instruction" should be followed. The Kaufman Assessment Battery for Children (Kaufman & Kaufman, 1983) is designed for the evaluation of "...learning disabled and other exceptional children...," but the authors stressed the importance of following directions and that for several of the subtests which involve timing (either stimulus presentation or response time), then "exactly" the amount of time specified should be followed. The reason for this is the need to develop rapport and an appropriate psychological environment, while stressing the importance of standardization procedures and that "any deviation from the prescribed procedures represents a violation of the ground rules, thereby rendering the norms of limited (and sometimes no) value" (p. 16). These authors emphasized that "a competent clinician is more interested in *why* the child earned a particular profile of scores, and *how* the profile can be used profitably, than in the specific empirical outcomes..." (p. 16).

The directions for administering the 8th Edition of the Stanford Achievement Test to hearing impaired students is based on the philosophy that "communicating the intent of the tasks required for the test is of paramount importance" (p. 6) and that "the method of communication to be used in the administration is the method normally employed in the instructional context with the students being tested (e.g., speech only, a combination of speech and signs, etc.)" (Gallaudet Research Institute, 1989, p. 6).

Few tests emphasize the importance of test instructions more than the Woodcock Reading Mastery Test-Revised (Woodcock, 1987). A stern warning is given that "the single most important principle to remember is that the *tests must be administered exactly as described in the test book*. To do otherwise invalidates the results from any standardized test" (p. 14). This might seem like a draconian approach as to the impact of test instructions on validity, but examiners should not blithely depart from basic standardization procedures without due consideration being given to the consequences.

The WRMT-R does allow for accommodations for students with disabilities when necessary (e.g., signing instructions), but that "when test procedures have been modified, however, the examiner must determine whether the results have been compromised to the extent that the published norms are no longer applicable (p. 18). The third revision of the Stanford-Binet Intelligence Scale (Terman & Merrill, 1973) also stressed the importance of adhering to standardization procedures and stated that "it cannot be too strongly emphasized that unless standard procedures are followed the tests lose their significance" and that "each individual subtest is an abbreviated experiment in which the conditions have been carefully set up" (p. 47). Dunn and Dunn (1981) provided considerable flexibility in instructions for the PPVT-R in that various response accommodations are allowed (e.g., a subject is given a stimulus word and then points to the picture representing the stimulus word), the time allowed to develop the necessary response is individualized, practice plates may be repeated, and the test is discontinued if the subject is unable to respond correctly to a cycle of three consecutive practice plates. The PPVT-R also has several versions of the basic instructions for younger, very immature and older (over age eight) individuals.

For most tests, the examiner is able to exercise a considerable amount of discretion with regard to test instructions, but if a test publisher explicitly prohibits modifying instructions because of its impact on test validity, then use of the accommodation and/or the normative interpretation of test performance should be seriously considered.

Test instructions offered by the producer are not always abundantly clear with respect to test accommodations. Often a test producer will indicate that not following administration procedures will detract from the test's reliability and/or validity. This might be the case, but this leaves the test examiner with the difficult task of determining what adaptations and modifications will significantly detract from the tests's reliability and validity, and what accommodations will allow a test to measure what it was designed to measure (after the effects of the disability have been minimized). A test user is guided by the test producer's instructions, and must make a "good faith effort" to conform to these instructions, while at the same time measuring the ability in question and not discriminating because of the student's disability.

Directions and disabilities. To a degree the nature of a student's disability will dictate how instructions must be modified. If a visually impaired student is taking a regular or large print version of a test, instructions should be read aloud, and the examiner should attempt to describe whatever visual examples are being provided. Also, sufficient time should be provided for the student to read directions and sample items.

For students who have auditory impairments, the examiner should face the student when speaking. As much as possible, the examiner should speak clearly and naturally. Exaggerated speech might distort rather than enhance communication, as will excessively loud speech. Eye contact is important when administering a test to a student with a hearing impairment. If a direction is given to read a sample item, eye contact should be made before the next instruction is given.

If a student requires directions in a foreign language, and the test itself is in English, the appropriateness of using the test must be questioned. If a student's English is not sufficient to understand or read the directions, poor performance on a test requiring English is a foregone conclusion. The need for non-English directions might be absolutely necessary, but this will not necessarily overcome the inappropriateness of a test in English or, for nonverbal tests, unfamiliarity with the general test format.

Adapting instructions. The requirement to administer tests "in conformance with the instructions provided by their producer"[4] might limit the use of such accommodations as the use of extra sample items and clarification of instructions. Often these types of adaptations will be allowed, or the scope of the adaptation might be indicated. The extensive elaboration of test instructions under the guise of clarification might be disallowed, but repeating instructions might be permitted. If a student is using sign language, an interpreter should be available to interpret test directions. Although tests frequently allow sign language to be used in presenting test instructions, this accommodation generally does not extend to the presentation of test items. For classroom tests, the teacher should make every effort to be alert for students who seem confused, are not quite sure what the response format is, or are unaware of possible time restraints.

Simplification. A goal for every test is to understand the instructions. However, an accommodation to "simplify test instructions" is often unclear as to what the examiner should do in order for the student to understand the task. If an arithmetic computational test is given to a Spanish-speaking student, the instruction should be given in Spanish rather than English but this is not really simplifying instructions. The use of the "simplify test instructions" guideline probably stems from the fact that many students referred for special education exhibit poor test performance and not understanding the test instructions is a part of the problem. For most standardized tests, if the student does not understand the instructions, the task itself is probably too difficult. Furthermore, changing or simplifying instructions might completely change how the task is conceptualized. The instructions and sample items might be simplified or changed to the extent that the instructions are no longer appropriate for what is actually being tested. If instructions are to be simplified, the *simplification* should be based on an explicit need and determined before the test is given.

Sample items. Providing extra sample items is sometimes recommended as a test accommodation. This is easier accomplished if a test is administered individually than in a group setting. As with simplifying instructions, if a student has difficulty with sample items, the test examiner must give serious consideration as to the suitability of the test. Problems such as this can be avoided by ample practice testing. For group testing, the test examiner should attempt to discern whether a student is able to understand and answer all sample items. If extra sample items are necessary, these should be kept to a minimum and should not interfere with general group testing; that is, a test accommodation for an individual should not be such that the needs (and patience) of students not receiving the accommodation suffer. In an individual setting, if a student has difficulty with sample items, an attempt should be made to determine whether the problem involves attention/motivation, comprehending the task, test difficulty or response mode.

Students requiring non-English tests can pose a difficult testing problem. If the primary language is Spanish, there might be someone with expertise who can provide suitable translation skills. However, if the language is a less than common language group, translation expertise might not be readily available. If a student does require an interpreter for the test instructions, and the test is English-normed, the usefulness of the test is suspect.

Feedback

During the test session the test examiner should be prepared to provide assistance when necessary. Many tests will encourage the proctor to move about the room, and to provide instruction clarification if there appears to be some confusion on the part of the student. Of course, this does not entail helping a student with answering test items, clarifying test item language, or giving any clue whatsoever as to what the answer to an item might be.

For individually administered tests, students should be given positive feedback and encouragement throughout the test. The difference between feedback to motivate the student to perform at a level commensurate with his or her potential and providing feedback as to the correctness of an item is sometimes a fine line. For example, saying "Very good," or "You're doing just fine" following an answer might be appropriate. Or the examiner might also provide nonverbal encouragement such as a smile, nodding, etc. However, if either verbal or nonverbal cues are used to encourage or suggest the correctness of a response, this can invalidate the test. For example, if the examiner nods or cajoles that the student is on "the right track" following correct responses, this could result in a strategy on the part of the student to try several responses until a favorable cue is received from the examiner before providing a complete response.

One advantage of individual testing is the ability to monitor performance. However, the advantages of one-to-one interaction can also completely invalidate results by unintentionally providing cues. For the PIAT-R (Markwardt, 1989) examiners are cautioned to "be alert to their own subtle behaviors that can inadvertently communicate the correctness of responses. Such behaviors include smiling at right answers, frowning or pausing at incorrect answers, and using an obvious system to mark the test record" (p. 6). This is sound advice, and an examiner does not help a student when the resulting score does not reflect the student's achievement or ability.

A distinction should be made between cuing alternatives and providing cues which can help deduce the correct answer. As discussed in Chapter 8, any intentional behavior (e.g., blink, finger movement) can be used to elicit independent and intentional responses. A situation might arise in which a student is not able to respond to an individual administered multiple-choice task. The instructions for the PIAT-R provide for the possibility of the examiner pointing "to each quadrant on the test plate in consecutive order" and eliciting a response. However, this is not an easy task, and the examiner must be extremely vigilant that when alternatives are cued that the correctness or incorrectness of alternatives are not indicated. For example, a slightly longer pause at the correct answer or a shorter pause at an incorrect answer might suggest the correctness of the answer. Of course, this problem is eliminated if a single-switch device is used so that alternatives are automatically scanned and the student is able to respond independently of the examiner (see Chapter 8).

Practice Tests

Practice tests provide an opportunity to acquaint the student with the task, to determine if the student requires other accommodations, and to otherwise determine whether the suitability of the instructions, the test, the facilities and location. Whatever test accommodation a student requires, the accommodation should be provided and evaluated during practice testing. This is the time to determine whether an accommodation is effective, or whether additional adaptations or modifications must be made.

Contrary to what some might believe, testing should not be an esoteric activity that is unrelated to curriculum and prior experience. Ideally, a test is a sample of items from a larger item population pool or domain of items. Consider a standardized achievement test which includes 5 primary addition fact items. Teaching these exact facts in the exact order shown on the test, and in the same format would be wrong. Tests must not be taught, but it is appropriate to sample from the general item domain used in the construction of the test. This is not teaching the test; this is sampling from the population of information from which a test was drawn.

The goal is to sample and measure the population of items (which, ideally, comprises the curriculum) and not to outwit the student by using an unusual or clever task. Old tests provide an excellent source of practice test items, although giving the complete version of an old test might be excessive. In addition, previously used tests are more likely available with statewide competency-type tests and teacher-made tests than with commercial standardized tests.

If a practice test is being used to prepare a student for a major test such as a statewide test, use materials which best simulate the actual test situation. If the statewide test uses an answer sheet to record answers, use a similar scoring sheet for a practice test. Correctly and efficiently using an answer sheet is especially important if items are skipped for later consideration. If a student skips item #6 and enters the answer for item #7 on the scoring sheet for item #6, all answers beyond this point will be incorrectly recorded.

Other test-taking skills can affect a student's efficient use of test time and should be developed via old tests or practice tests. The ability to change answers, mark answers clearly, use the correct pencil to mark answers, entering only one answer (usually), and erasing answers should be developed prior to administering a standardized test.

All too frequently test tasks take on an aura of infallibility. The reading curriculum consists of oral and silent reading, and then a multiple-choice test is used to evaluate reading. If a test task is different than what is used in the curriculum, a practice test can clarify the task, the domain of knowledge being assessed, and the required response for the task in question.

Practice test length. The purpose of using a practice test is not to generate normative scores, but to acquaint the student with the test, evaluate potential test needs, and to familiarize the student with the type of curriculum content being sampled. If the purpose is to acclimate the student to the task, initial practice tests or simulations might contain five or so items which are relatively easy. The first goal is to understand the task, and to experience some degree of success with the task. As the student becomes comfortable with the task, the number of items and item difficulty can be increased. If the eventual goal is to take a test comprised of 30 items, practice tests might be used with 5, 10, 20 and then 30 items.

Practice test directions. Practice test instructions should be as similar as possible to the actual test instructions. If the student is aware of the task and what is expected, there will be no need for extra sample items or enhanced directions which might distract the student (or other students) from actually taking the test. Practice test directions also provide an excellent time to determine other test needs. The ability to read directions independently and to understand such concepts as *none of the above* can be determined via a practice test.

Item familiarity. As said before, the item domain being tested should guide what is on a practice test. Because most commercial standardized tests are not constructed with a particular curriculum in mind, these tests should be examined for deficiencies in the regular curriculum. This is probably less important for students with disabilities participating in inclusionary settings than for students taking part in resource room programs and self-contained classrooms. One of the major weaknesses of self-contained classes is a tendency to create a unique curriculum to meet the needs of students. If the special education curriculum does not cover material in the regular or statewide curriculum, and a student is evaluated using tests which measure curriculum performance, the student is penalized before the first test item is given.

The task. As is the case with the content item domain, the test task should also be curriculum-based. The cloze procedure is a popular task used to measure reading, but for students who already have difficulties in reading, and who are unfamiliar with the cloze procedure, the task itself might be a confounding variable. If a test contains a task which is not ordinarily used in the curriculum, students should be aware of what the task is before testing. If a test uses the cloze to measure reading, and this task is not used in instruction or testing, time should be spent including the task in day-to-day instructional activities.

The response. Problems involving test responses should be clarified before actual testing. A practice test or test simulation should be used to determine whether the student can respond, understands what response is required, is unable to physically make the response, or becomes fatigued after 15 minutes of testing.

Test Strategies

For many students with disabilities, a test situation is unpleasant, unrewarding and a task to be endured at best. A variety of strategies might improve a student's test performance including problem solving, time management, reflection, organization, and guessing.

Testwiseness. Testwiseness was defined by Diamond and Evans (1972) as "the ability to respond advantageously to multiple choice items containing extraneous clues and to obtain credit on these items without knowledge of the subject matter" (p. 145). For students who are already having educational problems, inundating the student with infrequently-used test strategies might further confuse the student. True, a testwise person might discern that "all," "every," etc. in a distracter is less likely to be correct, or that for a classroom-made test, grammatical clues might indicate the correct answer (e.g., The animal is a 1. elephant 2. ant 3. cat). More exotic strategies abound such as selecting a certain alternative (e.g, always select *c* when in doubt or whatever), or selecting an item which has not been previously selected. No test is immune to testwise strategies, but most standardized tests are technically sound and test time spent considering myriad and infrequently-used test strategies can be better used focusing on test content and necessary test-taking skills.

Guessing. The one strategy which students with disabilities should be made aware of is the ability to guess...and to guess wisely. With the exception of admission tests such as the SAT, most tests do not use a correction formula for guessing. Even for a test which does correct for guessing, if one alternative can be eliminated as an incorrect answer, the student benefits by guessing, even at random, from the remaining alternatives. Thus, a student who is disinclined to guess is penalized (unless the student is terribly unlucky) for this trait. Consider an item where the student might have difficulty choosing between alternatives *a* and *c*, but alternatives *b* and *d* are obviously incorrect. Not answering this item when two alternatives are known to be incorrect is a poor test-taking strategy. On the other hand, if all the alternatives seem equally plausible, a guess would still be appropriate if no correction for guessing is used (and most achievement tests do not use such corrections).

If a correction formula for guessing is not used, students should answer all questions. However, students might misinterpret a guideline to guess to mean "not to consider all possibilities." Instructing a student to guess is appropriate when used as part of an overall test-taking strategy. The benefits of guessing are negated, and test performance can be negatively affected, if guessing becomes the method for responding rather than a strategy used in certain situations. Better phrasing for guessing might be to select the "best" answer to each question...but answer all the questions. If a student leaves many questions unanswered, an attempt should be made to determine whether this is the result of insufficient time, extremely difficult items, or a reluctance to guess. A disinclination to guess is often characterized by unanswered items throughout the test; while insufficient time or extremely difficult items result in many unanswered items at the end of the test. This, of course, assumes that the items are arranged by item difficulty.

Sensible strategies concerning guessing are best dealt with by means of practice test items. During a multiple-choice practice test session, the student might indicate that he or she does not know what the best answer is. At this point the examiner can help the student find an alternative which is incorrect, and then encourage the student to select the "best" answer from the remaining alternatives.

Well before taking a multiple-choice test, every student with a disability should be administered several multiple-choice items to discern test-taking skills. The examiner should observe the student's consideration of the stem and all alternatives, and then the student's ability to select the best alternative. Often times response latency will provide insight as to the intentionality of responses or the extent of reflection regarding the response. For students who are receiving test accommodations, many of the problems involving testwiseness and guessing can be dealt with effectively by using old tests, developing tests which simulate actual tests, or creating a pool of sample items to illustrate test tasks and strategies will help minimize the confounding effects of a unique test task.

The Test Environment

For students requiring test accommodations, considerable thought should be given to the test environment. Where to test the student, with whom the student is tested, and special testing personnel and facilities can all have a bearing on test performance. If a student normally uses a bookstand to do assignments for classroom tests, an attempt should be made to use this accommodation for all tests. Furthermore, the ability to use an accommodation in different settings should be determined before the accommodation is actually used.

Group Testing

If a test is normally given in a group situation, considerable effort should be made to allow a student needing a test accommodation to participate in regular group testing. Of course, when making this decision, consideration must not only be given to the student but to all students in the test environment. If an accommodation requires that test items be read to the student, this might be a considerable distraction to other students. Likewise, if a student requires extended time and a series of subtests are given, the overlap between those receiving and not receiving extended time and extended instructions could result in a very distractible test environment.

There are many occasions when a test accommodation can be used in a group setting, but the use of the accommodation might be misinterpreted by other students. If a student is allowed extra time to complete a test, while other students are required to stop at a designated time, other students might perceive the accommodation as being unfair. If a test accommodation is being used which might cause a distraction, a *brief* and straightforward explanation to the entire group prior to testing might be considered. Providing an accommodated test experience in a regular classroom is not necessarily an easy task, but group testing should not be excluded simply because a student has a disability. As with all other educational activities, there should be a reason for an individualized assessment and every effort should be made to test students with disabilities in the regular education environment "to the maximum extent appropriate."[5]

Individual Testing

Wright and Wendler (1994) reported that 13 percent of students administered the new SAT to determine time limits were tested individually. The reasons for individual assessment include accessibility, the need for special equipment, extra time, special instructions, a special test format (e.g., a reader is used), or for behavioral, attentional, or motivational reasons. Distractions to other students might be caused by time limit differences (e.g., different students are taking different tests or subtests), by the oral interaction of the examiner/examinee during an individual assessment, or by the behavior of the student (e.g., allowing the student to read aloud, or the student is disruptive in a group setting). Finally, the behavior of the student being assessed can be such that individual assessment is absolutely necessary. For a student who is unable to sit in his or her seat for even a short period of time, who "talks excessively," "blurts out answers," and "often interrupts or intrudes on others" (see criteria for hyperactivity-impulsivity in DSM-IV, American Psychiatric Association, 1994, p. 84) might have difficulty participating in a group test situation. For the Texas Assessment of Academic Skills "examinees may receive an individual administration of the assessment instrument and, in this setting, may read aloud as they work" (1994). Allowing a student to read questions aloud is not unreasonable (if that is what the student uses during the normal course of instruction and classroom testing), but it certainly would be distracting to other students, so that to provide this accommodation individual testing might be necessary.

If test norms are used, the administration should be in concert with the administration procedures cited by the test publisher. If a group test is given individually, it should not be administered as if it were a diagnostic test. Helping a student read each item, explaining the meaning of different alternatives, providing verbal praise following each item might be extremely useful diagnostically, but this is a radical departure from typical group test protocol. If an individualized test is needed (e.g., the PIAT-R, WIAT, WRAT-R), a test designed for this purpose should be used and a group test should not be used as if it were an individualized test. The goal of adapting a test to accommodate a student's disability is not to modify the test or to obtain diagnostic information, although both of these might be worthy goals for different reasons, but to use normal testing procedures with minimal accommodations.

Test Location

Test location is obviously a key element when testing a student individually. Many tests used in special education are given individually and require a quiet room away from the regular class. Factors which must be taken into account when considering the test setting include the type of test being used (e.g., group or individual), the need for special equipment (e.g, computer), and the accessibility of the location.

Home testing. For a student not able to attend school, the test setting might be the student's home or a hospital. This should not be a problem as long as the examiner is sure to bring all necessary equipment and materials. For classroom-type tests, a homebound teacher, care provider, tutor, parent might all be used to assess daily progress. However, standardized achievement tests should be given by the homebound teacher, the classroom teacher (which might be difficult to arrange), or teacher consultant. For most situations a parent or guardian should not be used to administer standardized tests.

Carrel. Although taking a test in a carrel or similar type of small enclosure might prevent distractions and thereby promote test performance is a possibility, there should be evidence that this type of accommodation is necessary. If a carrel is used, it should be because the student is distracted and not because the student is classified as having a disability (and not necessarily distractible). Just as important, a carrel should not be used as a test location site because of some abstract notion that it will be *helpful*. If a student can participate in normal group testing, the student is entitled to the opportunity to do so. This does not mean that a carrel is inherently inappropriate, but that every test accommodation should be based on student need.

Special room. The administration of a test might require testing a student in a separate location of which the following factors should be considered: (1) Accessibility: the test location should be accessible, and entry into the room should present no obstacles; (2) Availability: a room available at 9:00 A.M. does not mean that this will be the case at the time of actual testing; (3) Distractibility: testing in a chemistry classroom, social studies classroom (with maps galore) might create rather than eliminate distractions; (4) Inside Noise: lunchrooms are often questionable and **DO NOT DISTURB** signs will often have little impact on a hungry student body; (5) Outside Noise: this must be evaluated before testing and not in mid-testing when a whistle is heard beginning a full-court basketball game; (6) Lighting: a quick inspection and possibly a note to the custodian will generally remedy any problems in this area; (7) Personnel: be sure that all necessary personnel (e.g., an interpreter, scribe, reader) are aware of where and when the test is administered; (8) Furniture: if a table and chairs are needed, be sure the necessary items are available and appropriate; (9) Equipment: if special equipment is necessary, arrangements should be made before testing to ensure that the equipment is available delivered and working; and (10) Comfort: there might be a reason why an infrequently-used room is used infrequently. The appropriateness of the room temperature should be checked immediately prior to and during testing.

Diagnostic testing often requires considerable dialogue between the test examiner and student which can be distracting to other students. As indicated by the PPVT-R (Dunn & Dunn, 1981) test instructions regarding the test setting, many individualized tests require a separate location as part of the standardization procedures so that "the test should be given in a quiet room away from other people. Two chairs, one of comfortable size for the subject, and a table (or flattop desk) of appropriate height, will be needed. The room temperature should be comfortable, and ventilation and lighting adequate" (p. 5).

Accessibility

The importance of meeting accessibility standards is stated in Section 504,[6] but other factors besides physical access to a facility must be considered when evaluating the accessibility to a testing location. The amount of time needed to arrive at the test site and the need for assistance can delay a student from arriving at the designated time. The time required from going to point A to point B in a wheelchair, in spite of the design of the facility, might be considerable. Extra time must not only be considered when taking the test, but to reach the test location where the test is being given.

For students who are tested individually, a special testing time might conflict with other classes or activities. If testing is conducted outside of the regular classroom, the classroom teacher must be notified as to when the testing will occur. More importantly, a time must be sought which will have minimal impact on regular classroom instruction.

For students with mobility problems, the test location should be wheelchair accessible. In addition, for some students, the room might require a table and desk rather than an all-in-one desk for test taking. For students with health problems being tested in a lab situation, a stool might be useful for reducing fatigue. The American National Standards Institute (1986) has developed guidelines relating to accessibility for persons with physical disabilities. Such factors as wheelchair passage width (a minimum of 36 inches), doorway width (a minimum of 32 inches), accessible routes, necessary seating and work space for persons in wheelchairs, space to maneuver, accessible bathroom facilities, stairs, elevators, Braille elevator buttons, handrails, ramps, adequate lavatories facilities, are all factors which can effect the test situation.

Transportation

A local educational agency must "provide special education and related services designed to meet the needs of private school handicapped children residing in the jurisdiction of the agency."[7] Rothstein (1990) made a distinction between direct services which may not be provided at parochial schools, "and diagnostic services, which may be provided at the school or reimbursed if provided at the religious school" (p. 166). Although a "public agency is not required by this part to pay for the child's education at the private school or facility... the public agency shall make services available to the child."[8] Whether a student is evaluated at the private or public school site, the examiner might be required to travel to the private school or have the student transported to the public school. If the examiner tests the student at the private school, decisions concerning when and where to test should be made in conjunction with private and public school personnel well before the testing date. If the student must travel to the public school for diagnostic services, the logistics of transportation (which includes scheduling, time to go from school A to School B, personnel accompanying the student, and necessary equipment and adaptive devices) must be thoroughly planned beforehand.

Environment

For group and individual testing in a separate room, the suitability of the location must be evaluated before testing. Noise level within and outside the room should be evaluated. Lunch rooms and libraries are sometimes available for testing, but the location should be available without interruption for the duration of the testing. A vacant room next to the main office might be ideal late in the afternoon when school has been dismissed, but might prove to be a hub of commotion at the time of actual testing. Likewise, a room that is little used, and little heated, or where the temperature and humidity assume tropical proportions might provide a less than ideal test environment. During test administration, periodic comfort *checks* might be appropriate.

Lighting should be sufficient to avoid visual discomfort and in working order. This is especially important when testing in a nonclassroom location. If glare is a problem, moving the chair or desk so that the light source is overhead or behind the student is usually all that is required. Barraga and Erin (1992) suggested that for students with visual impairments "teachers should let children try many different lighting conditions to determine those that are optimal" (p. 166).

Enhancing lighting and reducing noise level are typical accommodations, but for some students just the opposite might be useful to promote a calm testing atmosphere. For example, turning down the lighting and background music/noise might be useful for reducing test anxiety.

Equipment

Students will have two types of equipment needs: environment- and test-related equipment. Environment-related equipment includes items which have no direct bearing on the test, the test format or mode of response. Examples of this type of equipment include special chairs, tables, bookstands, vaporizers, dehumidifiers, air purifiers, sound buffers, partitions, special lamps, and some magnification (e.g., glasses) and amplification devices (e.g., hearing aid) and other unobtrusive devices designed to facilitate test performance (e.g., visor cap). The test examiner should consult with the student prior to testing, and once testing has begun, to ensure that the student has all necessary equipment, the equipment has been adjusted to meet individual needs, and the equipment is working. Needless to say, the student will also need actual testing time so that the number of inquiries by the examiner (e.g., Is everything OK? Do you need anything?) must be kept to a minimum.

Environment-related accommodations are adaptations which are unrelated to the test or testing, while test-related equipment accommodations can have a substantial impact on test performance. Examples of equipment in this category include Braille devices, augmentative communication equipment, special paper, computer equipment, and magnification and amplification devices which alter the test format. Using a screen enlarger to increase the point size of a test changes the test format and, in all likelihood, will require more time. Using a calculator, computer or typewriter when not ordinarily allowed entails a major test modification. Test-related equipment is discussed in more detail in Chapter 8. However, even though a test examiner might have minimal knowledge of the equipment being used, the examiner should be aware of the allowability and availability of all approved equipment-based accommodations.

Seating

Preferential seating should be given to those students who might better understand instructions by being in close proximity to the test examiner, when lighting is a factor (e.g., the glare from a window), when accessibility is a consideration (e.g., room for a wheelchair is made near the room entrance), or if a student requires monitoring. The American Association for the Advancement of Science's publication Barrier Free in Brief (1991) suggests that "mobility impaired students are not relegated to a doorway, a side aisle or the back of the room" (p. 24) and that "common sense" will often provide a suitable accommodation (e.g., unbolting a fixed seat to make room for a wheel-chair). In most instances, special seating arrangements involve nothing more than reserving a desk at or near the front of the room.

Of course, the most preferential seat might be someplace other than the front of the room. If accessibility is a problem, a seat (or place) near the entrance might be best; if a student is using an interpreter, a seating arrangement which minimally distracts other students might be useful. If a student has an aide, a location in the room where the student and aide will not distract other students should be considered. If a student has frequent bathroom needs, a seat near the door might be the least distracting location.

If a student does have a disability which requires a seating accommodation, the student will not automatically identify his or her need prior to testing. A classroom teacher who is aware of a student's IEP should be aware of necessary accommodation, but if the test proctor is someone other than the student's teacher, there is no assurance that the accommodation will be implemented. If this situation occurs, the student must be prepared to request the necessary seating or other approved accommodations.

Proctor Role

When testing a student individually the examiner is generally aware of the specific test accommodations the student requires, but this is not always the case when a student requires an accommodation in a group setting. In a group setting, the test proctor must be aware of required test accommodations and be able to assist in the implementation of the accommodation if necessary. A major problem that can occur is a request for an accommodation without prior notification or authorization. A student might request extra time to complete a test, but a test proctor would be remiss to allow this without authorization. Likewise, a student should not be allowed to use a calculator or other aid unless there it is authorization to do so. Some accommodations will seem obvious (e.g., using an interpreter to sign instructions), but explaining the accommodation to the test proctor before the test is a matter of simple courtesy.

For a group test, the experience of the proctor will range from a thorough knowledge of the individual testing needs little to or no knowledge of special education or required test accommodations. Prior to testing the proctor should be made aware of students requiring IEP or Section 504 accommodations, the need for special seating or equipment, the allocability of aids, the use of special tests or forms, special administration instructions (e.g., recording answers in the test booklet), extended time limits, and the need for special personnel (e.g., translator).

Attention

For many students receiving special education and related services, poor attention and motivation can significantly impact test performance. Many factors can cause inattentive test behavior including lack of interest or motivation, fatigue, daydreaming, focusing on something other than the test (e.g., home life), personality conflict, a test task or test which is disinteresting or downright unpleasant, or a very difficult or very easy test. If poor attention during testing is a factor, especially if the inattentive behavior warrants an accommodation, there are several strategies which can be used to maximize attention. First, remove potential distractions and/or find a more suitable test environment. Second, individualize testing so that the examiner can provide additional encouragement, provide breaks when necessary, and promote on-task behavior when testing become tedious or bogged down. Third, the examiner should attempt to maintain a steady tempo. This can cause somewhat of a dilemma in that on the one hand the examiner must carefully explain the task and allow for a response, while on the other hand the examiner should not dawdle or become distracted by irrelevant behavior (e.g., the student wants to discuss unrelated topics).

For certain tests (viz., cassette, Braille, large print, single-switch) additional testing time is necessary. However, when attention is an important variable, minimizing the amount of time a student is tested, coupled with using strategies to maximize attention, is very important. The proctor or examiner should be aware that inattention can be a confounding factor, especially when the task itself requires a considerable amount of effort.

For the student who has a problem attending to a test task, pretest planning is essential. Giving a student two hours to complete a test when the student's attention span is fifteen minutes is more a test punishment than an accommodation. There are a variety of strategies which can be used to promote attention including the following: (1) Environment: remove distractions; (2) Individualization: administer the test one-to-one; (3) Rapport: develop and maintain good test rapport with the student; (4) Interest: make the test and task as interesting as possible; (5) Purpose: if the goal is to test to derive a normative score, don't interrupt the student (e.g., as with impromptu with remedial or diagnostic interventions); (6) Praise: give encouragement and praise, but not answers; (7) Clarification: explain the task and what is expected; (8) Involvement: involve the student in the test as quickly as possible; (9) On-task: don't be distracted by irrelevant responses; (10) Success: use sample items to reinforce task success; and (11) Time management: maintain tempo and provide breaks

Examiner Rapport

The ability of the test examiner to develop rapport is extremely important when assessing students with disabilities. If a reasonable high level of interest is expected, the test examiner must exhibit a degree of interest in the test and what is being tested. If the examiner appears bored and disinterested, the student will probably exhibit similar characteristics. As best as possible, the student should be at ease and tested in a comfortable and relaxed atmosphere. This is best accomplished by carefully explaining the test, answering all questions, and not being critical or demanding. During the test the examiner should provide encouragement, while at the same time being sure that the student is not given an unfair advantage.

Creating a nurturing and nonthreatening test environment is a goal for all test situations. A lack of attention or motivation can affect test performance. If this is the case, the test examiner must not be hurried, yet the test instructions and test items must be given with a degree of alacrity. This is especially the case for individually administered tests. Very often a student begins a test with enthusiasm, but items are presented so slowly that before the test is completed, the student is no longer engaged in the task.

There is a limit to the extent to which an examiner can or should attempt to make a test into a thoroughly enjoyable experience in that all tests are not intrinsically enjoyable, and many tests require considerable focus and good work skills on the part of the student. The examiner needs to engage the student, calmly explain the task, smile, don't yell, don't threaten, clarify questions and problems the student might have (but do not give the answer), and provide praise and encouragement. If the examiner demonstrates a sincere interest in the student and testing, the student will perceive this and act accordingly. If the examiner is uninterested, dispassionate, and indifferent to the student and the test, expect a similar response on the part of the student.

When a test is administered to a student requiring test accommodations, the examiner must focus on the purpose of the assessment. Often the situation requires the examiner to administer the test as expeditiously as possible. This means that the purpose is not to remediate problems which might be detected (e.g., impromptu speech and/or language remediation), but to give the assessment as quickly and efficiently as possible. The exception to this is when a test is given diagnostically. However, even in this situation, if the goal is to give an assessment in its entirety, frequent interruptions will jeopardize this goal. Diagnostic questioning and impromptu remediation might seem necessary, but to the student it might be tedious and bothersome.

Meeting with a student prior to testing for five or ten minutes will provide the examiner with an opportunity to become familiar with the student's level of motivation, interest, language, readiness for testing, and the suitability of the tests which are about to be used. If a student is difficult to understand, Hargrove and Poteet (1984) suggested that extra time be spent with the student in prior conversation in order "to become accustomed to the student's speech and level of communication" (p. 305). This is an excellent suggestion.

Examiner Training

Consultation from persons with expertise regarding a student's disability and necessary test accommodations is essential when the student's needs are not within the test-user's "range of professional experiences " (American Psychological Association, 1985, p. 43). Many problems which arise when testing students can be avoided by a relatively brief workshop for teachers and administrators relating to test administration and accommodations. Even if a teacher is not administering a test to a student requiring an accommodation, understanding what is allowed and disallowed during testing will help foster a better understanding of the appropriateness and use of test accommodations.

Qualifications. The qualifications of an examiner can be an issue when a student requires a test accommodation such as individual testing. Although tests must be "administered by trained personnel,"[9] the meaning of "trained" depends on the test and the personnel administering the test. For classroom tests, an aide under the guidance of a teacher would generally be able to administer classroom tests with necessary accommodations. For statewide competency tests, teacher certification might be a requirement. In Texas (Texas Education Agency, 1997) substitute teachers and "teachers who hold teaching permits or alternative certificates that have been authorized by the Texas Education Agency (TEA) may serve as test administrators" for the statewide competency test (Texas Assessment of Academic Skills)." In addition, "training is required for all test administrators." For many tests used in special education, formal test training is generally not necessary but familiarity with the test and test administration is suggested. The PPVT-R (1981) recommends that "practice in administering and scoring the test, preferably under the supervision of an experienced examiner, is encouraged" (p. 5). Certain standardized tests (viz., Stanford-Binet & WISC-III) cannot be administered and interpreted by untrained and unlicensed personnel, while a test such as the Kaufman Assessment Battery for Children (Kaufman & Kaufman, 1983) cautions that test administration "requires a competent, trained examiner, well-versed in psychology and individual assessment" (p. 4).

At the very least, the test examiner should be familiar with the test manual which details how the test should be administered. If an aide is used to administer a test, the permissibility of administering a specific test by specific personnel should be determined at the state and local level, and whether such administration is in conformance with the test instructions. Most importantly, regardless of the type being used, training should be provided to administer tests without and with accommodations.

For tests which are given individually, the test examiner should practice administering the test to a student with no disability before using the test with a student requiring a specific test accommodation. Most important, personnel might require specific training so that tests are administered without inadvertent modifications. Administering a group test individually might be necessary, but the validity of the test would be undermined if cues or feedback were given which suggested the correctness of answers. This problem might be avoided by providing a brief training session and guidelines for administering tests for all personnel involved with special education and related services.

If several modifications are routinely used within a school, a brief workshop can be useful for developing a standardized approach for applying the accommodation. For example, the procedure for having a test transcribed into large print, and a reasonable turnaround time, can be discussed. If some students require readers, important factors relating to reading printed tests can be discussed such as reading speed, reading rhythm, answering questions, rereading items, not providing inadvertent cues, and proving sufficient time to answer items.

ENDNOTES

1. 34 C.F.R. §300.532(a)(3)
2. 34 C.F.R. §300.532(c)
3. 34 C.F.R. §300.532(a)(3)
4. 34 C.F.R. §300.532(a)(3)
5. 34 C.F.R. §300.550(b)(1)
6. 34 C.F.R. §104.23(c) which cites the *American National Standards Institute accessibility standards.*
7. 34 C.F.R. §300.452
8. 34 C.F.R. §300.403 (but recently modified by IDEA-1997 so that on-the-premises services *may* be provided as per Section 612(a)(10)(B)(i)).
9. 34 C.F.R. §300.532(a)(3)

Chapter 6

TEST FORMAT ACCOMMODATIONS

A test format accommodation results in a substantive change to a test (e.g., print size), how the test is administered (e.g., extended test time), or the response required by the test-taker (e.g., oral responses are allowed). Reading printed test items to a student with a disability is invariably a substantial change in how the test was originally standardized. Transcribing a test into Braille will probably change, to some extent, what the original version of the test measures although the magnitude of the change depends on the transcription of the items into Braille. As with all accommodation, a valid format modification is one which mitigates the effects of a disability without changing what the test measures. Presenting fewer items on each page in order to reduce test clutter alters the test layout, but the accommodation might have no impact on test performance. When making a format modification, changes must be limited to only those necessary to reduce the effects of a disability. On the other hand, extended time (see Chapter 7) does not alter the test itself, but if rate of work is part of what the test measures, this format modification would substantially change what the test measures.

Table 6.1 lists various types of format accommodations in terms of the test format, test administration, and response accommodations. Very often two or more of these accommodations are used in combination, or a primary accommodation (e.g., oral testing) mandates a secondary accommodation (e.g., extended time) because of the primary accommodation task. Braille, cassette and scripted tests require additional time because of the format. Or a student might use a Braille or large print version of a test, have a reader to orally present items, be permitted to respond orally and be given extended time to complete the test.

159

Table 6.1 Format Accommodations.

Test Format	Administration	Response
Layout	Test time	Oral
Large print	Within-test breaks	Braille
Braille	Oral presentation	Sign language
Cassette	Sign language	Bubble format
Item format	Combined Input	Adaptive response
Translation	Foreign language	Transcriber
Item difficulty	Scripted tests	Facilitated

Teacher support. Because format modifications often require time to prepare and implement, support for the classroom teacher is essential. The classroom teacher must have support in terms of who will make the modifications (e.g., who will make the actual large print classroom test), who will administer the modified test, and how the test results will be interpreted and used.

The classroom teacher should be consulted prior to the implementation of a format accommodation, and the role of the classroom teacher should be clarified, as well as all other support services which are used to implement the accommodation. For classroom-made tests which require modification, the amount of lead time necessary to make such modifications should be clear. If individual testing is required, who will do the testing and where must be decided. If a test accommodation requires a unique format (e.g., reading content questions), how this will be done and who will do this must be determined.

Standardized Test Modifications

Modified Standardized Formats

A modified standardized format is a test which has been specifically modified to accommodate a student's test needs. The modified test formats are developed and provided by the test publisher or state agency. Transcribing a test into Braille, using a large print version of a test or reading a test verbatim are examples of modified test formats. If available, a modified format provided by the test publisher will limit validity problems caused by changing test format.

College admission tests such as the SAT and ACT have been most conscientious in providing modified test formats (viz., large print,

Braille, cassette, or script) while statewide competency tests tend to be very idiosyncratic with respect to allowable test accommodations and available research. In spite of the large number of commercial tests available, relatively few are available in modified formats. One exception is the 8th Edition of the Stanford Achievement Test (SAT-8) which has been adapted for use with deaf students (Schildroth, 1990) by using screening tests to assign deaf students to the eight SAT-8 difficulty levels (ranging from grade levels of 1.5 to 9.9), and by providing a variety of normative data for interpreting the performance of deaf and hard-of-hearing students.

For students with visual impairments, the SAT Form J has been renormed by eliminating visual-based items so as to better reflect the abilities of visually impaired students when compared to students form the general school population (see Bradley-Johnson, 1994, p. 156). The American Printing House for the Blind (APH)[1] offers the Stanford Achievement Test (Primary 1, 2 & 3; Intermediate 1, 2 & 3; advanced 1 & 2) in large print and in Braille. In addition to the Stanford Achievement Test, the following large print tests are available from APH: California Achievement Test (levels 1.6 through 11.2), Cognitive Abilities Test, Comprehensive Test of Basic Skills (Grades 1 through 12), Metropolitan Achievement Tests, Iowa Tests of Basic Skills (Covering grades K through 7), Survey of Basic Skills, and Test of Cognitive Skills (Grades 3 through 12). Large type versions of the Brigance Diagnostic Comprehensive Inventory of Basic Skills, the APH Tactile Supplement, and the Otis-Lennon School Ability Test are also available from APH.[2]

Alternative Standardized Format

If a modified standardized test is not available, an alternative test might be necessary. If a school district uses an achievement test which does not have a corresponding Braille version, a different test which does have this format might be selected. An alternative test might be necessary in order to meet a specific test need (e.g., maintaining a student's interest) because of norm limitations (e.g., the test which is being replaced has restricted norms), the alternative test has a task which best meets the student's needs (e.g., using the PPVT-R to assess the verbal ability), or because a special normative interpretation of performance is wanted.

When considering an alternative test, the purpose of testing should be very clear. If the test goal is to obtain diagnostic information, test selection will be based on the test which will provide the desired diagnostic information being sought. If the test goal is to obtain normative information which is most comparable to the regularly used test, the alternative test should approximate the test which it is replacing while providing the necessary format, task and response accommodations.

Alternative content and task. Except when a specific task is required, task and content comparability are important factors when considering an alternative test. If the regularly used test is inappropriate, an alternative test should be selected which best measures the content domain in question (i.e., the domain being measured by the regularly used test), and which uses a similar test task. There are a number of reasons why a cloze task might provide useful normative and diagnostic information, but if the regularly used test entails a traditional passage/question format, a cloze format might not be the best alternative test. Here a distinction must be made between selecting a suitable alternative test and a useful diagnostic test. The cloze test might provide useful diagnostic information, but if the goal is to select an alternative test to make a normative statement about the student's reading performance on a schoolwide test, an alternative test which best approximates the test is appropriate.

There are occasions when an alternative test might be selected because of the uniqueness of the content or task. For a student with an auditory impairment, a nonverbal rather than verbal task might be used to measure intellectual functioning. For students with expressive language disorders, a test which measures receptive language might be necessary (e.g., the PPVT-R). For student's with visual impairments, verbal tests are frequently used in place of nonverbal tests and tasks (e.g., only WISC-III verbal subtests are given).

Individually administered tests. In special education individually administered tests (e.g., WRMT-R, PIAT-R) are routinely used as part of the overall educational evaluation. There are several good reasons for this practice such as the wide difficulty range of these tests, a corresponding wide normative range, and increased interest/motivation associated with an individually administered test. As useful as individual tests are in special education, they should not be the only source of evaluation and diagnostic information, and should be used when regular school tests cannot be used or in conjunction with schoolwide tests. Test results from a wide-range test are not the same as the results from a group test because of content, norms, and general administration differences. A percentile rank of 35 in reading on a individual test might be equivalent to regular test performance or might provide a completely different estimate of reading ability.

The individually administered wide-range tests described below rely on national norms, while many group achievement tests provide both national and/or local norms. The difference can be substantial. If a student attends a school with above average students in comparison to the national average, national norm scores will be higher than local norm scores; if the student attends a school with below average students in comparison to the national average, national norm scores will be lower than local norm scores. If there is a difference between national and local norms, and because many tests might not have local norms (e.g., wide-range tests and IQ tests in particular), national norms should be used to compare scores from different tests. There will no doubt be differences between two different tests with two different national samples, but in view of the sampling sophistication of the tests described below, this is more appropriate than comparing tests based on national and local norms.

Table 6.2 describes several individually administered tests which are often used in special education. All of these tests are psychometrically sound, can be used with a wide-range of students, and each can provide important evaluation for better understanding a student's educational needs.

Table 6.2 Individually Administered Tests.

Test[a]	Use
PIAT-R	Very useful wide-range screening test of achievement comprised of six subtests involving mathematics, reading, general information and writing.
WRAT3	Requires very little time to administer, content is so-so (reading, spelling, arithmetic subtests), but norms are wide-range and sound.
WIAT	Comprised of eight subtests involving reading(3), mathematics(2), listening comprehension, oral expression, and written expression. An attractive test when used in conjunction with the WISC-III.
DAB-2	Includes listening and speaking subtests, in addition to reading, writing and mathematics.
KTEA	Two versions (comprehensive and brief forms) are available which measure different aspects of reading, spelling and mathematics.
Brigance	Very popular because of excellent content selection, but the inventories do not provide extensive norm-based data.
WRMA-R	Much used measure of reading, but the tasks for the different subtests might be different than what appears in a school's curriculum.
GORT-3	An excellent measure of oral reading and this, or a similar test, should be used whenever a student is suspected of having a reading disability.
KeyMath-R	The illustrations are outstanding, 14 subtests, and has good clinical usefulness. One drawback is an insufficient number of items for several subtests.
TOWL-2	Because there are so few measures which concentrate on written language, this test is frequently used in special education.
PPVT-R	Excellent assessment of receptive language using a nonoral (e.g., point to a picture) format.

[a]**PIAT-R**: Peabody Individual Achievement Test-Revised (Markwardt, 1989); **WRAT3:** Wide Range Achievement Test 3 (Wilkinson, 1993); **WIAT:** Wechsler Individual Achievement Test (Psychological Corporation, 1992); **DAB-2:** Diagnostic Achievement Battery-2 (Newcomer, 1990); **KTEA:** Kaufman Test of Educational Achievement (Kaufman & Kaufman, 1985); **Brigance**: Brigance Diagnostic Inventory of Basic Skills (Brigance, 1977) and the Brigance Diagnostic Inventory of Essential Skills (Brigance, 1981); **WRMT-R:** Woodcock Reading Mastery Tests-Revised (Woodcock, 1987); **GORT-3:** Gray Oral Reading Tests-3 (Wiederholt & Bryant, 1992); **Keymath-R:** KeyMath-Revised: A Diagnostic Inventory of Essential Mathematics (Connolly, 1988); **TOWL-2:** Test of Written Language-2 (Hammill & Larsen, 1988); **PPVT-R:** Peabody Picture Vocabulary Test-Revised (Dunn & Dunn, 1981).

LEP and ESL Assessment[3]

If a student has no English-speaking skills, limited English proficiency (LEP) or acquired English as a second language (ESL) or where a bilingual environment is a factor in the evaluation of ability, a bilingual specialist should be part of the multidisciplinary evaluation team. This is necessary if "tests and other evaluation materials are provided and administered in the child's native language or other mode of communication, unless it is clearly not feasible to do so."[4] In addition, if there is a difference between the language normally used by the student and parents, the evaluation of the student should "be in the language normally used by the child and not that of the parents."[5] Depending on the nature of the evaluation and the student's native language, an evaluation of cognitive and academic skills commensurate with an English-speaking evaluation might not be "feasible." If possible, an examiner with expertise in the student's native language should be a part of the team.

Determining needed test accommodations for a student whose primary language is not English, or where more than one language is spoken, is difficult. Before the effects of a disability can be considered, a test must be available in the student's primary language. Extended time for a student whose primary language is not English might be a valid accommodation for certain tests, but it does not circumvent the inappropriateness of using an English-based test with a student not proficient in English.

Extemporaneous or impromptu translations of tests (e.g., items are translated during testing) might provide useful qualitative information as to ability and test needs, but the results cannot be used to derive standardized scores. A written translation of a test provides some measure of accountability and consistency, but the effect of the translation on test validity is problematic and doing so might be discriminatory. For example, assume that in comparison to the student's cultural group, the student has average cognitive ability. Translating a test into the student's native language, and then using regular test norms might reflect cultural differences rather than a forthright evaluation of cognitive ability.

The use of reference materials by an LEP student for most standardized tests is not allowed because the material might explicate the test language, change the test difficulty, change what is being measured, and possibly provide answers to test questions. If reference material is allowed, extended time will also be necessary if one of the student's tasks is translating via the reference material. If a test is not standardized, the use of reference material might be allowed if such material is allowed during the normal course of daily instruction. In Texas (Texas Education Agency, 1994) the use of English or foreign-language reference material is not allowed for the statewide competency examination, but reference material is allowed during end-of-course examinations:

> A limited English proficient (LEP) student may use a dictionary that provides translations of English words if such a dictionary is used as part of his or her regular classroom instruction.

and

> A limited English proficient student may have words on the test translated into his or her native language if this assistance is part of his or her regular classroom instruction. In providing a student with translation assistance, only native-language equivalents for English words or phrases may be given. The translator must be careful not to provide interpretations that would allow the student an advantage in arriving at a correct response.

The difficulty involved concerning the evaluation of students with limited English proficiency is an obvious concern in the IDEA Amendments of 1997 which acknowledge special education placement inequities involving these students:

> The limited English proficient population is the fastest growing in our Nation, and the growth is occurring in many parts of our Nation. In the Nation's 2 largest school districts, limited English students make up almost half of all students initially entering school at the kindergarten level. Studies have documented apparent discrepancies in the levels of referral and placement of limited English proficient children in special education. The Department of Education has found that services provided to limited English proficient students often do not respond primarily to the pupil's academic needs. These trends pose special challenges for special education in the referral, assessment, and services for our Nation's students from non-English language backgrounds.[6]

One condition for the evaluation of a specific learning disability is the provision that the disability is not the result of "environmental, cultural, or economic disadvantage."[7] When first considering this proviso, one might conclude that it is overly restrictive but the intent is to eliminate discrimination because of environmental, cultural, or economic factors. If a student has limited English, the student most definitely has special instructional needs, but this does not necessarily signify a disability, and treating this need as a disability might ignore actual needs and preclude appropriate services (e.g., ESL services).

Before a determination can be made that a student has a disability when language is a confounding variable, and before a test accommodation can be specified, information is necessary to determine language proficiency in both the student's native language (or first language) and English, and cognitive and achievement proficiency in both languages.

If a student does not have a disability in his or her primary language, the existence of a disability in English for a student with limited English-speaking skills is certainly suspect.

An even more complex situation is the possibility that a student does not have a learning disability in his or her native language, but does in English. If a disability in the student's native language cannot be determined, the student must be given the opportunity to demonstrate proficiency when given appropriate instruction. If an LEP student requires special education or related services, one of the services might be English language instruction. However, in order to evaluate academic progress, test accommodations in the student's native language, in English or in both might be required. Unfortunately, tests (much less test accommodations) might not be readily available or even in existence.

The abuses of using English-version tests[8] with bilingual or non-English speaking students have been so egregious that examiners are often reluctant to administer such tests even when the test can provide useful information. If an English-version test is given to a LEP student and the student performs satisfactorily, this is a very important information in terms of understanding the student's potential. However, if an English-version test is given to a LEP student and the student does not perform satisfactorily, the only conclusion which can be drawn is that limited proficiency in English might be a factor.

LEP assessment. When selecting a test in the student's primary language, consideration must be given to whether the test is a translation and uses English-based norms, whether the test has been restandardized in the primary language (e.g., norms are based on Spanish-speaking students participating in bilingual programs in the

United States), or whether the test is a nonstandardized inventory-type measure used to evaluate language and/or academic proficiency. Some statewide tests are available in Spanish, and the Tenth Mental Measurements Yearbook describes a variety of assessments in Spanish (e.g, the Ullman ESL Achievement Test for Beginning ESL Students and the Woodcock-Muñoz Language Survey, Riverside Publishing Company). For school use there is a Spanish version of the Eighth Edition of the Stanford Achievement Test for grades K-12 entitled Aprenda 2: La Prueba de Logros en Espanol (Psychological Corporation), the Spanish Assessment of Basic Education, Second Edition (Hampton-Brown Company, 1992), and the Riverside Performance Assessment Series (Riverside Publishing Company, 1994). In addition, there are Spanish versions of several tests used in special education (e.g., the Brigance Diagnostic Assessment of Basic Skills-Spanish Edition).[9] Unfortunately, there are relatively few tests which provide a normative assessment of school achievement in languages other than English and Spanish.

There are several tests which are designed to measure the ability of ESL and bilingual students but most are on the order of inventories rather than tests of intelligence and academic achievement. To a large degree, this is not necessarily the fault of the developers but due to the fact that sampling and generating meaningful LEP normative data is a very difficult task. Not only are there huge geographic and socioeconomic differences associated with different non-English speaking groups, but the diversity of non-English speaking groups makes the development of a coherent normative sample all but impossible. Brown's review (Tenth Mental Measurements Yearbook, 10:136) of English as a Second Language Oral Assessment-Revised characterizes many of the problems with LEP inventories. This reviewer concluded that "in sum, at first glance this test is attractive. However, on closer inspection, it turns out to be a relatively naive product, the use of which would be inappropriate from a serious language tester's point of view."

If a test is available which has been normed in the student's native language, than this test might provide relevant information. For bilingual and non-English speaking students, an evaluation of cognitive ability, often necessitates the use of nonverbal measures.

Nonverbal ability. For students with LEP, nonverbal assessment is often an important source of data. Nonetheless, a nonverbal or "performance" test does not necessarily mean that the test is void of language. If test instructions are in English and there are several different tasks, the test might provide a good measure of nonverbal cognitive ability but not necessarily for students with limited English proficiency. The Test of Nonverbal Intelligence, Second Edition (TONI2) (Brown, Sherbenou & Johnson, 1990) is an untimed test involving figural matching, analogies, classification and processions which require minimal language instructions and motor response (e.g., pointing) and is described as being useful for students "whose test performance may be confounded by language and motor impairments arising from such conditions as aphasia, hearing impairments, lack of proficiency with spoken or written English, Cerebral Palsy, stroke, head trauma, and lack of familiarity with the culture of the United States." The Kaufman Assessment Battery for Children (Kaufman & Kaufman, 1983) Nonverbal Scale is comprised of five subtests (face recognition, hand movements, triangles, matrix analogies, spatial memory and photo series) which are "provided to assess the mental processing of hearing-impaired, speech- and language-disordered, and non-English-speaking children" (pp. 2-3).

An evaluation of school achievement using curriculum-based measures translated in the student's native language is often necessary to measure present levels of performance. However, if a student has limited academic skills, but has reasonable cognitive ability (as measured by a nonverbal test), and information indicates that the student has had limited educational experiences, this would preclude the identification of a learning disability.[10] This does not mean that the student is not learning disabled, but only that the most obvious reason for the student's present level of performance might be environmental factors and not the result of a disability as defined by IDEA.

Literacy assessment. For a student with limited proficiency in English who is referred to the multidisciplinary evaluation team for possible classification and corresponding programs and services, appropriate assessment in both English and the student's native language is essential. The vast majority of students who are referred to the multidisciplinary evaluation team have difficulties in reading. Before a determination can be made that a student has a disability in reading English, the determination must be made as to the student's ability in his or her native language. Even if standardized test information is not available, qualitative information should be obtained to assess literacy skill in the student's native language.

Identifying an individual who is proficient in the native language of a student referred to the multidisciplinary evaluation team is extremely important. This is not only necessary to evaluate the student in his or her native language but also to provide a description of whatever is used to evaluate or report results to the parent "in the native language of the parent or other mode of communication used by the parent.[11]

Format Modifications

Although there are occasions when the format of a standardized test must be modified, this labor-intensive activity, coupled with copyright restrictions and validation issues, is best suited for teacher-made tests. Because of the time and effort required to make test format changes, format changes should be minimized and used only when necessary. Extra space between lines on tests might be a helpful test enhancement for all students, but who will make this accommodation, with what tests, and the validity of the accommodation must be considered.

Minimize Accommodations

Test accommodations should be minimal and should have a definite rationale. A format of accommodations should not be indicated for the sake of doing something, or to say that a test accommodation has been made if it is completely unrelated to test performance or student need.

Modifying reading passages so that complete sentences are placed on a single line might be cited as a modification, but this would be unnecessary if the student did not demonstrate a need for this accommodation. A format accommodation might improve a test, but an improvement which all students could benefit from. The goal of making a test modification is to test ability without invalidating the test; the goal is not to make a *better* test. In New York (New York State Education Department, 1995) a cautionary note is given that "test modifications should not be excessive" and that "they should alter the standard administration of a test to the least extent possible." (p. 6).

If a test modification does not impact test performance, it should not be used or its use reconsidered. If a test accommodation entails reducing the number of items per page, an assumption is made that placing fewer items on a page will contribute to the student's ability to participate in testing on an equal basis with others. The need for making this accommodation might be because the student begins answering one item then goes on to the next, answers items completely out of sequence, misplaces answers, or combines answers for different items. There are an infinite number of reasons why placing fewer items on a page might be useful, but there must be a reason for making this accommodation. Depending on the importance of the accommodation, a practice test might be used to determine the usefulness of the accommodation, or the accommodation might be used for a limited period of time (e.g., three months).

In most situations item layout is not going to have a drastic effect on test performance. However, if there is something about the layout that can be identified and related to specific test behavior(s), and subsequent investigation reveals that the accommodation does impact performance, then the accommodation would be justified.

In terms of the impact that a test can have on the results, format accommodations fall into five major categories: (1) layout modifications, (2) transliterations, (3) translations, (4) language-mode accommodations, and (5) reduced-difficulty tests.

Layout

A layout accommodation should have minimal effect on the difficulty of the test. The reasons for changing the layout might be to meet the visual needs of a student (e.g., large print), focus on a specific task or item, or enhance a student's ability to respond. Every layout modification should have a specific purpose. Generic accommodations, accommodations which are made unrelated to a specific test need, are designed to make a test "user friendly." For example, Greenberg (1980) discussed several test modifications for New Jersey's assessment program: An arrow instead of the words "GO on to the next page," item-bubble identifier consistency, enlarged type, dark line between items, items centered in boxes, stop signs at the end of sections, vertical item choices, large bubble and space between bubbles. These might be excellent ideas for improving a test for use with all students, but there is probably no single test format which can be used to meet the very individualized accommodation needs of students with disabilities.

Modifying the item spacing and/or margination can be useful accommodations for students who are easily distracted by printed material or intimidated by an ominous test task. Unfortunately, determining the degree of distractibility and intimidation is not easily done. Every student might profit from a less crowded and easily readable test format. However, the test accommodation task is to determine if an accommodation will reduce the effects of the disability.

Tests should have a reasonably uncluttered appearance. One appeal of tests such as the PPVT-R, PIAT-R and Keymath-R is the exceptional item layout of these tests. In contrast to many group tests, each of these tests is extremely attractive, uncluttered, and easily used. For classroom tests an uncluttered appearance can be accomplished by using a simple font (e.g., Courier, Times Roman), a point size of 10 or 12, wide margins (e.g., 1.5 inches on all sides), double spacing between lines and triple spacing between items, left justification to eliminate gaps between words, a vertical format for multiple-choice alternatives, and bottom centered page numbers to allow students the ability to move through the test with some ease, will provide an acceptable test layout (see the guidelines below).

Highlighting. Several techniques can be used to highlight questions and/or answers including large print, shaded or highlighted boxes, color, arrows, stop signs, etc. The difficulty with highlighting tests is that the accommodation may or may not meet the specific needs of a student. Student-supplied highlighting (e.g., using reading windows, rulers, place markers, marking the test booklet, marking answers left incomplete, marking items needing reconsideration, underlining words or sections of text, using a highlighter, etc.) solves this problem. Of course, the method used to highlight responses should in no way suggest the correctness of the answer (e.g., pertinent test information is "highlighted" which helps identify the correct answer). In Texas, a student is allowed to "place a colored transparency over the test" (Texas Education Agency, Chapter 3, 1996) although no guidelines are provided to determine when this accommodation would be needed. Although text can be highlighted, "highlighters or color pencils" are not allowed because this might interfere with machine scoring (Texas Education Agency, 1997). Generally speaking, if a highlighting technique is used in day-to-day instruction, in spite of the questionable validity of the accommodation, it should be allowed during testing.

Single item format. Easel format items have been shown to be very useful when testing students with disabilities. Presenting items individually provides a very uncluttered and easily controlled testing environment. For most students with disabilities, this type of test modification has more diagnostic import than general test utility for learning how a student responds and for developing test-taking skills and strategies. However, if a student has a physical disability and/or expressive language disorder, this type of task (or a language-board equivalent as discussed in Chapter 8) might be useful for evaluating student progress. Easel format items can be used to illustrate different types of items and tasks on an individual or group basis. When used diagnostically, the examiner can question the student concerning the stem and responses, and evaluate the student's test-taking strategies such as the ability to guess or why a certain alternative was selected or was not.

If used to measure academic performance, constructing individual test plates is labor-intensive work and who will do the test development, how it will be done, and for what type of test must be considered. An example of easel test plate is shown below (see tests such as the PIAT-R, PPVT-R and KeyMath-R for excellent examples of easel-item plate test questions).

Jon had two feet of rope. He used 12 inches. How many feet of rope were left.	
1	2
3	4

Test difficulty. When modifying the format of the test, test difficulty should not be changed. Unless a test is used as practice test or diagnostically, the number of items, the number of alternatives, the difficulty of items, and the language of items should not be changed. If a science test is transliterated to Braille and an exact transliteration of these items is impossible, the items should be replaced by means of an oral item or by a similar item which can be transliterated.

For norm-based tests, reducing the difficulty of items (e..g, by changing the language) creates an entirely new test and existing norms no longer apply. This does not necessarily mean that the test is easier or more difficult, but that the test is different than the original version.

A test modification can and will change item difficulty, but this should never be the intent of a modification. Reading a content test to a student likely changes the test difficulty, especially if the student has a reading disability. However, in this situation, an assumption is made that content is being evaluated apart from reading skill.

The item difficulty of a test is also changed by reducing the readability or the conceptual level of the item. This is very similar to out-of-level testing described in Chapter 2. If a test item contains the word *constitution,* using a substitute word or phrase (e.g., "a set of laws," or "laws that are written") might be a useful instructional tactic but this is not necessarily an acceptable test accommodation. Diagnostically, the test results might be useful, but if the goal is to determine whether the student has mastered subject content presented in the regular classroom, an overly simplified version of the subject matter would compromise the purpose of testing.

If a content test is read to a student, the vocabulary and syntax should be read exactly as written. However, if the content test is signed, this presents a problem. The only way to communicate specific content/technical words is to fingerspell. Yet, if the student is being signed the test because of poor reading skills, the student will probably have difficulty *reading* fingerspelled words. For example, reading the fingerspelling representation of the word *reservoir* contained in an item is probably more difficult than being able to see the word in print. But if the task is to understand the verbal concept of *reservoir,* using a sign for this word might result in an easier item or change the character of the item. A test accommodation can not only result in an easier task, but might clearly indicate the correct answer. If a spelling test is signed to a student, fingerspelling the target word would obviously result in the correct answer.

Large Print Applications

The availability and flexibility of personal computers and printers provides ample opportunity to generate highly individualized large print test accommodations. Large print applications are used not only with students having visual impairments, but also with students who are distracted by cluttered test formats and for very young children. The National Braille Association Manual for Large Type Transcribing (NBA, 1973) offers the following guidelines for large print formats (1) a point size 18 or greater; (2) a heavy sans serif (Gothic, plain, or block letter) typeface; (3) at least 6 characters per inch (cpi) for 18 point type; (4) a space of at least 75% of point size between lines; and (5) the use 0f off-white paper.

When determining the large print needs of a student, the best approach is to experiment with different fonts, point sizes, and type-face characteristics to generate text that best meets each student's individual needs. This is easily accomplished by creating test items using different typeface characteristics, and then having the student provide feedback as to which item is most readable. For one student 18 point Times Roman Bold might be best, while for a second student a non-bold 12 or 14 point typeface might be adequate. The goal should be to select a point size and font which best approximates the original test format being enlarged, while meeting the visual reading needs of the student.

As with all accommodations, a large print modification should be based on demonstrated rather than assumed need. Barrage and Erin (1992) cited several problems with using large print such as inconvenience, more adaptive motor control on the part of the reader and expense. These authors noted that "the use of enlarged materials, such as books with large type, is now considered a last resort, less desirable than either the reduction of reading distance or the use of optical device" (p. 164).

An obvious consideration regarding the use of large print is the amount of residual vision. A 1960 study by the American House for the Blind (Walker, 1960) of 14,125 visually impaired students studied revealed a very pronounced linear relationship between the use of large print and level of vision; that is, the use of large print decreased as level of vision decreased. The use of large print is related to the degree of residual vision, and that the characteristics of print should be designed to meet these residual needs.

Fonts

A general rule is to avoid elaborate fonts and to use the simplest font available. With the availability of a vast number of fonts with personal computer systems, the task of selecting a font can be daunting. For most large print applications, a sans serif typeface (a simple typeface with no flourishes) is preferred. Frequently available fonts such as Helvetica, Times Roman, Arial and Courier will be more than adequate; while fonts such as Playbill (too stylistic), Braggadocio (too bold), Script (hard to read) should be avoided.

Proportionality. Fonts can be either proportional (each character occupies the same amount of space) or nonproportional (the space occupied by each character depends on the character width). Courier is an example of a proportional font, and Times Roman an example of a nonproportional font. In terms of readability, nonproportional fonts have a "book-like" quality, while proportional fonts beckon us back to the days of the typewriter. For mathematics items a proportional font is often easier to use, while for reading applications a nonproportional font can enhance the readability of the typeface. The following illustrates the difference between proportional and nonproportional fonts:

This is 18-point Times Roman bold.

This is 18-point Courier bold.

Point size. Point size refers to the size of the typeface. Each point is 1/72 of an inch in height and is measured from the top of the tallest ascender (e.g., h, l) to the bottom of the lowest descender (e.g., p, q). A point size of 18 is equivalent to 1/4 of an inch, while a point size of 24 is equivalent to 1/3 of an inch. Although a point size of 18 is used with many large print modifications, Carr (1989) described three large print point sizes depending on grade level: Grades 1-3: 18 point; Grades 4-7: 14 point, and grades 8-12: 12 point. The following illustrates different point sizes for Times Roman.

Table 6.3 Nonproportional Times Roman Point Sizes.

Point Size	Times Roman Sample Text
12	**This is a standard point size.**
14	**Used as large print for some texts.**
18	**Basic large print point size.**
24	**This is a very large point size.**

Large print spacing. The space between lines is also measured in points and is referred to as the leading (as in the metal *lead*). To avoid a crowded appearance, large print lines need suitable spacing between lines. The simplest line spacing solution is to set the spacing to 1.5. If desired, the exact amount of leading can be specified, but this will depend on the font, point size and word processor being used. The line spacing leading for different point sizes is approximately one-half the point size so that the line spacing for 18 point should be 9 point, and the line spacing for 36 point should be 18 point.

The recommended letter spacing for 18 point is six characters per inch (cpi). The number of characters per inch may not be a major variable, but should be considered if improved letter spacing will increase the readability of the text and avoid a crowded typeface appearance. For point sizes other than 18, the number of characters per inch is limited by the point size. A point size of 24 allows 4.5 cpi, a point size of 30 allows 3.6, and a point size of 36 allows 3 cpi.

Mathematics Problems

Large print mathematics problems can be useful creating highly visual, uncluttered, and approachable test items. The following mathematics problems are in 18 point bold Courier which provides easy-to-read problems and helps eliminate number alignment diffi-culties.

```
    4              5              8
  + 2            + 5            + 9


    3              7             35
    5              4           -  9
  + 1            + 9


 $55.60           25          34 ÷
 +  8.50         X  6
```

Computer display accommodations. With the availability of personal computers, the test accommodations can include font, point size, color and item format. Computer testing can entail both closed- and open-ended tasks. Multiple-choice items can be presented in a single-switch format (see Chapter 8), items can be presented via a text file, or a task involving written expression can be developed. In terms of display accommodations, the format, font, point size, background and foreground color can be changed to meet specific test needs.

There are several methods for generating large print screen displays. First, the point size of more advanced word processors can be set so that the actual screen point size is enhanced. Second, depending on the system being used, a zoom component is often available which can be used to enlarge text a specified amount. Third, there are freeware (no cost), shareware (a cost if used), and commercial large-text word processing programs which allow point sizes ranging from 18 (about .25 inch screen characters) to 180 points (2.5 inch screen characters). In addition, large-print word processors often allow for the adjustment of character width and foreground/background colors (e.g., black characters on a white background or vice versa). Other computer accessibility options are discussed in Chapter 8.

Oral Test Accommodations

Reading Tests

In spite of the fact that the regulations state that "test results accurately reflect the child's aptitude or achievement level...rather than reflecting the child's sensory, manual or speaking skills (except where those skills are the factors which the test purports to measure),"[12] IEP's are sometimes written with a generic accommodation that tests be read to students. Reading a reading test to a student is contrary to the regulations, potentially discriminatory, most often contrary to the purpose intended by the test publisher, and definitely misleading.

Of the vast number of reading tests which have been constructed, few, if any, have ever suggested or recommended that a test be read to the student. Of all the instructions which demand conformance,[13] the *reading* required by reading tests seems the most obvious. Needless to say, this practice completely undermines test validity[14] and completely changes what the test measures.

An even greater problem than changing what a test measures when a reading test is read to a student is the potential for discrimination.[15] The phrase *except where those skills are the factors that the test purports to measure*[16] means that a test can reflect a student's impairment if that is what the test measures. This is included so that appropriate programs and services can be provided in relation to the student's ability in reading. Reading a reading test to a student might result in service not being provided (e.g., remedial reading) because the resulting score would not reflect the student's disability in reading. Suggesting that a student in the fifth grade is able to read at the seventh grade level, based on a score derived from a reading test which has been read to the student, is a gross misrepresentation of ability. The immediate effect of appearing to be able to read at or above grade level might provide a degree of immediate satisfaction but the long term effects of this illusion can be devastating. If a student's reading ability is falsely inflated, the need to participate in necessary remedial programs might be contraindicated, the ability to eventually develop or demonstrate competency denied, and participation in programs where the reading is required precluded.

If norms are used when a reading test is read to a student, the resulting scores are so misleading that virtually all instructional and remedial decisions will be problematic. Excluding a student from reading instruction and activities because the student has not been given an opportunity to demonstrate reading ability (or ability to develop this ability as a result of remediation) is discriminatory; excluding a student from a service or program because the student's ability is artificially inflated because of an egregious change in what the test measures is equally discriminatory.

Reading a reading-test might have some inclusionary or diagnostic value. If a student is having difficulty in reading comprehension, reading a comprehension passage might provide useful information concerning the student's cognitive processes. However, under no circumstances should this type of test administration result in a normative evaluation of reading performance or to suggest a normative level of reading competence.

Oral Reading Need

A student might need a content test read because of a reading, visual or physical disability. The need for a reader for a student with a disability depends on the severity of the disability and not the classification of the disability. Willingham et al. (1988) stated that in relation to the SAT performance of learning disabled students, the "data appear inconsistent with the assumption that this group, as a whole, suffers on test performance because of a reading problem." (p. 169).

For students with visual disabilities, if the student is not able to use large print or Braille, reading a test might be the only method to evaluate content ability. For students with physical disabilities, the inability to use a finger to select or to scan text material might create a very difficult reading task, and the use of a reader might be necessary for the student to read the text in an organized fashion.

If a content test is read to a student, there should be evidence of a severe reading disorder. Although the student might well be able "to gain meaning from printed material," reading ability must be impaired to the extent that actual content knowledge is not adequately measured. There is no need to overrely on IQ when determining the need for oral testing. A student with an IQ of 70 will probably exhibit below average reading performance, even though the primary problem is not *reading* but a more general *language* deficit as evidence by the low score. A student with a very low IQ score might demonstrate little understanding of the content from oral testing, but oral testing might be the most appropriate and direct method for evaluating content knowledge the student does have. A test accommodation does not ensure average test performance, but provides a fair method for exhibiting average performance.

The most effective way to determine whether a content test should be read to a student is to first administer the test in the usual manner, then with the oral reading accommodation using an old test or practice items. The practice test should parallel the actual type of test which will be used as much as possible. Although most content tests will require reading to some extent, the degree to which reading is a factor and how the student is able to cope with that reading will vary from test to test and disability to disability. A student might be able to read a column matching task, but have difficulty with lengthy text on a social studies test. A blanket guideline that all content tests should be read might be unnecessary and ignore the need and/or ability of the student to participate in regular educational assessment.

Providing the student with a copy of the test might be beneficial if the student is able to co-read the test with the reader, or at least follow the reader as the test is being read. Following the reader as the test is being read is obviously beneficial in that the student will then be able to refer to the stem and alternatives when selecting or formulating an answer. A student who cannot refer to the test is obviously at a disadvantage in that the student must rely on auditory memory and having the reader re-read items and alternatives. Providing a student with a copy of the test might not be helpful if the student is focusing more on the reading task or attempting to read than the content. If the student is engrossed in the reading task and oblivious to the content, reading the test without the accompanying text might provide a better measure of content ability. In most situations, a copy of the test should be available for the student to follow as much as possible. This is especially necessary if items contains graphs, charts or diagrams. In addition, being able to refer to item text is important for items requiring comparison and reflection. However, if a student's reading ability is extremely low, providing the student with a copy of the printed text might measure "attempted reading" rather than the target content.

Again, although an oral administration is a substantial departure from a print testing, one major goal is to maintain the validity of the test. In other words, if the test is designed to measure a specific content area (e.g., social studies, science, etc.), considerable effort on the part of the examiner must be devoted to measuring this content and not inadvertently measuring the ability of the student to pickup on examiner cues.

Oral Reading Format

There are two approaches for reading a test to a student: Verbatim reading in which the reader reads the exact test, and scripted tests which provide the exact format for reading the test (which might be somewhat different than the actual test). The SAT uses a scripted test for readers for students needing this accommodation so as to better standardize administration procedures.

When giving a test orally, the examiner must take into account a number of factors. For the Texas Assessment of Academic Skills guidelines: (1) the examiner and the examinee should use the same form of the test booklet, (2) questions and answers may be read as frequently as needed, (3) verbal or nonverbal assistance is not allowed, and (4) a neutral voice inflection is maintained during reading. A rise in pitch or a pause when reading an item might identify the correct answer. In addition, factors relating to pronunciation, clarification and general assistance should be determined beforehand. Requests for repeating questions or alternatives, how many times questions will be repeated, and time limits for responding (or waiving time limits) should be determined prior to testing.

The following provides a general guideline for reading content tests to students: (1) Difficulty: test difficulty should not be changed; (2) Assistance: the reader should not explain items, define words, or clarify concepts; (3) Time: provide sample time. At least double the normal amount of testing should be set aside for oral testing; (4) Literacy: an attempt should be made to evaluate the student commensurate with their primary mode of communication; (5) Practice: the examiner should practice administering the test orally; (6) Consistency: the method for presenting items/alternatives should be consistent; (7) Pronunciation: potential problems concerning pronunciation should be clarified; (8) Cues: avoid giving cues which might indicate the correctness of an answer such as by inflection or an inadvertent visual cues; (9) Presentation: the method for repeating questions should be determined beforehand; (10) Text: whether a copy of the printed version of the test should be available to the student really depends on the student's reading ability.

When reading a content test as a test accommodation, the need for the accommodation should be evaluated on an annual basis. The purpose of the accommodation is not to eliminate the necessity of developing reading or independent test-taking skills but to fairly measure content knowledge. Reading tests to a student should be used only when necessary and not as a matter of convenience. If the student is able to read Braille or large print, tests should be presented in this format when appropriate.

Recorded Tests

The advantage of a recorded or cassette version of a test is standardization and the ability to eliminate possible cues which the proctor might inadvertently give the student if the test is read. The disadvantage of cassette testing is that relatively few tests are available in recorded form, an extraordinary amount of time is necessary to make recorded test formats, and the task can be confusing to some students. May (1994) reported that for the SAT the script version is created before the cassette because there are more issues when creating the latter. For the cassette version, tone-indexing is used to allow the student to work through different parts of the cassette. For examiners and teachers developing an oral test, a cassette format certainly has a standardization appeal but developing this type of format is a time-intensive task and might not be practical for most test situations.

Sign Language

There are occasions when an interpreter is necessary in order to evaluate a student with a hearing impairment. This might involve interpreting or transliterating instructions. The difference between an interpretation and a transliteration is not always clear, but basically an interpretation conveys the meaning of the communique, while a transliteration is, more or less, a letter by letter or word-by-word translation. For example, fingerspelling could be used to give a letter-by-letter transliteration of the text, but signing, with or without fingerspelling, would be used to convey the meaning of the text.

The Registry of Interpreters for the Deaf has recognized the responsibility of interpreters and transliterators and has developed a Code of Ethics. One important element of this code is to convey the meaning of the communication, and do not add, help or advise. If the interpreter is a member of the Registry of Interpreters for the Deaf, the ethical responsibilities of the interpreter should be known. However, an interpreter might be an aide proficient in sign language, American Sign Language or some combination of signs, fingerspelling and gestures. Asking a student to repeat incorrect responses, providing comments following responses or offering what is thought to be "helpful" information might jeopardize the integrity of the test. Also, the interpreter must be aware that facial expressions can reveal the correctness of an answer. For example, a science test is signed to student who is substantially below grade level in reading. For each correct alternative, the interpreter's facial expression might change slightly which then provides a subtle but discernible cue. Although the intent is not to help the student, and the fact that facial expressions are an important in conveying sign language nuances, the end result is a test which does not accurately reflect the student's knowledge.

The ethical responsibility of an interpreter/transliterator applies to all who record responses. This includes those who record oral dictation, record multiple-choice responses, or participate in any manner in the transliteration, interpretation or recording of responses. As discussed with facilitated communication (see Chapter 8), ignoring basic ethical responsibilities can compromise the integrity of a testing situation and the validity of the test. The Code of Ethics of the Registry of Interpreters for the Deaf states that "interpreters/transliterators shall render the message faithfully, always conveying the content and spirit of the speaker using language most readily understood by the person(s) whom they serve. Interpreters/transliterators shall not counsel, advise or interject personal opinions."

ENDNOTES

1. Two very useful catalogs: *APH Catalog of Instructional Aids, Tools, and Supplies and APH Catalog of Accessible Books for People Who are Visually Impaired.* This catalog has an excellent collection of large print and Braille academic tests. APH, 1839 Frankfort Avenue, P.O. Box 6085, Louisville, Kentucky 40206-0085.

2. The APH Catalog of Accessible Books for People Who are Visually Impaired lists the various tests and prices for both large type and Braille formats when available).

3. McLoughlin and Lewis (1990) provide an excellent chapter relating to bilingual assessment and special education (pp. 407-449).

4. 34 C.F.R. §300.532(a)(1)

5. 34 C.F.R. §300.12 (Note 1)

6. IDEA Amendments of 1997, H.R. 5, Section 601(c)(7)(F)

7. 34 C.F.R. §300.7(b)(10)

8. In *Diana v. State Board of Education* (C-70-37 RFP, 1970) the placement of students in special education classes using English-version tests with hispanic children was discriminatory and based on language differences. See *Larry P. v. Riles*, 495 Federal Supplement, p. 926-992.

9. The ERIC Clearinghouse on Assessment and Evaluation test locator, a joint project in conjunction with the Educational Testing Service, has a large database describing tests and can be accessed by http://ericae2.educ.cua.edu//testcol.htm

10. 34 C.F.R §300.7(b)(10)

11. 34 C.F.R. §300.505(b)(2)

12. 34 C.F.R. §300.532(c)

13. 34 C.F.R. §300.532(a)(3)

14. 34 C.F.R. §300.532(a)(2) which states that tests must be "validated for the specific purpose for which they are used."

15. 34 C.F.R. §104.4

16. 34 C.F.R. §300.532(c)

Chapter 7

SCHEDULING AND TIME MODIFICATIONS

The time restraints involved when taking most tests are the result of administration and standardization needs (e.g., completing tests within a reasonable period of time) rather than the needs of the individual test taker (e.g., a student reads or works at a slower rate than other students). Of course, the individual test needs of students, the need to develop valid tests,[1] and the need to obtain what Mehrens and Lehmann (1973) referred to as "samples of behavior under uniform procedures" (p. 376) are not easy to disentangle. Although not having sufficient time to complete a test can be disadvantageous, allowing students extended or unlimited time can bring other variables into play such as fatigue, increasing disinterest, and distractions which can affect test performance.

Standardized tests generally have fairly strict guidelines as to the amount of time allowed for each test or subtest, and a thorough reading of the test manual is often necessary to determine exactly what freedom an examiner has with respect to response time. For the Wide Range Achievement Test-Revised (WRAT-R) (Jastak & Wilkinson, 1984) 10 seconds are allowed to read each word, but "refusals to read within times limits" is not always recorded as failure in that students are encouraged to attempt or otherwise guess at the word being read. Most individually administered tests employ item time limits in order to assess the complete range of the student's knowledge before disinterest or frustration occurs stemming from item difficulty or the length of testing. The instructions for the PPVT-R state that "the subject may take any reasonable amount of time per item to make a choice, since this is a test of power, not speed. However, if a minute has passed and no choice has been made, encourage the subject to "choose" before going on to the next item. The Peabody Individual Achievement Test-

187

Revised (PIAT-R) (Markwardt, 1989) is also described as a power test, but after 30 seconds on the mathematics subtest and 15 seconds on other subtests students are encouraged to give a response. For the PIAT-R written expression subtest, students are given 20 minutes to respond. This provides a reasonable amount of time to complete the items, and maintain a degree of test-taking rhythm on the part of the student. For the revised Keymath (Keymath-R) the need "to establish a fluid, efficient pace across items" is coupled with "temporary pauses when a student appears in need of a 'psychological breath'" (Connolly, 1988, p. 11).

Extended time is a widely-used test accommodations, yet for many students the need is not to provide extended time but to provide an appropriate amount of time to measure the ability in question. A student reading a Braille test might require double the amount of normal testing time, while an unmotivated or highly distractible student might be better evaluated by shorter test periods. For a student who is distractible or unmotivated, providing extended time might actually exacerbate the student's distractibility and lack of motivation thereby increasing test error. This possibility is considered in the instructions for the administration of the WAIT (Psychological Corporation, 1992) where examiners are encouraged to complete testing in one session, but "some children especially younger children, may need to be tested in two sessions because of fatigue or inadequate motivation" (p. 7).

Power and Speed

A comfortable-time limit is described by Nunnally (1967) as "the amount of time required for 90 percent of the persons to complete a test under power conditions" (p. 565). For a pure power test an unlimited amount of time is available to complete the test so that the mean of the number of items unattempted is 0. For a pure speed test no test taker has time to complete all the items which are of "trivial difficulty," so that the mean of the number of items wrong items is 0. In other words, time is not a factor for a power test, but increases as the speed component of the test increases. For a pure speed test, the ability to respond in a certain time period is not incidental to what is being measured, it is the whole purpose of the assessment. Indeed, for a pure speed test, the best test is the most reliable test which can be determined by finding the time limit which best discriminates among scores (i.e., the time limit which yields the highest standard deviation). Most tests fall somewhere in between being a pure power or speed test, with greater emphasis being placed on the power rather than speed.

Determining speededness. The simplest method for determining the speededness of a test is to consider the number of items completed. If all students are able to complete test items within the allowed time limit, the speededness of the test is probably minimal. If there is considerable variance in the number of items completed by students, speed is probably a factor. Anastasi (1982, p. 122) suggested comparing the variance of items completed to total test score variance to calculate a simple index of speededness. For example, assume that the standard deviation of a 40-item test given to 10 students with learning disabilities is 8 and the variance is 64. If all students completed all test items, the index of speededness would be 0/64 or 0. However, if the completion rates for the students were 20, 22, 25, 28, 30, 35, 36, 40, 40, and 40, the standard deviation of items completed 7.269 and the variance 52.83, the ratio between the items completed and total test score variance would be 52.83/64 or .83.

For a student with a disability who receives extended testing time, an assumption is made that the test is a power test and that extended or unlimited testing time is in keeping with the power makeup of the test. Indeed, the appropriateness of the extended time modification directly corresponds to the power of the test. If all students have sufficient time to complete[2] a test so that few or no items are unattempted, and a student with a disability is not able to attempt all items, extended time would seem to be in keeping with the power character of the test.

Extended time does not necessarily result in an easier task. If a student has limited reading ability and answers content questions by means of a reader, the cognitive processing required by this task is not necessarily easier than that required by a student who is able to use a standard reading format. As discussed later in this chapter, presenting items orally or by cassette can be very time-consuming tasks which creates a different, but not necessarily easier, memory demands.

Unfair advantage. Although the emphasis is generally on power in psychological and educational assessment, certain tests emphasize a speed component more than others. For example, a student taking a 10-item reading vocabulary test might not benefit from unlimited time, but unlimited test time for a reading comprehension test in which reading speed is a significant variable might have considerable impact on the student's test score. A test might claim to be a power measure, but if students with no disabilities are able to attempt only 85% of the test items, and students with disabilities are given unlimited time to attempt all items, the result might be an unfair advantage for the student with the disability. If a test is somewhat speeded (e.g., the average number of items completed is 75% or so), then students with disabilities should be given the amount of time necessary, in addition to the allotted time, to answer at least 75% of the test items or a percentage comparable to the completion rate of students without disabilities. But to give a student an appreciable amount of time beyond what other students receive might significantly inflate a student's score.

When a test is speeded, a time modification can compromise the standardization procedures and the underlying validity of the test. There is probably no perfect solution to the problem of determining a fair and valid time limit for a test. The only practical approach seems to be to consider the completion rates of students without disabilities on a given test, the speed and power character of the test, the time restraints imposed by different disabilities, and what seems to be a fair amount of time to complete the test for a student in consideration of these variables.

Efficiency

The ability to take a test within a specific period of time is in itself a skill. Test-taking efficiency entails the ability to work at a rate which produces the highest score, while test-taking inefficiency results from not being able to use time effectively (e.g., either too much or too little time is given to questions) or not allocating time so that the maximum number of questions correctly known are answered within the given time limit. In other words, an efficient test-taker is one who can allocate the minimum amount of time in order to answer the maximum number of questions correctly. If a student feels undue pressure to answer all the questions as quickly as possible, the student might need to develop a better sense of how much time can be devoted to individual items within the time restraint. One time management strategy is to first answer all items known before reattempting more difficult items so that easier items do not go unattempted. Regardless of the amount of extra time given to complete a test, a student must be able to manage his or her time efficiently.

For students with disabilities, extended testing time might affect a student's test-taking efficiency. If a student becomes disinterested after 10 items, doubling the testing time may do little more than compound the disinterest. One of the advantages of administering a test individually is to lend an element of efficiency. Woodcock (1973) stated that "quick and efficient test administration will help maintain the attention and interest of the subject" (p. 13).

Directions involving speed and the need to work efficiently can range from a general guideline to respond "fairly promptly," to an encouraging "Work quickly," to an emphatic "STOP!" after a specified time period. The PIAT-R (Markwardt, 1989) is referred to as "an untimed power test, not a speed test" (p. 6), but students are given "sufficient time to reach an answer, but not unlimited time" (p. 6). This might seem to be contradictory, but this does illustrate the complex relationship between speed and power. If the goal is to allow a student an opportunity to answer all or most items, yet the student becomes engrossed or preoccupied with a single item, the ability or motivation to consider other items might be impaired. In this situation, an element of speededness, as evidenced by a very liberal item time limit, might be necessary to promote test power.

Nunnally (1967) described a student's *preferred rate of response* (p. 562) or the speed an individual likes to respond which is related to the student's motivation. Assume a 20 item vocabulary test is given to two students, and that one student has a disability, the other does not, but both know the 20 vocabulary items. If the student with the disability takes 60 seconds to respond to each item, and the other student 30 seconds, the student with the disability has a 30 second longer preferred rate of response. Given 20 minutes to complete this test, both students will have sufficient time to complete all items and both will have the same final score (all other things being equal). If, however, a 10-minute time limit is imposed, even though 10 minutes is sufficient time for a student with no disability to complete the test, this limit might result in the assessment of the student's preferred rate of response in addition to testing the knowledge of the 20 vocabulary items.

Underestimating a student's preferred rate of response can result in an underestimation of performance if a time-limit is imposed. When a test format such as Braille, cassette testing, or using a reader is used, there can be a dramatic increase in the student's rate of response.

Even though two students both use Braille, each will probable have different Braille skill levels, and a different preferred rate of response which require different time limit needs.

A student's preferred rate of response must be differentiated from both a longer rate of response dictated by the test format and by item difficulty. For all students taking a group test, the items will usually take on a unique item difficulty character. For example, one item is very easy for one student but very difficult for the next. If a test being given is a pure power test, extended time could be given in spite of a high level of item difficulty. But most tests are not pure power tests and rate of response is part of what the test measures. This might be an unwanted byproduct of what is assessed, but to change this might substantially change what the test measures.

The use of extended time based on item difficulty is generally not a problem unless speed is a factor being measured. A mathematics test might have a speed component, but extending the test time might not have a drastic effect on test performance. However, if the test task is to answer 100 primary addition facts within five minutes, speed is being measured. The rationale might be for students to demonstrate primary fact recall rather than using a number line or counting to correctly identify fact sums. Allowing a student extended time for this type of task would not be valid because time is a part of what is being measured.

The use of extended time because of a reading disability depends on what is being measured. If reading is incidental to the content being measured, and knowledge of content rather than rate of response is being tested, extended time might be warranted; if items are read to a student because of a reading disability, this format might necessitate extended time. However, extended time is not a valid accommodation for reading tests when completing the reading task is what the test measures. A student might require extra time for a content test because of reading, but not for a reading test which measures reading ability within a certain time frame.

The use of extended time when reading is a factor is further confounded when a test accommodation increases item difficulty. If a student has extremely limited reading skills and must answer test items via a recording or reader, the oral presentation of items might actually result in a more difficult task than the regular version of the test (e.g., not being able to review, compare or consider a series of printed choices). In addition, the time requirements are not necessarily the same when students are read questions, depending on whether the student has the accompanying test text (a usual practice) or whether the student can benefit from reading the text.

Motivation and Fatigue

For some students with disabilities motivation and fatigue are additional variables which must be considered. Most students are able to maintain a reasonable level of motivation throughout the test. If a student has an attention deficit, the length of the test might increasingly measure this deficit. On a similar basis, for a student who is Other Health Impaired, who "has limited strength, vitality or alertness,"[3] the length of the test will affect performance. If a student has twice the amount of time to complete a test, fatigue resulting from both physical and mental exertion might become an increasingly significant variable. If after 10 minutes a student is not able to attend or the student is fatigued so that consideration of test items is affected, the student is limited not only by the imposed time limit but by the effects associated with attention/fatigue factors. If during the extended time of testing a student appears tired, listless, unmotivated, or disinterested, the usefulness of the extended testing period must be questioned.

Another factor to consider when time is a salient variable is the relative difficulty of the test and the degree of success a student will initially experience. Guilford (1954) hypothesized that "it is likely that the easier the task, the greater relatively the effect of increased motivation" (p. 368). The ability to begin assessment at a relatively easy difficulty level is another advantage of individually administered tests (e.g., the PIAT-R, PPVT-R, etc.). If a small increase in the total amount of testing time is not a factor (i.e., the student becomes increasingly disinterested or fatigued), beginning the test at a very easy difficulty level, even though this will increase total testing time, might be advantageous in terms of student interest and motivation.

There is no formula or rule of thumb which can be used to specify the most appropriate time limit. As noted by Ragosta and Wendler (1992) in the development of comparable time limits for the SAT, "the amount of extra testing time needed by examinees with disabilities differed both by disability group and by the test format used" (p. 3). For many tests, a time limit is an inextricable part of the standardization process and changing this limit changes, to some degree, what the test measures. A time limit, in and of itself, might be contrary to the well-intentioned power character of a test, but eliminating time limits is an unlikely solution because motivation and fatigue would become increasingly important, students finishing at various times would be highly distracting, and the administration of subtests (e.g., starting times, giving instructions) would be difficult problems to surmount.

Extended Time and Validity

Extended time is a major format accommodation, but the extent to which validity is affected depends on the power of the test, the content being tested, the task, and the format. Wild and Durso (1979) evaluated the effects of extending the time for an experimental version of the GRE from 20 minutes to 30 minutes and found that there was a small gain of less than 1 point on a 26 item test for all groups studied.

Centra (1986) examined the SAT scores of 1,793 disabled students who took both the standard (timed) and nonstandard (untimed) administration of the SAT. Of these students, approximately 80 percent took the timed SAT first (N=1453). The results showed that SAT-Verbal scores were 57 points higher and SAT-Mathematics scores were 60 points higher when the nonstandard format was used. When the nonstandard format was taken first (N=340), SAT-Verbal scores were 17 points higher and SAT-Mathematics scores were 16 points higher than for the standard administration scores. Overall, "the average gains over scores earned in a timed administration were generally between 30 to 38 points higher on the SAT after growth in student ability, practice effects, and errors of measurement were taken into account" (p. 327). The reason cited for the increase was that the nonstandard administration of the SAT was less speeded and therefore students were able to complete more items than when the timed administration was used.

Bennett, Rock and Kaplan (1985) examined the psychometric characteristics of the SAT for nine disability groups. The speededness of the test was evaluated by using two indices: the percent of students completing 75% of the test and the percent of students completing the last test item. The results revealed that "no disability group is consistently disadvantaged by lack of time" (p. 17) and that some groups might actually receive more time than necessary.

Braun, Ragosta and Kaplan (1988) examined the SAT scores, high school grade point average and first year college averages of students with and without disabilities. The results of this study caused the authors to specifically question the use of extended test time for LD students in that "it is mainly in the learning-disabled group of examinees that our research findings suggest an association between longer SAT testing and overprediceted college performance" (p. 169). The mean SAT-verbal score was higher for LD students taking the special version (412) in contrast to LD students taking the normal version (385), yet high school grades and eventual college performance during the first year was lower for the first group. One conclusion from this study was that, with the exception of hearing impaired students whose college performance was underpredicted, SAT scores overpredict college performance of students with disabilities. The authors concluded that "to increase validity, a more accurate match needs to be made between the extra time needed to compensate for disability and the amount of time given" (p. 130).

Bennett, Rock and Jirele (1986) evaluated Graduate Record Examination scores for visually impaired students (N=151) who took the test using a large print version with extended time (VIL) and visually impaired students (N=188) who took the national timed administration (VIN). The mean verbal, quantitative and analytical scores for the large print/extended time group (VIL) were 513, 512 and 559, as compared to mean scores of 486, 507 and 503 for the students participating in the national timed administration (VIN). The scores for the national reference group (N=441,654) were 499, 526 and 524. These data suggest somewhat higher scores by the VIL group, but the reasons for this might be the extended time, the use of the large print format, the combination of the large print format and extended time, or a sampling artifact. For example, the time and format accommodations associated with the VIL group might have attracted very serious and higher scoring students as opposed to visually impaired students who took the timed national administration.

The issue of validity regarding time modifications involves not only the effect of modifying time standardization procedures, but the appropriateness of time modifications for specific disabilities. The Standards for Educational and Psychological Testing (American Psychological Association, 1985) suggests that "empirical procedures should be used whenever possible to establish time limits for modified forms of timed tests rather than simply allowing handicapped test takers a multiple of the standard testing time. Fatigue should be investigated as a potentially important factor when time limits are extended" (p. 79). In spite of this advice, attempts to empirically determine appropriate time guidelines for disabled individuals is scarce and often involve admission tests such as the SAT and GRE. Ragosta and Wendler (1992) concluded that "based on six years of data and almost 30,000 timing records from special administrations, the old rule of thumb for testing students with disabilities seems to have been a fairly accurate estimate" (p. 5). This rule of thumb, doubling the amount of testing time, was found to be appropriate for most disability groups, but for visually impaired students using Braille or cassette required approximately 2.5 times the allotted test time, and deaf and hard-of-hearing students required somewhat less time than double the amount of normal test time. Bradley-Johnson (1994) also reported that "reading Braille and large print takes about 2 to 2.5 times longer to read than regular type," and that "the time varies depending on the medium, the material, and a students's visual problem" (p. 51).

Because of the potential impact on validity, a test publisher might prohibit a time extension. If the test instructions state that "the time allowed to complete each test should never be extended," and if the examiner wishes to comply with IDEA regulations[4] that tests "are administered by trained personnel in conformance with the instructions provided by their producer," time extension would seem inappropriate.

Time Adaptations and Modifications

The only regulatory guideline concerning time is the requirement that "modifications may include changes in the length of time permitted for the completion of degree requirements"[5] which acknowledges the possibility that a disability can interfere with a student's rate of work. Nonetheless, a time accommodations must, as with all test accommodations, strike a balance between the need to test the student's ability rather than disability and maintaining the test's validity.

A time accommodation can involve a relatively minor adaptation (e.g., the time of day, or the day of the week) which has minimal impact on test validity, or a major test modification (e.g., unlimited test time) which can significantly affect what the test measures and the student's normative performance. Time accommodations can be categorized into four areas: (1) scheduling, (2) time management, (3) extended time, and (4) reduced time. Scheduling accommodations require the standard amount of testing time, but when the student is tested is a focus of concern. Time management accommodations involve strategies which can be used by the student or examiner to ensure that the time allocated is used efficiently. Extending the amount of time to complete a test is probably the most commonly used test accommodation. For some students extra time is deemed necessary because of processing (e.g., reading) or format needs (e.g., oral testing, cassette, Braille). When this occurs, extended time is secondary and the result of the primary format accommodation task. The need for reduced time becomes necessary when a student is unable to attend, is not motivated, or where the test task simply overwhelms the student.

Although seemingly diametrically opposed to one another, a student might require both extended and reduced time. Experience might show that a student is not able to attend to a task (any task) for more than 15 minutes. Yet, within this time frame, the student might require additional time to complete each item. For example, a student might be able to respond for no more than 15 minutes, but might require additional time for each response within that 15-minute time period.

Of the time accommodations which can be made, scheduling is often the least restrictive. For standardized tests, extending the test time may or may not be permitted by the test publisher and will probably have the greatest impact on test validity. Unlike extended test time, if a reduced test time period is needed, this is often achieved by using individual tests, deleting subtests, or using one or more time management strategies. The following describes various scheduling, time management, extended and reduced time accommodations:

Table 7.1 Time Adaptations and Modifications.

Scheduling	Time Management	Extended Time	Reduced Time
Time of day	Time strategy	Extended time	Eliminate items
Day of week	Time cues	Student-determined time	Eliminate subtests
Multiday testing	Item pacing	Examiner judgement	Modified test format
Between-test breaks	Difficulty management	Waive time	Critical-range testing
Within-test breaks	Response strategies	Disability-based time	Individualized testing
Fixed time periods	End-of-test strategies	Comparable time	Exemptions

Scheduling

Scheduling involves determining the appropriate place to test, the most opportune time to test, and using test breaks to promote test performance (e.g., the use of test breaks). When a test break is used, the amount of test time is not changed, but the total test time is distributed over an extended period of time. The only guideline provided by the regulations concerns admission tests and states that tests "are offered as often and in as timely a manner as are other admission tests,"[6] and are administered in accessible facilities. For all tests, scheduling should be timely in that giving a test at a very inopportune time when the student is unmotivated or inattentive, will not meet the needs of the student.

There are a number of ways in which scheduling can be used to enhance favorable conditions for testing. The day of the week, the time of day, the amount of time between subtests, the number of subtests administered each day can often be controlled to best meet a student's testing needs. Experience will provide some guidance as to what might be the best time of day or specific day for testing. Although a morning test time might be the ideal for most students, experience might indicate that a student requiring a test accommodation is more responsive in the afternoon.

For group and individual testing an attempt should be made to adhere to the normal testing schedule. What an examiner must look for are those circumstances which, when combined with the student's disability, substantially interfere with test performance. If a student is extremely inattentive on Mondays, beginning testing the following day might be a minor albeit worthwhile delay. Although additional free time might be available before major holidays for individualized testing, the advantages of the individualized test format might be contraindicated by the holiday atmosphere. Changing the time when a student is evaluated is not inconsequential and can deny a student an opportunity to participate in a very important educational activity.

The time of day can also be an important variable when administering a test to a student with a disability. A morning assessment might be more conducive for optimal test performance than an afternoon evaluation. The importance of when to test increases if there is evidence that a test fails to adequately measure a student's ability at a specific time of day. If reading ability is always tested in the latter part of the morning, and the student seems less attentive at this time, assessing the student at an earlier time might be warranted. Likewise, testing a student immediately after lunch might assess post-lunch drowsiness as well as whatever the test purports to measure. There is no absolute guideline as to the best time of day for assessing a student, but input from the classroom teacher, parents and the student can be extremely useful.

Between-test rest periods. Most tests comprised of a series of subtests allow for a break between testing and a typical rest period might be five minutes or so. For a student with a disability this could be extended to 10 minutes when tested individually, or an increase in the between-test break could be given to all students in a group test situation. Between-test breaks are especially important when a student is being tested individually. Rather than going from subtest to the next without interruption, engaging the student in conversation and establishing rapport will often provide a much needed break from the test situation.

If previous testing experience reveals that a student's attention decreases as the amount of test time increases or the student becomes fatigued or noticeably frustrated (e.g., grimacing, tapping, talking to oneself), a lengthened test break might be essential. Test directions might suggest the length of time between tests, but this is often in the form of a recommendation and not a strict guideline.

Within-test rest periods. During testing, distractibility, irritability, frustration, or more specific behaviors (e.g., rubbing eyes, facial expressions, fidgeting) might indicate that a short pause or break is necessary. As discussed above, the ideal time to provide a break is between subtests, but the student's behavior might indicate that a within-test break is necessary.

If items for a subtest are not arranged by difficulty, a very brief pause in testing might be useful if a student is obviously frustrated and the assessment effort of questionable value. If the subtest items are arranged by item difficulty (which is more than likely), a pause or interruption in testing might detract from the problem-solving rhythm the student has developed by proceeding from easy items to more difficulty items. As a general rule a within-test break is more suitable for students who are being tested individually, or in a very small group, and where a student can be instructed to put his or her pencil down for a minute or so and then resume the task.

Multi-day testing. Security is one of the a primary reasons why multiday testing is often not allowed. Statewide and admission tests which are secured often prohibit multiday testing. If multiday testing is allowed, and fatigue and/or inattention are important variables, this might be useful. Some achievement tests strongly recommend that the complete test battery not be administered in one day. There is, however, at least one potential drawback when a series of subtests are given over an extended number of days in that the student's frame of mind and test readiness might be decidedly different on the subsequent testing days. However, this might result in relatively minor performance fluctuations in comparison to the test error which will occur if the majority of subtests are given when the student is extremely unmotivated or inattentive.

Fixed-time periods. A frequently-used test accommodation is to indicate a specific additional amount of time to complete a test. The SAT allows an additional 90 minutes of testing time for students with documented learning disabilities, and for students using formats other than the regular SAT edition. Each test must be completed "the day it is started."   The College Entrance Examination Board (1994) reports that students with disabilities complete each 30 minute section in about 45 minutes. For a test such as the SAT, time management is a critical factor and "a student with a learning disability may benefit from assistance in allocating the total time of 4.5 hours" (p. 4).

For IEP specified accommodations, specifying a fixed period of time for testing might result in extended test time, reduced test time, or it might have no affect on the amount of time allowed to complete the test. The following statement might be used to indicate the length of each test session:

Test should be administered in periods of _____ minutes.

If 20 minutes is normally given to complete a test, administering the test in a 30 minute period would be to extend the time for *this* test. However, if no distinction is made between the test for which the time extension is intended and other tests, this might be used as a general guideline for all tests. If a test requires 35 minutes to complete, but the "accommodation" allows only 30 minutes, interrupting the student with five minutes remaining in order to honor a specified test accommodation might do more harm than good.

There is always the possibility that the intent of a fixed time period accommodation is not to extend the amount of each test session, but to ensure that because of attentional, motivational or physical factors, testing does not exceed a certain period of time. If this is the case, and a student is to be tested for no longer than say 15 minutes each session, then the first consideration should be to select tests which do not exceed this time period. Temporarily interrupting a student after 15 minutes of testing because of a predetermined fixed time limit, as described above, might have a negative impact on test performance. If a test requires 15 minutes of testing time, the items are of increasing difficulty, administering the first half of the test at time A and the second half at time B might be disadvantageous for a student when taking the more difficult half of the test.

Time Management

Group and individualized testing situations provide an opportunity to assess a student's time management needs. Every student will approach a test somewhat differently so there is no *right* way to take a test. What the examiner is looking for are factors which might help explain the student's time accommodation needs.

For all tests, both open- and closed-ended, the examiner should attempt to determine whether the disability is somehow preventing the student from completing the test in the allotted amount of time. For example, the physical test response might interfere with the primary test task. Even if a student is allowed to use a computer/typewriter to respond, limited keyboard proficiency might interfere with the conceptual organization of the answer. If the primary goal is to evaluate written language (e.g., language mechanics, vocabulary, sentence construction, composition) rather than handwriting, and the student has difficulty with fine-motor coordination, this difficulty can detract from the primary area being assessed.

During the test there are several factors which might be considered when evaluating the time management needs of a student. Does the student answer items too slowly or too quickly? Is too much time spent on difficult items? Does the student answer items in an organized and systematic fashion? Does the student become inattentive or frustrated during testing? Does the student consider all parts of the question? Does the student require extended time because of the physical test response? Does the student fail to complete all test items?

Often the time management needs of a student are difficult to discern but for every test the completion rate should be compared to students without disabilities. One goal should be to discern whether there was insufficient time because of item difficulty or because of the student's rate of work. In other words, would the student's completion rate be comparable to other students if extended time were given. For a standardized test, this can be determined diagnostically by determining normative performance based on items completed during the allotted time period, and then allowing the student to complete the remaining items. This technique can be used to provide an extended time accommodation which results in a comparable completion rate.

Time strategies. Most group tests employ a total time-limit, but the amount of time allocated to each item is critical. A student must be aware of a test's time limit and a reasonable amount of time which can be devoted to each item. Whether the test is open- or close-ended, a multiple-choice test or writing an essay, developing a plan for completing the test within the allotted time is essential for efficient test taking. If a student is not able to complete a test regardless of the amount of time given, specific practice might be devoted to learning this skill. For example, five, ten, then fifteen item practice tests might be given within corresponding time frames (e.g., 5, 10 and 15 minute periods).

Time cues. During testing, if time management for a student with a disability is a problem, developing self-monitoring skill is important. If the student is able, a watch/clock should be made available. For a student with a visual impairment, a talking clock might be necessary. If necessary, one or two time reminders by the examiner during testing and five minutes before the end of the test period might be appropriate. This might be done orally and/or writing the amount of time remaining on the chalkboard. The goal is not to create added anxiety but to periodically announce the amount of testing time remaining and write the remaining time on the board. For a student with a hearing impairment, rather than needlessly interrupting the student, the examiner should note the student's progress, and indicate the amount of time remaining by using the appropriate mode of communication. Anxiety-producing enjoinders to "Hurry up!" or "Work quickly!" are vague with respect to actual time remaining and should be avoided.

Item pacing. Individually administered tests employ some variant of test pacing; that is, the student is allotted either a specific time or "reasonable" amount of time to complete each item. For students with very poor time management skills, where too much time is expended on too few items under a time-limit condition, pacing is one method for presenting a viable range of items within the time limit. For students with time management difficulties, test pacing using sample items, either individually or in a small group situation, can be a very important intervention for developing test-taking skills. For very difficult items which cannot be answered quickly, students should be taught to mark or highlight test items not readily known in the test booklet and/or on the answer sheet, go on to the next item, and then return to the more difficult items.

Extended Time

Extending the amount of time to complete a test is probably one of the most widely-used test accommodations. Willingham stated (1995) that "seven of 10 students taking a nonstandard test use the regular form, with extended time usually being the only variation of any consequence" (p. 177) when taking the SAT. This is obviously specific to the population of students taking a college admission test, but extended time, either as the sole accommodation or with other adaptations and modifications (e.g., using a reader, cassette recording) is a frequently-used accommodation.

Gajria, Salend and Hemrick (1994) found that 64 general education teachers surveyed to evaluate 32 test modifications ranked "allocate more time to complete test" (90.6%) as one of the more frequently-used modifications. Interestingly enough, time modifications were not judged as highly in terms of perceived integrity (79.7%). This, of course, highlights the major dilemma when considering modified time limits: To what extent do the time modifications impact the validity "for the specific purpose for which the test is used" and to what extent does the time accommodation depart from "the instructions provided by their producer."[7]

If the time required to complete a test is excessively long (and this is relative to each student), fatigue, attention and motivation become influential factors; if the test time or test length is reduced, the test might not measure what the complete test measures. Extending the amount of time to complete a test is often perceived as a simple and straightforward method for accommodating a student's needs. But this is not always the case. As the time required to take a test increases, there is probably a corresponding effect on such factors as fatigue, attention and motivation. Unfortunately, there is no way to determine what exactly the effect is or to what degree fatigue increases and attention and motivation decreases.

Ragosta and Wendler (1992) made an interesting observation that "most test-takers would like to have the extra testing time allowed for people with disabilities" (p. 1). These authors also stated that "not all people with disabilities require special test accommodations, and not all people who require special accommodations need extra testing time" (p. 1). Although modifying the time required to complete a test is often used, this accommodation of and by itself may or may not be appropriate depending on the test and student's disability.

Extended test time is appropriate whenever the test task itself requires additional time (e.g., Braille, tape recording), or when the student is not able to work at a normal rate of speed. If a student is thought to have the ability to answer additional items correctly, but does not attempt these items because of insufficient time, extended time might be an appropriate accommodation. The appropriateness of the extended time accommodation is also related to the concept of comparable testing. If students without disabilities do not have sufficient time to answer all questions, there is no reason why students with disabilities should be given the time to do so. For a test which is even moderately speeded, the amount of extended time will be unfair to the extent that the amount of time allocated allows the student to attempt either less or more questions in comparison to others.

If the regular test task is being used, the need for additional testing time will depend on the test taking speed of the student and the student's ability. If test-taking speed is affected by poor reading skills, but the student is able to demonstrate proficiency when given additional time, extended testing time is an appropriate accommodation if reading is not being measured. When an extended time accommodation is used, and the additional time is not needed, the unused time should be noted. This might provide useful information for modifying this accommodation in the future, or for discontinuing the accommodation entirely. Differentiating whether diminished test performance is the result of attention/motivation factors, item difficulty, or a combination thereof is a difficult task. After the regular testing period, and during the extended testing time, a student might be disinterested because the items are simply more difficult. If the test contains fewer items, this same behavior might occur. In other words, a student might appear tired, listless, unmotivated and disinterested when dealing with difficult items or items for which the student is unable to answer.

One method for determining whether extended testing time is being used productively is by observing the student and analyzing the student's responses after the regular test period has elapsed. If during the extended test period, the student is able to demonstrate some level of successful performance, the extended test time might be useful. If, however, the student is functioning at the chance level on a multiple-choice test, or simply not responding to open-ended test questions, the need for the extended test time should be reconsidered and other means for managing time evaluated.

Unlimited Time

From the standpoint of standardized testing, if extended time is needed but to an unknown degree, selecting untimed tests is an excellent idea, but there is not an abundance of these types of standardized tests from which to choose. Bradley-Jonhson's (1994) advice regarding test selection for students with visual impairments to "avoid any that are timed if possible" (p. 51) is good but not generally practical.

If a test does have time limitations, specifying an unlimited amount of time to complete the test might provide the student with an unfair advantage, might result in a fair assessment of the ability being measured, or might bring into play fatigue and motivational factors which might depress test performance. There will probably be a point during a test when a student has had sufficient time to consider test items in a way that is comparable to that of students without disabilities and this is the ideal amount of time which should be given.

Often times an extended time accommodation specifies that the student is given extra time "until the student can no longer sustain the activity." This, of course, is a judgement decision made by the test proctor or examiner. This decision should be based on the amount of work completed, sustained rate of work, response latency, attention, and an interest by the student to continue with the task. If a student has answered all the items, and then rechecked each answer, this is probably comparable to the amount of time required by a student without a disability, and testing might be terminated. If a student is not attending to the task, or the student stops working, often asking the student whether she or he would like to continue will be sufficient to terminate testing. If a student is given unlimited time to complete the test, the proctor should be aware of the student's progress, attention, and desire to continue working. If the student's rate of work is extremely slow, but consistent, the student should be allowed as much time as needed if an unlimited amount of time has been specified in the student's IEP or Section 504 Plan.

Comparable Time Limits

Willingham, Ragosta, Bennett and Braun (1988) stated that "the primary source of noncomparability that is directly associated with test scores is the amount of time available in test administrations. That lack of comparability is, in principle, correctable by setting time limits in nonstandard administrations so that handicapped and nonhandicapped examinees are equally likely to finish the task" (p. xi). The phrase "equally likely" is very important in that *all* students might not complete a test, but *most* are likely to complete the test. Regardless of the time limits available, *all* students with disabilities might not be able to complete a test.

Ragosta and Wendler (1992) attempted to develop comparable time limits for students with disabilities, but made a distinction between time *needed* and time limits which are consistent with the restraints placed on students in the normal population of SAT test takers. In order to do this they examined the SAT scores of 17,180 students with disabilities who took the SAT from 1986 to 1988. The average testing time for the five SAT sections was 150 minutes. The administration of the regular SAT for the five disabilities ranged from 217 to 363 minutes. The regular SAT format total test times ranged from 217 to 250 minutes, the large print format ranged from 258 to 293 minutes, the cassette version ranged from 262 to 352 minutes, and the time for the Braille version was 363 minutes. In terms of time, the Braille version required the most time (363 minutes), the cassette version was next, followed by the large print version and then the standard version which required the least amount of extended time.

Ragosta and Wendler used the amount of time needed to complete the SAT by nondisabled students as an estimate of the time which should be allowed to take the test. Using data based on the percentage of the general population, 64.4% of test takers completed 100% of either the mathematical or verbal subtests (i.e., students who completed the last item of each section was used as an index of overall test completion), and that 54.4% of test takers completed the entire test. The amount of time required by different disability groups to complete the SAT using the 54.5% (conservative estimate of needed time) and 64.4% (a more liberal estimate of needed test time) was then determined. For example, for the physical disability group using regular print (N=721), the amount of time required to complete the SAT by 64.4 percent of the students in this group was 286 minutes, or an increase in the allotted time of 136 minutes. For the LD group using regular print, which was the largest group studied (N=10,999), the time required to complete 64.4% of the test was 270 minutes or an increase of 120 minutes from the allotted time. For the LD group using cassette (N=2,282), 293 minutes was required to complete 64.4% of the test. Overall, students with visual impairments using cassette or Braille required the most extra time, and hearing impaired students the least amount of extra time. For students with visual impairments to complete 64.4% of the test, Braille (N=913) required 412 minutes, cassette (N=156) 402 minutes, large print (N=913) 294 minutes, and regular print 282 minutes. Students with hearing impairments using regular print required the least amount of time to complete 64.4% of the test (245 minutes).

A reasonable goal regarding extended test time is to provide a fair amount of time and not necessarily an extended amount. In the development of the 8th Edition of the Stanford Achievement Test for hearing impaired students (Gallaudet Research Institute, 1989), extended time is related to the mode of communication and not to the general category of hearing impairment. The instructions state that "for the non-dictated subtests, the time limits given in the directions for administering must be followed *exactly*. For the teacher-dictated subtests the time limits listed are approximate" (p. 6). Here, the time limit is governed by student need or mode of communication. Overall, the need for extra time depends not only on the disability, but certain characteristics within the disability group. For example, the SAT study above does not differentiate between hearing impaired and deaf students, onset of hearing loss, and type hearing loss, all of which might warrant more or less time.

Reduced Time

Unlike extended time, the need to reduce the length of testing often necessitates the use of an alternative test which has less demanding time requirements. A number of factors might warrant reduced testing time such as if the student is easily disinterested or fatigued, or where the test format results in an inequitable amount of test time (e.g., a special test format requires twice as much time to complete).

There are several situations when reduced testing time is necessary. First, when a student is not able to attend to a test task regardless of on-task reminders and high interest strategies the examiner might use. For these situations when the student is able to perform but will not stay on task, reduced test time might be necessary in order to obtain a valid assessment of the student's ability. Dunn and Dunn (1981), in discussing the administration of the PPVT-R, noted the possibility of perseveration and responding too quickly and described this tendency as being "seen with young children as they approach their ceiling, and are getting a bit tired and discouraged" (p. 18). Of course, if a student perseverates or exhibits no reflection in the selection of answers, this might indicate that the test is either beyond the range of the student's ability (e.g., giving 8th grade multiple-reading test to a student reading at the second grade level), a tendency to perseverate on most tasks, or a complete lack of interest in being tested or the test itself. In these situations, the problem is not the amount of test time but the test task or test.

When attention deficit is a factor, a plan to reduce the amount of test time might be an important consideration. The DSM-IV (American Psychiatric Association, 1994) describes difficulty sustaining attention, avoiding tasks that require mental effort, and being easily distracted by extraneous stimuli as criteria associated with attention deficit disorders. Friend and Bursuck (1996) indicated that students with attention deficit/hyperactivity disorders "perform better on short passages than on long ones" (p. 187) in reading thereby suggesting that reduced time on task might be appropriate. On the other hand, these authors stated that "in math, students should be given extended periods of time to complete computational work since their attentional problems interfere with their efficiency in this type of task" (p. 187). Indeed, depending on the student and the type of attentional disorder, both strategies might be appropriate. If a student's attention steadily decreases over a period of time, short tasks would seem appropriate. If the students attention waivers throughout the task, rather than following a downward trend, extended time might be quite effective.

Another occasion when reduced test time is required occurs when the student's health precludes normal test periods. Because of a health impairment, the student might not have the physical capacity to function at a normal rate or at his or her normal performance level after a specified period of time.

Finally, as mentioned previously, reduced and extended test time are not mutually exclusive. A student with an attentional problem might attend to a test task for no more than 10 minutes, yet might require a longer than usual period of time to respond to each item within that 10-minute time frame. For a student who has a physical disability and requires three times as much time to respond than what is usually given, the increased total test time might need to be subdivided into a series of reduced test periods because of fatigue factors. A student with a disability who requires 12 hours to complete a test is obviously at a disadvantage because of the sheer length of total test time, and this should be taken into consideration when evaluating the overall time accommodations needed by the student.

Wide-range Tests

There is an obvious relationship between item difficulty and time so that a more difficult test will require more time. Rather than approaching the problem by the amount of time needed to complete a test, another strategy is to reduce the number of items or to change the difficulty of the items (e..g, by changing the readability of a reading passage, using easier items). These types of medications cannot be used for standardized tests. If test difficulty is changed, test norms become meaningless and probably misleading. Although providing extra time can influence test performance, test items and alternatives of standardized tests should never be simplified, reworded or otherwise modified.

Rather than changing the length of the test, a better strategy is to select a test which has the most desirable length characteristics. Group standardized achievement tests used in grades 1-12 often require anywhere from 3.5 to 6 hours to administer the entire battery of subtests. For some students, the need to better manage time is more important than the need for extra time. If a student is given a 30 item test, and expends the majority of test time on only several items, regardless of the total amount of time given, extending the total test time is not the needed accommodation.

Wide-range achievement tests obviate a student's inability to efficiently manage time by evaluating the student's critical ability range, examiner-controlled item pacing and developing examiner-examinee rapport via individual assessment. A student's ability is assessed by determining basal and ceiling levels which serve to bracket the student's critical ability range. The basal level is based on the number of correct responses within a set of responses, and the ceiling level on the number of incorrect response within a set of responses. The following table provides basal and ceiling guidelines used by several wide-range individually administered tests. For most tests, discontinuing testing because the examiner believes the student is not attending can have a negative effect test performance. Wide-range tests often provide guidelines for evaluating performance within the student's critical response range so that testing is discontinued when item difficulty for the student reaches a certain point. For example, for the PIAT-R the basal item is the point where five consecutive correct responses have been made and items below this point are not given. The ceiling item is the point at which five out of seven responses are incorrect and items above this point are not given. The student's score is the ceiling item minus the number of errors.

Table 7.2 Basal and Ceiling Guidelines.

Individualized Wide-Range Basal and Ceiling Guidelines		
Test[a]	Basal	Ceiling
PIAT-R	5 consecutive correct responses	5 errors in 7 consecutive responses
PPVT-R	8 consecutive correct responses	6 errors in 8 consecutive responses
WIAT	Varies: many subtests require 1 of 5 responses correct	Varies: e.g., Spelling: 6 consecutive errors; Reading Comprehension: 4 consecutive errors
KeyMath-R	3 consecutive correct	3 consecutive errors
WRAT-R	Credit given if pretests not given or necessary	Reading and Spelling: 10 consecutive errors
WRMT-R	6 consecutive correct	6 consecutive errors

[a]**PIAT-R:** Peabody Individual Achievement Test-Revised; **PPVT-R:** Peabody Picture Vocabulary Test-Revised; **WIAT:** Wechsler Individual Achievement Test; **WRAT-R:** Wide Range Achievement Test-Revised; **WRMT-R:** Woodcock Reading Mastery Test-Revised.

Because wide-range tests often assess a critical range by means of basal and ceiling scores, and encourage item pacing and item responses during administration, these tests generally require a short period of time to administer. For the Keymath-R, the author suggested the test can be administered in 30 to 40 minutes for students in the primary grades, and 40 to 50 minutes for older students. This is similar to the Wechsler Individual Achievement test (WAIT) (Psychological Corporation, 1992) which requires approximately 30 to 50 minutes in the primary grades, and 55 to 60 minutes for older students. The Woodcock Reading Mastery Tests-Revised (WRMT-R) (Woodcock, 1987) requires approximately 30 minutes to administer the four reading tests and 40 to 45 minutes to give all six subtests.

When the need for reduced testing time is a factor, wide-range tests provide excellent measures to gather pertinent information in a reduced period of time. From a technical standpoint, these tests are well-standardized, have excellent manuals, and yield a variety of scores and indices for interpreting performance. Nonetheless, there are two disadvantages associated with wide-range tests: First, performance and scores on these tests is not always comparable to the performance of students taking much lengthier group achievement tests. Second, although the internal consistency coefficients of these tests are quite respectable, one criticism of wide-range tests is limited content sampling. To a large degree this is an unfair criticism in that the wide range of content allows the test to be given quickly and efficiently and to thereby meet a very definite need in special education.

The criteria for determining basal and ceiling scores for wide-range achievement tests cannot be used with a classroom multiple-choice test which is given individually to a student. For example, a 25 item group multiple-choice test is given to a student individually and the examiner stops testing after five out of seven responses are incorrectly answered. Although one might reasonably assume that if the items are arranged by difficulty, that this is a reasonable point to terminate testing, this will result in a deflated score when compared to other students who were able to attempt (albeit guess) all test items.

Reduced Test Length

Schulz, Carpenter and Turnbill (1991) discuss "changing the format of materials, directions or assignments" (p. 171) such as by accommodating a student's special needs by subdividing assignments into smaller units or by reducing the length of the activity. This is certainly a consideration which should be entertained when selecting a wide-range achievement test, and when constructing teacher-made tests. When constructing reduced-length tests, care must be taken to provide a reasonable sampling of the test content and not simply reduce the test length by eliminating the "difficult" items.

Usually the only justification for eliminating items is when the test format is modified and certain items cannot be used with the new format (e.g., Braille). Even when this is done, the remaining items should be renormed. For most standardized tests, eliminating test items (as opposed to entire subtests) is not possible and doing this will make the resulting scores uninterpretable. For classroom tests it is possible to eliminate items providing that the items eliminated are selected randomly (e.g., eliminating only difficult items would change what the test measures).

Eliminating subtests. Eliminating items is always a dubious task unless a complete reconsideration of standardized scores is undertaken. If a disability is caused by a chronic health problem which precludes extended test time, subtests could be administered over an extended period of time or subtests could be deleted. If the first option is not viable because of test security, or a belief that administering a test over an extended period of time might be unfair, subtests could be eliminated. Which subtest(s) to eliminate can be determined by evaluating the primary purpose of testing for the student. If standardized information is lacking for reading, administering subtests relating to reading vocabulary and reading comprehension would be appropriate. Every subtest can provide useful information, but knowing how a student performs on a test such as reading comprehension might be far more important than performance on a subtest involving language mechanics (e.g., punctuation).

Most group standardized achievement test batteries include several content-based tests such as mathematics, science and social studies. The importance of these tests depends on the degree to which the test samples the actual school/district content, and the availability of other standardized information. If a student is required to take statewide competency tests in science and social studies and a group achievement test having these subtests, but the amount of time the student can be tested is at a premium, the "high-stakes"[8] tests might be used in lieu of the group achievement test counterparts.

Test discontinuation. As important as attention is, there will be occasions when nothing will motivate a student to perform at his or her potential. If a student does not want to be tested, or is completely uncooperative and will not be tested, consider a break, delay or postpone testing. If all attempts by the examiner to solicit meaningful responses are to no avail, the continuation of testing will not only generate potentially misleading results but also might reinforce undesirable test behaviors. Many students might elect not to be tested if given a choice so that discontinuing a test might be more of a reward than punishment for some. If possible, the examiner should use other strategies before testing is discontinued such as a test break or going to a different location. As best as possible, the decision not to test should be made before rather than during actual testing. However, if a student is not cooperating, or exhibiting indifferent or random responses, terminating the test might be appropriate. The exception to this is a large group test in which students with disabilities are expected to demonstrate a certain skill or mastery level. Discontinuing a test while a student is taking a high-stakes test should be a last resort and only used if the student's behavior is unacceptably disruptive or inappropriate.

Test exemptions.[9] Obviously, a test exemption represents the most restrictive time modification possible: no time is expended administering the test to the student. A test exemption can involve a specific test (e.g., the California Achievement Test), test content (e.g., reading), type of test (e.g, standardized test), or an entire testing program (e.g., statewide competency testing). A test exemption, although necessary, is nonetheless a potentially discriminatory accommodation. Not taking a test might preclude inclusion in certain programs, receiving a benefit such as a degree or certification, or being deprived of a service.

A test exemption might be necessary because the test is beyond the ability level of the student, or the skill or knowledge being tested is within the student's ability range but a modification or alternative test is not possible. In the latter case, other evidence is used in place of the exempted test(s). For example, an achievement subtest which measures auditory vocabulary (e.g., "Point to the picture of the clock.") would be unfair to a student with an auditory impairment. Because signing the words to the student would be tantamount to creating a new test (of which the norms for the regularly administered version would not apply), exempting the student from this subtest might be appropriate.

As much as possible, an attempt should be made to limit test exemptions. A usual criterion when making a test exemption is the extent of regular classroom participation. If a student participates in regular classroom activities over 50 percent of the time and participates in regular classroom testing, a test exemption from standardized tests might be disallowed. Another criterion that might be used is whether a student is in a diploma or certificate program. If the student is in a certificate program, there might be no need to participate in the state testing program. Nonetheless, if a student is able to benefit from a test in any way, the student is entitled to an opportunity to receive such a benefit.

ENDNOTES

1. 34 C.F.R. §300.532(a)(2)
2. There is a distinction between having an opportunity to attempt all items and actually attempting all items. A student might have an opportunity to answer a given item but not do so for a variety of reasons.
3. 34 C.F.R. §300.7(b)(8)
4. 34 C.F.R. §300.532(a)(3)
5. 34 C.F.R. §104.44
6. 34 C.F.R. §104.(42)(b)(3)
7. 34 C.F.R. §300.532(a)
8. What Phillips (1993) refers to as "any assessment activity that is used for accountability" (p. xviii).
9. Test exemptions are also discussed in Chapter 1 in relation to the hierarchy of least restrictive test accommodations.

Chapter 8

RESPONSE ACCOMMODATIONS

Response Adaptations

A response accommodation can entail either an adaptation or test modification and can impact validity in different ways. A response adaptation should not affect the format of the test, does not change the test response, or how response is recorded. Practicing the response task prior to actual testing, clarifying what response is required, or providing a comfortable setting (e.g., a table rather than desk) are all aimed at facilitating the student's ability to respond but without changing the test or the actual response required by the test publisher.

Response environment. Changing the environment (e.g., using a table or slant board rather than desk) provides an indirect method for facilitating a student's response, and should have little impact on test validity. Most response adaptations go hand-in-hand with general test adaptations. Enhancing the lighting, testing in a room in which instructions can be heard, providing a room with a vaporizer or a comfortable room temperature might have a positive effect on the student's ability to respond. For students in wheelchairs, the test location should provide suitable work space, a comfortable workspace height, and sufficient knee space (see American National Standards Institute, 1986, p. 62) so that the student can respond. For some students, a straight-back chair or other seating arrangement might ease the student's ability to respond. For students who are visually impaired, a bookstand might lessen fatigue and facilitate responses. And for students with physical disabilities, the examiner might be required to open test materials, position the test or answer sheet, turn pages or record responses. If physical assistance is all that is required, the examiner/aide should only provide the minimum assistance necessary to accomplish the response task. The examiner should not indicate the answer, help formulate or select the correct answer (see the section on facilitated communication at the end of this chapter), or indicate the correctness of an answer which has been given.

Response skill. If a student has difficulty recording multiple-choice answers on a grid or scoring sheet, the reason might be that the student is unfamiliar with the task, is not attentive to the task, or has difficulty with the motor response. For these possibilities, one response modification might be to allow the student to record the answers directly in the test booklet. However, rather than modifying the response required by the test, a more productive long-term approach might be a test adaptation which develops this specific test-taking skill prior to testing. If the response required by a test is unique (e.g., a column matching task or a reading cloze task), the student should be provided with ample practice prior to testing. Other skills which can be taught include how to record answers, changing answers, erasing answers and even using appropriate test-taking materials (e.g., pencils, scrap paper if allowed, etc.).

For many students the problem is not how to respond but not attending to the response task. If a student misrecords one entry on a scoring sheet, this is probably the result of a lapse in attention rather than a complete misunderstanding of the response task. The test needs are decidedly different for a student who misrecords most answers than for a student who misrecords a single answer, even though the result might be a spuriously low score for both students. For a student who does not understand the response task, teach the task; for a student who is not attentive to the task, develop this skill; and for a student who has difficulty recording responses because of a motor disability, recording answers in the test booklet might indeed be the most appropriate response accommodation. For many students requiring response accommodations, the real need is response practice rather than changing the require response.

Quality of response. Although a student might know how to respond to the response task, a student might not comprehend the dynamics of the test task. A hasty response might result because the student believes there is insufficient time, while a very slow and cautious response might result because of an unawareness of time restraints. For the student who responds too quickly, the problem might be either a misinterpretation of the available testing time, or because of item difficulty, inattention, disinterest, or impulsive behavior. As with the student who is overly cautious and whose slow response rate does not allow sufficient time to attempt all items, impulsive responses might occur with nontesting tasks and has nothing to do with the amount of time given to respond. The quality of a student's response is related to planning, organization and reflection, all of which are essential for providing a systematic and coherent response.

The only way to determine the cause of the student's behavior is a one-to-one evaluation. If a student responds with seemingly little reflection, when the student is asked why a response was made so quickly, the reply might be that "I have to hurry" (which suggests a time management need), or "This answer seems right" (which might indicate a lack of reflection if entire questions are never considered), or "I don't care" (which might suggest a motivational problem). Determining the cause of a response difficulty is often found by simply asking the student why a specific response was made and then following the student through the entire question/response sequence. This, of course, should be done diagnostically and not during a test which will result in a normative score.

Response Modifications

A response modification might involve a relatively minor change in the test response such as allowing a student to use a felt marker to record answers, or to record answers in the test booklet rather than using a multiple-choice bubble. Although both of these modifications might require responses to be recorded on scoring sheets, the impact on validity of these accommodations should be minor.

However, allowing a student to answer questions orally or using an interpreter to respond could have a substantial impact on the test's validity such as when a response modification helps the student select or formulate the correct answer. A proviso for every response accommodation is that the accommodation should not indicate or suggest the correctness of the answer, help the student to find the correct answer, or indicate that a questionable response is incorrect (and thus suggest the correctness of the answer). Examples of inappropriate accommodations include a reader who emphasizes the correct answer when reading test alternatives, eliminating multiple-choice alternatives or simplifying the conceptual difficulty of the response task, changing the criteria for interpreting response correctness (e.g., the sign for "bad" is recorded as a correct response for the printed word "grievance"), editing a student response while recording the response, or creating the answer for the student when facilitating responses.

Although a primary concern is that a response accommodation not give a student an undue advantage, the reverse can occur; that is, a response accommodations, albeit necessary, might result in an undue disadvantage. A single-switch task in which a form of matrix scanning is used to formulate a written response can be difficult to learn and time-consuming to use. Task difficulty was discussed by Barraga and Erin (1992, p. 145) who noted the advantages of using a Braille writer over that of slate and stylus writing in that slate and stylus writing requires writing mirror image symbols of readable Braille cells and writing from left to right.

Even when a student is allowed to provide an oral response, this does not mean that the task is easier. A student might be allowed to orally respond to items, and the examiner records answers, but this might deprive the student of an opportunity (or an inclination) to review answers. For a student with a severe physical disability (e.g., as a result of a spinal cord injury) but who has high-level language skills, an oral response might be a suitable replacement for a writing task if the response is recorded verbatim, the student spells all technical words (if spelling is a criterion), and the recorder rereads material, makes changes, but provides absolutely no language or conceptual assistance. The task approximates a writing task if the student is allowed to see, direct and edit what the examiner writes, rather than the examiner simply taking dictation. Although the oral response might be comparatively *easier* than the actual writing task, the conceptual component of the accommodated task might be just as high or even higher.

Receptive/expressive accommodations. Often a test accommodation will require input and output using the same format. If a student uses Braille input, a Braille response is required; if items are signed, signed responses are allowed; if items are read to the student, the student is allowed to respond orally, and if the test is in large print, test alternatives will be in large print.

There are three situations when the receptive/expressive modality might be different. First, the general question format might be acceptable, but the student is not able to perform the required test response. For example, a student is able to read test items but must respond orally or use a communication board. Second, a modified response might result in a better assessment of what is being measured than the regular test response. If Braille is used to measure reading comprehension, reading the questions to the student after the student has read the Braille text and then allowing for an oral response might be a better measure of "Braille comprehension" than requiring a Braille response. This, of course, depends on the student's Braille skills and the exact purpose of the test (e.g., a Braille response might be a part of what is being measured). This is not to say that reading a paragraph in Braille and allowing for oral answers is actually better or preferable than an all Braille task, but that if the focus of the assessment is comprehension, a variety of responses might be considered.

Third, a specific type of response might be necessary for diagnostic purposes. There are several standardized tests which are primarily used because of the type of response required. For a student with an expressive language disability, the inability to provide an oral response can detract from an assessment of the student's receptive language. A test such as the PPVT-R (Dunn & Dunn, 1981), which entails an oral task followed by a series of pictorial alternatives for each item, can help minimize the expressive language necessary to demonstrate receptive language performance. A multiple-choice reading test might be preferable to a test which requires open-ended responses if the student has expressive writing difficulty.

Response simplification. Providing a simple and easy-to-make response can be a useful response accommodation. If a student does not understand the bubble task, is clearly not able to record answers using the bubble format, or there is a mobility or coordination problem, marking answers in the test booklet might be an effective accommodation. Simplifying the response task should not be confused with simplifying the test or content. If a test is open-ended, the task cannot be changed to a multiple-choice format because this task is easier than an open-ended response. Likewise, the language of alternatives or the number of alternatives cannot be changed to produce an easier test.

Response clarity. If a response accommodation is made, the student and examiner should know exactly what the modified task is. A generic respond-in-any-manner accommodation is a vague instruction and should be avoided. Consider a visually impaired student who is proficient with Braille and responds in Braille. If the test examiner is not proficient in Braille, and a respond-in-any-manner accommodation

were in effect, oral responses might be used because it is easier to interpret and score rather than because this mode of response best meets the
student's test needs.   A respond-in-any-manner accommodation can
also change what a test measures. If a student is told that he or she can
respond in any manner when taking a writing test, a student might
decide that the best *response manner* is to orally dictate answers which
might not be an acceptable response mode.

Highlighting modifications. Response highlighting should not help
a student determine the correctness of an answer, but is designed to help
the student focus on salient elements of the response task. For a writing
task, providing bold-lined paper will not affect the assessment of
ideation, language or spelling, but might help the student organize the
response which is being made. A student might have written three sentences which are quite acceptable, but if the sentences overlap and are
visually disjointed on the page, this will not only affect the student's ability to correct mistakes but for the reader to adequately evaluate the
response.

When reading questions and alternatives, a variety of highlighting
can be used. A student might be allowed to use a ruler, marker, or reading window to read text and/or alternatives, or to align scoring sheet
numbers and corresponding answer bubbles. If these types of aids are
used during the normal course of instruction, they should be allowed
during testing. There are a variety of additional accommodation aids
which can be used to highlight the response such as felt marker, thick
pencil, colored pen/pencil, ruler or reading mask to facilitate reading
item alternatives. Of course, highlighting can suggest the correctness of
an answer such as when the modification involves highlighting verbs,
words or keywords, especially when what is highlighted is the answer.

Simplifying the appearance of the response task is intuitively appealing. Presenting alternatives in large print does reduce the amount of
information on a page because of the size of the print, but if large print
alternatives are used, the entire test should be in large print. If a student
has difficulty recording answers using a traditional bubble format, a
large bubble format might serve to both highlight and simplify the
response task. For standardized and classroom tests, large print answer
sheets are easily constructed in a variety of formats with most word
processors.[1]

Listing alternatives on a single line rather than having sentences
wrap around to a second line might be useful if the student has diffi-

culty with line-to-line reading. Of course, to be consistent the entire test would need to be formatted in this way and not just the item alternatives. Consider the following alternatives which are preceded by a brief reading comprehension story. There are several ways in which the alternatives can be displayed and highlighted as shown below.

The story is mainly about

    a. a fishing boat which was lost at sea in a storm
    b. a large passenger ship which came to the assistance
       of a fishing boat
    c. a fishing boat which came to the assistance of a
       passenger ship
    d. a Coast Guard ship which came to the aid of a passenger
       ship

The alternatives can be written so that each is on a single line. Obviously, the length of the alternative or the sentence determines the feasibility of this adaptation.

The story is mainly about

    a. a fishing boat which was lost at sea in a storm
    b. a large passenger ship which came to the assistance of a fishing boat
    c. a fishing boat which came to the assistance of a passenger ship
    d. a Coast Guard ship which came to the aid of a passenger ship

Large print can also be used to delineate alternatives. However, as shown by the following example, using large print might preclude the placing of alternatives on a single line (if both accommodations have been specified):

The story is mainly about

a. a fishing boat which was lost at sea in a storm

b. a large passenger ship which came to the assistance of a fishing boat

c. a fishing boat which came to the assistance of a passenger ship

d. a Coast Guard ship which came to the aid of a passenger ship

If a student has difficulty with line-to-line reading or separating alternatives from one another, providing some type of demarcation (e..g, drawing a line) between alternatives, or between the stem and alternatives might be used but this is can be a very involved task and before a standardized test is modified in this fashion, a student should have demonstrated a definite need for the modification. Because of the time and effort required to make this type of extensive accommodation, there should be a demonstrated need that the accommodation is necessary and will mitigate the effects of a disability. Overall, developing extensive and unique layout accommodations cannot be done with most tests and a generic recommendation for this type of modification is inappropriate. For a standardized test, a large print version might be available. Although the standardized test can be highlighted (e.g., drawing lines between alternatives), this might be more distracting than no highlighting, depending on the print size, line spacing and number of items per page.

Equipment-Aided Responses

The availability and working order of equipment should be determined at least a day before actual assessment, and immediately prior to the assessment. Not having necessary equipment, equipment that is not working, or equipment glitches can preclude a meaningful assessment. Also, the need to repair equipment just prior to testing a student probably raises the anxiety of the student (and that of the examiner/repairperson). For everyone who has worked with electrical equipment ranging from overhead projectors to computers, most have suffered the frustration of not being able to find an outlet, having a cord that is too short, or a software program that fails to load, run or show the slightest hint of life. Equipment difficulties will occur prior and during testing, but a modicum of preparatory work on the part of the examiner will keep these problems to a minimum. This is especially critical when the test response is computer or equipment dependent. If the examiner is even moderately familiar with the equipment, preparing for what might be considered *typical* equipment failures is certainly wise. Having extra batteries for a hard-of-hearing student requires some knowledge as to the type of aid used by the student. Checking circuits for loose wires is easy to do, and those vexing equipment failures resulting from the not-plugged-in plug is best remedied before professional repair help is sought.

Students with disabilities who require special equipment must be encouraged at the time of testing to indicate if equipment is lacking or not in working order. Table 8.1 illustrates the types of equipment which might be used during a test to allow, permit or enhance a student's response.

Table 8.1 Types of Test Accommodation Equipment.

Abacus	Enlarged keyboard	Ruler
Adaptive firmware card	Expanded keyboard	Screen enlarger
Adjustable keyboard	Felt-tip pens	Sensor switches
Adjustable workstations	Friction pads	Sound buffer
Alternate computer keyboard	Head controlled mouse	Special chairs
Alternative communication	Headphones	Special tables
device	Keyboard overlay	Special lamps
Batteries (extra)	Keyboard guards	Special desks
Bold-lined paper	Kurzweil reader	Speech synthesizer
Bookstands	Language master	Stylus
Braille Rulers	Large print clock	Switchboard
Braille paper	Large display calculator	Switches
Braille Eraser	Letter board	Talking calculator
Braille slates	Letter/language board	Talking typewriter
Braille 'n Speak	Light talker	Tape recorder
Braille number line	Magnifiers	Telescopes
Brown glaze paper (for	Mouse adaptations	Text-to-speech software
Braillers)	Number line	Touch 'n Talk
Calculator	Optacon	TouchWindow
Cassette foot/pedal switch	Optical scanner	Turntable desk
Cassette tapes	Page marker	Trackball devices
Closed circuit television	Page turner	Tread switches
Color transparency	Paper holder	Type 'n Speak
Communication board	Pencil holder	Typewriter
Computer notebook	Perkins Brailler	Ultravisor screen
Computer	Placemarkers	Unicorn keyboard
Computer switch interface	Power pad	Vaporizer
Crammer abacus	Raised lined paper	Variable intensity lamp
Dehumidifier paper	Raised print clock	Visor cap
Echo synthesizer	Reading stands	Voice activated systems
Embossed paper	Reading windows	

If necessary, certain equipment items must be ordered or signed-out. If equipment must be moved from one location to another, this will require planning. If electronic equipment is being moved, care must be taken so that the equipment arrives intact, and the person responsible for moving the equipment should be aware of what precautions should be taken. Other large equipment items might be dedicated to a particular place or room (e.g., optical scanner) so that the student must come to the equipment and not vice versa. Finally, a determination must be made that the test site is able to support whatever equipment is being used (e.g., electric outlets near the table used for testing).

Computer-Aided Responses

A computer can be used to bypass problems associated with the response task (e.g., penmanship), to simplify or clarify elements of the task (e.g, using a Spellcheck), or simplifying the task itself as is done with single-switch response accommodations. For a student with a disability, a large portion of the student's test-taking effort might be given to the physical process of responding rather than the conceptualization of the response (e.g., concentrating on vocabulary, syntax and ideation). If a computer can remedy this problem, a computer response is appropriate. However, as is often the case, a computer does not always provide the most suitable test accommodation solution. If the student lacks the necessary keyboarding experience, a computer task might further detract from measuring the student's writing ability when a relatively fluid response is advantageous (e.g., as when writing). Some students might have touch-typing skills, but many will rely on hunt-n-peck typing and attempting to write a coherent sentence, much less organized paragraph, can be a formidable task if finding each letter is a major task unto itself.

Whenever computer keyboarding is part of the response, keyboarding skill can influence performance. If the student is spending an inordinate amount of time with the task of keyboarding (selecting letters), writing performance (viz., syntax, ideation, etc.) might be affected. For some students simply selecting an alternative identifier (e.g., selecting alternative **A** as the answer) might be a difficult task if the student has limited keyboard experience.

Computer technology is becoming an increasingly important vehicle for providing test accommodations. As the technological innovations increase, so does the ability of software packages to reduce the conceptual effort required to complete computer-based response tasks. Computer enhancements which allow a student to meet test criteria should be disallowed. If spelling is a criterion, the spellcheck capability should be deactivated (e.g., by renaming the pertinent file names or removing the spellcheck) unless there is a specific reason for not doing so. If the purpose of the assessment is to evaluate vocabulary and grammar, spellcheck, Thesaurus, and grammar-check capabilities should be disconnected. If a calculator is allowed, the capability of the calculator should be specified (e.g., a programmable calculator might be disallowed but a simple four-function calculator might be permitted). Most calculators have a square root function, but if an item measures the ability to find a square root, the use of a calculator to determine the answer should not be used. Talking calculators are useful for students with disabilities, but if the assessment involves the ability to calculate, the use of a talking calculator (or any type of calculator) should not be allowed.

Screen enhancements. Many computer systems have accessibility options for person's with disabilities. These include such features as sticky keys which allow a user to press the **Alt**ernative, **Ctrl** (Control) or shift key and then a second key without holding both keys simultaneously, and a repeat rate option so that random or repeated key strokes are ignored. These options, in addition to large point fonts, can be used to create test files/materials to facilitate keyboard responses.

Response Assistance

For the most part, aids which can result or suggest the correctness of an item are not allowed. The are several exceptions to this such as the use of a calculator for mathematics problems. However, even when a calculator is allowed, it should only be for problems in which computational skill is not the primary ability being tested. If needed, a calculator can be used with the SAT and ACT tests, but a calculator should not be used by a student taking a statewide competency test or school achievement test which measures, in part, computational skills. For an aid such as a calculator, the effect on test performance and test validity is generally not known. If a student has considerable difficulty with computational problems, the probability that the student has developed higher-level mathematics problem-solving skills seems unlikely. The benefits of using a calculator is the ability to reduce problem-solving time and careless mistakes, difficulties which are characterized by all students and not just students with disabilities. Depending on the test and item, the possibility also exists that a calculator might distract the student from the underlying problem-solving task in the same way that a student using a word processor to write a composition might be distracted by inadequate keyboarding skills.

There is some data to support the notion that using a calculator will improve test performance. Lawrence and Dorans (1994) examined the effects of using a calculator with over 90,000 students who took the SAT. Approximately half were allowed to use a calculator and the other half were not. The results revealed that the group using a calculator (N=46,637, M=12.13, SD=6.23) received somewhat higher scores than the group (N=45,765, M=11.23, SD=6.07) which did not use a calculator (t=27.04, P<.001). The authors noted that for specific test items "the skills measured by the item administered with a calculator are quite different when the item is administered without a calculator" and several items were reported to be easier with a calculator than without. When asked to compare the number of seconds in 24 hours to the number of minutes in eight weeks the item was easier with a calculator. In any case, for high-stakes tests such as the SAT, a calculator might make the task somewhat easier. For students using a calculator to answer straight-forward computational problems (e.g., 839+426), an extensive research study should not be necessary to conclude that a calculator will, on the average, improve both the speed and accuracy of the response.

Test Accommodation Aids

There are three general categories of aids which a student can be given during a test: (1) minimal-impact aids which have little or no impact on the content being measured; (2) response aids which help a student respond; and (3) problem-solving aids which might be used to determine the correctness of an answer or increase the probability of finding the correct answer. The following table gives several examples of the different types of response test aids:

Table 8.2 Using Aids.

AID	Example
Minimal-impact aids	Magnification devices Reading aids (markers, reading windows) Writing aids (felt marker, thick pencil, colored pen) Hearing amplification
Response aids	Examiner recorded response Examiner interpreted responses Word processing for writing Synthesized speech Adaptive technology
Problem-solving aids	Examiner help Using calculators Spellcheck and word processing aids Speech recognition Manipulatives, arithmetic tables and number lines Reference materials

The response adaptations previously discussed are mostly minimal-impact aids, and have little or no effect on the response task, but assist the student in dealing with the task and making the necessary response. Allowing a student to use a placemarker to read or track answers is not going to help the student determine the correctness of an answer, or allowing a student to use a bubble magnifier might make both the test and response task possible, but has minimal impact on test validity. The primary concern for the examiner regarding minimal impact aids is to ensure that the aid is available, in working order, and is being used.

Unlike minimal impact aids, response aids provide direct help or assistance from the examiner in order for the student to respond. If the examiner records or interprets responses, or equipment is used which substantially changes the character of the response, the validity of the accommodation must be carefully examined so that the modified response does not permit a student to inaccurately demonstrate ability. This is a difficult task and requires a concerted good faith effort on the part of the examiner to evaluate the purpose of a test when such an aid is being used, and how the aid might or might not affect validity. If a student is allowed to record answers in the test booklet or use a felt marker to record answers, if a scoring service is used to tabulate results and generate individual reports, someone will be required to rerecord the responses on a scoring sheet. Prior to doing this, there should be strict guidelines as to how responses will be rerecorded. For example, a student might use an X over a corrected bubble response if a felt marker is used. In this situation, the response would not be recorded. On the other hand, if multiple-responses are made, all would be rerecorded and not just the response which is correct.

If assistance is given to help a student respond, the assistance must focus on the physical response and not on the correctness or quality of the response. If the examiner is required to record responses, a standard method should be used. For example, the scoring sheet is placed in front of the student and the examiner records responses as indicated and then returns to a neutral position. When recording answers, the examiner should not tap with a pencil, anticipate answers or otherwise indicate the correctness of responses, or encourage students to change or reconsider a response. The possibility of providing information as to the correctness of an answer increases with the amount of assistance given. Indicating the correctness of an answer is probably less likely if only alternatives are read by the examiner than if the examiner reads and tracks with a pointer or finger as each alternative is read.

Finally, if the examiner does provide aid, the assistance should be only what is required. Providing aid is not the time to do a diagnostic assessment, encourage guessing, or develop test-taking strategies. Providing aid should only entail what is necessary to respond, and not aid which reflects the knowledge, ability or test-taking skill of the examiner. This is the essential difference between examiner aid and examiner help: the former allows a student to show his or her response, while the latter incorporates the ability of the examiner to respond either in part or in whole.

If a scribe is used to record dictated responses for a content test, the exact response must be recorded. If the response also measures spelling, then this must be included in the student's response (e.g., spelling all content words). If a test accommodations involves the use of a notetaker to record problem-solving strategies (e.g., the student directs the notetaker through the problem-solving steps or the development of a composition), the notetaker must not provide feedback concerning the correctness of the answer, assistance in formulating answers, or cues or prompts which somehow might suggest the correctness of the answer.

Recording Oral Responses

When assessing the content ability of students with physical, sensory or learning disabilities, an oral response might be necessary. For students who have difficulty with the response required by a test (e.g., as a result of quadriplegia), an oral response is a logical solution and should have minimal effect on what the test measures. If test items are read to the student, an oral response would be consistent with the task. For a student with a visual impairment, an oral response might be used in conjunction with oral assessment, Braille or large print.

When oral responses are recorded, an effort must be made not to give clues. For example, asking the student following an incorrect response, "Are your sure?" and then allowing an alternative response might indicate the correctness of the answer. The examiner must practice reading alternatives and recording responses. Obviously, a change in inflection or pitch, as is the case with reading questions, or an unintentional pause or facial expression while reading an alternative might help the student determine the correctness of an answer.

Tape recording responses. Tape recording an oral response does eliminate the immediate influence of an examiner, but increases the difficulty of the test task. The first problem of concern is whether the student is allowed to control the recorder or whether a continuous recording of the response is made. If the student is allowed to control the recorder, the student must not only be able to use the recorder but know how to edit responses (e.g., rerecording responses, erasing segments of a response) if allowed. If a continuous recording is made, an examiner must still evaluate the response which might be difficult because of the quality of the recording, the volume, or the speech or language of the student. Although the examiner should provide minimal aid when evaluating oral responses, an advantage over recorded responses is the ability to solicit interpretable speech and language which cannot be done when a tape recording is made.

Although tape recording responses does present several problems when the recording is used as the only source for interpreting a response, a tape recording can provide a useful backup for an examiner when a student's speech or language is difficult to interpret. If speech or language is a problem, the examiner should become accustomed to the student's speech and language prior to testing.

Speech recognition. Advances in speech recognition technology allow users with sufficient disk memory to dictate test responses. Speech recognition software *learns* a student's speech and language although the accuracy of the recognition depends on the learning capability of the system and available active and user-specific vocabulary. This type of aid is ideal when the task is to determine content knowledge via short-answer or essay-type tests. Of course, speech recognition would be inappropriate if the task were to spell content-specific vocabulary. The use of speech-recognition systems to assess writing ability is problematic and entails the same difficulties as when a scribe is used to record responses (with the exception of spelling). The attraction of a speech-recognition response format is the ability to respond without a recorder or direct examiner assistance; the disadvantage is a computer-aided oral response which is far from identical to that of a written response.

Recording braille responses. A visually impaired student might use a Brailler or provide responses via a computer. If so, provisions must be made to transcribe the Braille responses for evaluation. This service is often available through a specialist or itinerant teacher service. If the responses are multiple-choice, the teacher, consultant-teacher, or special education teacher might be able to transcribe choices to a scoring grid.

Recording signed responses. Sign language is somewhat of a misnomer in that there are a variety of techniques which a student might use to communicate. Students with hearing impairments will likely use a combination of oral responses, sign language and fingerspelling. The exact language format for administering tests should be decided before testing (e.g., combined communication, sign language, American sign language, exact signed English, fingerspelling). Regardless of the final response format selected, the examiner should attempt to closely follow regular-test item format. To accomplish this, the examiner must be familiar with the student's communication system and acceptable responses must be determined beforehand. If the task is to name a very abrasive substance used in grindstones, and the answer is *carborundum* the only acceptable answer might be to fingerspell the word or use a sign specifically for that word. Whether a characteristic of carborundum (e.g., the sign for *hard*) would be an acceptable response would depend on whether the task was to know how to fingerspell the target word, or to indicate a general idea as to the meaning of the word (of which the sign for *hard* might or might not be acceptable).

For many statewide tests sign language is only allowed when giving directions. For the 8th Edition of the Stanford Achievement Test (SAT-8) designed for use with hearing impaired students, "the method of communication used in the administration of the SAT-8 should be the same method normally used in the classroom with the deaf students being tested" (Schildroth, 1990, p. 5). When interpreting responses, care must be taken not to query the student for elaboration and to therefore guide the student to the correct answer, or to provide feedback which might otherwise help the student determine the correctness of an answer.

Augmentative Communication

Augmentative and alternative communication (AAC) refers to all communication techniques and accommodations which improve, enhance, supplement or replace speech, writing and nonoral communication (e.g., fingerspelling) sign language, gestures.[2] For a student not able to respond using speech, writing, signs or gestures, a variety of techniques are available which simplify the response task. Whatever technique or device used, three factors are essential when assessing a student using augmentative communication: (1) the identification of a consistent response behavior, (2) response intentionality, and (3) response independence.

First, if the student's task is to exhibit a response when the examiner points to one of four alternatives, a meaningful and consistent response on the part of the student must be identified. This could be a foot movement, nod, blink, muscle contraction, puff, turn of the head, clenched fist, or whatever. Before a meaningful evaluation can be made, the student must be able to exhibit one behavior which can be used to make the response. When at least one consistent behavior has been identified, most academic and cognitive abilities can be assessed.

Second, the student's behavior must be intentional. Giving a student an elaborate electronic language board, only to have the student randomly poke keys, probably does little more than to reinforce random behavior. If the student seems to respond randomly, such as by repeated responses, not looking at the communication apparatus, immediate responses, the behavior might not be intentional. If behavior is not intentional, the task is likely too difficult or completely disinteresting to the student. A multidisciplinary team might be interested in evaluating the writing skills of a 16-year-old student with cerebral palsy. A letter board or some type of assistive technological device is given to the student, but the responses appear to be meaningless. Does this mean that the student has a writing disability in addition to cerebral palsy? Not necessarily. In this instance, an evaluation of the student's reading ability might indicate similar behavior, or given a very simple discrimination task, the student might not be able to select the letter which is different (e.g., **A A B A**). In this situation, a determination must be made that the student can do simple discrimination tasks (viz., readiness tasks) before reading, and be able to read before a determination can be made that the student has a writing disability.

Third, the ultimate goal of all augmentative and assistive communication is response independence. That is, the goal should be for the student to respond with no physical help or other cues. Initially, guiding a student through a response might be appropriate. And providing verbal cues might be necessary to help the student understand the task (e.g., "press the switch."). However, the only real test of response intentionality is an independent response. As discussed below, one of the major criticisms of facilitated communication is questionable response independence.

Letter boards.   Single-switch scanning (which is discussed in below) is often associated with computer-related technology but the concept underlying scanning is readily available using picture, letter or word boards. A letter or word board is easily constructed to allow a student to select answers, alternatives, or to construct written answers. The following is a simple true/false communication board in which the student selects one of the elements or a recorder points to each element (viz., cued responses) until the student indicates a selection by some type of intentional behavior (e.g., finger or shoulder movement, eye blink).

YES	NO

The above concept is easily modified for use with a five-alternative multiple-choice task. Assume that a student is not able to respond using a traditional bubble format or even to enter selection directly in a test booklet because of a physical disability. If the task is to answer the following:

$$-17 + (-8) = \quad \text{A) } 25 \quad \text{B) } 9 \quad \text{C) } -9 \quad \text{D) } -25,$$

an **ABCD** letter test board is easily devised whereby the examiner scans each identifier with a finger or pointer until the student indicates a response by a nod, finger movement, blink or some other identifiable, consistent and intentional behavior:

A	B	C	D

Rather than using a closed-ended multiple-choice response, an open-ended number array can be used to select answers.

0	1	2	3	4	5	6	7	8	9

The complexity of the communication board is increased by using a more detailed board configuration to answer questions in an open-ended format for tasks requiring alphabetic or numeric responses.

A	B	C	D	E
F	G	H	I	J
K	L	M	N	O
P	Q	R	S	T
U	V	W	X	Y
Z	.	!	?	NEW

Single-Switch Accommodations

For students who have physical disabilities which prevent oral or written responses, or the use of a computer keyboard, a single-switch response format can be used to respond to test items in a multiple-choice format and to generate open-ended responses (e.g., writing, open-ended problem-solving). As shown by the following single-switch task, a problem is presented followed by four alternatives. Each alternative is scanned via the computer by means of a cursor to the left of each alternative. The amount of time each alternative is scanned depends on the individual being tested, but an initial scan period might be three seconds or so. Variables such as the type of scan, the speed each alternative is scanned, the time between scans, and the type of switch behavior required (e.g., the student must engage and then release the switch before a response is recorded) often can be set to best meet student's response needs.

When the student decides to select one of the alternatives, a switch connected to the computer is engaged while the alternative is being scanned. The device might be a simple tread switch which requires the student to press a lightly tensioned plate, but there are many switch options available such as a mercury, puff, plate or sensor switch which senses muscle tension. The only requirement for a single-switch task is the ability to identify a movement which can be made intentionally and consistently by the student.

$$
\begin{array}{r}
6 \\
+8 \\
\hline
\end{array}
$$

13
■ 14
15
16

The switch task is easily modified to assess a wide variety of skills, ranging from spelling, word meaning, reading comprehension, or content area knowledge. The following is an example single-switch reading item (where an incorrect alternative is being scanned). This type of item is easily modified to accommodate a wide range of disabilities and language levels by customizing the screen character size, providing feedback, using auditory cues, and using a speech synthesizer.

> **Grass is green and sugar is**
>
>   1) red
>   2) white
>   3) blue
> ■ 4) green
>   5) salt

Single-switch writing. Many single-switch tasks use a multiple-choice format to scan a set of items so that a switch is engaged in order to make a selection. Variations of this technique can be expanded to produce very complex responses. Matrix scanning can be used in a variety of ways in conjunction with a single-switch task. The simplest scanning technique is to scan each element of the matrix in sequential order. For a writing task this can be very time consuming in that the student must wait for a letter to be scanned in order to make a selection.

An alternative to element matrix scanning is to use some type of row-column scanning technique as shown below. The alphabet is displayed using five screen lines. Each matrix row is scanned to first select an array of characters. This could be done by first positioning a scan to the left of each row, or by inverting the row of characters during each scan. A second scan is then used to select the specific letter or character in that array.

To select a character two switch movements must be made: row selection and then the specific character selection from that row. Although row/element scanning is more efficient than element-by-element scanning, the task can be difficult to conceptualize.

```
        A     B     C     D     E     F

 ■      G     H     I     J     K     L

        M     N     O     P     Q     R

        S     T     U     V     W     X

        Y     Z     *     .     ?    NEW

Word:
```

To spell **HELLO** the letter **H** is selected by first engaging the switch when the second row is scanned. As soon as the second row is selected, each element of the row is scanned sequentially until a letter is selected or, in this case, the letter **H.** This procedure is repeated until the desired word or message has been selected and displayed. When this technique is used with a speech synthesizer, each letter is synthesized as the letter is selected, and then entire word or message is synthesized when the * symbol is selected. Matrix scanning can include a variety of options such as upper- and lowercase characters, printing, filing and editing capabilities, and a full range of keyboard or ASCII characters.

```
        A     B     C     D     E     F

        G     H     I     J     K     L
              ■
        M     N     O     P     Q     R

        S     T     U     V     W     X

        Y     Z     *     .     ?    NEW

Word:  H
```

Single-switch bubble. The following program illustrates how a single-switch interface can be used to respond to a traditional multiple-choice format. Questions are presented orally or using visuals, and the student engages the switch when the desired alternative (e.g., **ABCDE**) is scanned. As each alternative is scanned, a sound cue is provided to indicate the alternative number (e.g., two beeps indicate that alternative 2 or **B** is being scanned). Following a single-switch response, an X is marked in the bubble and several notes are played. After the Esc is pressed to exit the program (by the examiner), item feedback is displayed. This program illustrates the basic principle of scanning multiple-choice alternatives. A more extensive program would allow a student to move backward and forward to change responses.

Table 8.3 Single-Switch Bubble Program.

```
10 REM SINGLE-SWITCH BUBBLE
20 REM
30 DIM ANSWER(100)
40 STRIG ON
50 KEY OFF
60 SCREEN 1
70 DELAY = 1
80 ITEM=1
90 Y = 70: X = 50
100 CLS
110 IF STRIG(1) < 0 THEN 110
120 COLOR 0,15
130 GOSUB 530
140 LOCATE 13: PRINT TAB(2);ITEM
150 FOR L=1 TO 5
160 LOCATE 8,2+7*L:PRINT CHR$(64+L)
170 LINE (X,Y)-(X+40,Y+50),,B
180 IF L=1 THEN 190
190 X=X+55
200 NEXT L
210 Y = 70: X = 50: A = 1
220 START = TIMER
230 LINE (X,Y) - (X+40,Y+50),,BF
240 FOR K = 1 TO A
250 SOUND 523,5: SOUND 32767,2
260 NEXT K
270 IF STRIG(1) < 0 THEN 380
280 KY$ = INKEY$: IF KY$ = "" THEN    310
290 IF ASC(KY$) = 27 THEN ITEM = ITEM - 1: GOTO 460
300 GOTO 380
310 IF TIMER - START > DELAY+2 THEN 330
320 GOTO 270
330 LINE (X,Y) - (X+40,Y+50),0,BF
340 LINE (X,Y) - (X+40,Y+50),,B
350 GOSUB 530
360 X = X+55: IF X > 300 THEN 210
370 A = A+1: GOTO 220
380 LINE (X,Y) - (X+40,Y+50),0
390 LINE (X,Y+50) - (X+40,Y),0
400 FOR K = 1 TO 3
410 SOUND 500+50*K,5
420 NEXT K
430 ANSWER(ITEM) = A
440 GOSUB 530
450 ITEM = ITEM + 1: GOTO 90
460 WIDTH 80
470 SCREEN 0
480 PRINT "Answers": PRINT
490 FOR K = 1 TO ITEM
500 PRINT K" = "ANSWER(K),
510 NEXT
520 END
530 START = TIMER
540 IF TIMER - START > DELAY THEN RETURN
550 GOTO 540
```

Morse code. The ability to use Morse Code is another example of a possible test response accommodation which is difficult in and of itself. The ability to use Morse Code requires not only the ability to conceptualize the relationship between a series of dots, dashes and letters, and a degree of reading proficiency, but also requires the physical ability to use a switch to enter the necessary dots and dashes. Appendix B provides an example of a Morse Code program which can be used to enter keyboard characters via a single-switch format.

Facilitated Communication

Facilitated communication (FC) is based on the methods developed in Australia while attempting to devise an alternative communication system for a student having cerebral palsy. The technique has subsequently been used with persons having a wide range of disabilities, including autism and mental retardation. The essence of FC involves providing physical support while the communicator uses a keyboard or letter board. This assistance might involve having the facilitator provide hand support directly to the hand of the student who is using the keyboard, letter board or some other communication device. Or, if less support is required, the facilitator might simply provide support to the FC user's forearm, shoulder, etc. The controversy surrounding FC stems from the possibility that physical support might result in the facilitator authoring responses rather than the FC user. Critics of FC believe that the facilitator is doing the "pointing" or communicating. There is no doubt that if a student was seemingly unable to read, write and had minimal receptive communication skills, the use of a test accommodation (viz., FC) which allowed the student to pass tests in everything from English to Chemistry would be a marvelous accommodation if it were so.

The FC debate centers about a single question: To what extent does the physical assistance provided by the facilitator involve "manipulation" rather than "support"? In short, are the communications that result from FC authored by the communicator or facilitator? Shane (1994) asserted that the underlying theoretical foundation for FC rests on a belief that apraxia, a neurological based deficit that does not involve cognitive ability, explains the FC capability of persons classified as autistic. Proponents of FC believe that the underlying problem concerns the task of responding and not the cognition required by the task. If this is so, FC might be able to bypass this deficit. Shane discounted that apraxia allows persons classified as having autism to effectively use FC based on extant literature, and noted that "...there is no scientific or clinical evidence that the speech of a person who is autistic contains the speech characteristics generally associated with apraxia of speech" (p. 12).

Actual data which calls to question the validity of FC range from common sense observations to controlled investigations. For example, there are situations when persons being facilitated fail to attend to the communication device (viz., keyboard) thereby suggesting the messages are being authored by the facilitator.

Many of the problems associated with FC, especially when considered as a means for providing test accommodations, is the belief by FC proponents that FC cannot be validated by traditional assessment techniques because of word-finding difficulties (i.e., the person being facilitated might know a test answer, but is unable to communicate that answer without a cue), and the belief that testing will undermine the trust between the facilitator and communicator. Paradoxically, the rationale for this belief is based on facilitated communications; that is, FC is used to show that FC should not be tested.

Shane discussed what he referred to as "the most perplexing and difficult to defend aspect of facilitated communication" (p. 21): The ability of persons with no previous literacy skills to exhibit high levels of literary and written proficiency. The FC position regarding unexpected literacy seems to be that this is the result of a combination of vicarious learning (e.g., being in the vicinity of cereal boxes, watching television) and hyperlexia. Shane's criticism of FC literacy is based on the improbability that so many disabled persons would exhibit this behavior, the unlikely developmental occurrence that a large number of very young children diagnosed as autistic would exhibit sudden literacy, and the characteristics of hyperlexia and savant skills.

In the final analysis, FC does offer several interesting strategies which might enhance a student's test performance. However, regardless if a student is assisted by FC or some other technique, the following factors should be taken into consideration: (1) Independence: a student cannot be tested until an independent response is possible; (2) Intentionality: a student's test responses must be intentional; (3) Assistance: physical support should be minimized and faded as soon as possible; (4) Authorship: test for authorship by "message passing" or "single blind" testing; (5) Literacy: completely unexpected literacy must be viewed with considerable caution and makes the task of determining the authenticity of FC authorship imperative; and (6) Observation: if the communicator is not attending to the task, authorship should be questioned.

If FC is used to test a student, a determination must be made as to authorship of facilitated test responses using a single-blind technique. One FC validation strategy is to show a letter, number, word etc. to the communicator but not to the facilitator. The facilitator is then requested to use FC to retrieve the letter, number, word etc. that was shown. As with all accommodations which provide undue assistance to a student, the results can be highly discriminatory in that the test might result in a student being denied a necessary benefit or service. If a student is thought to be capable of reading Shakespeare, but actually has no reading ability whatsoever, the appropriateness of allowing a student to participate in a literature class which required advanced reading skills would deprive the student of an opportunity to develop more appropriate basic reading or functional skills.

ENDNOTES

1. Generic large print answer sheets are available though the American Printing House for the Blind Catalog of Instructional Aids, Tools, and Supplies. See also the APH Catalog of Accessible Books for People Who are Visually Impaired for materials relating to specific tests.

2. The National Institute on Disability and Rehabilitation Research (NIDRR) is an excellent source for information relating to augmentative communication and assistive technology.

Chapter 9

TEST SCORE ACCOMMODATIONS

Following the administration of a test, there are a variety of techniques which can be used to report a student's ability and interpret test performance. Standard scores can be used to develop a coherent psychometric profile; norms can be selected to better interpret student performance; and various test score indices can be used to determine the need for test accommodations.

Although test scores and indices might imply a great deal of precision, there is simply no way to understand a student's test performance without a thorough understanding of the test and the underlying normative frame of reference. The apparent statistical precision of scores, which is sometimes misleading, does not absolve the examiner from understanding the test, the scores, and, most important, the student.

Because "tests and other evaluation materials include those tailored to assess specific areas of educational need and not merely those which are designed to provide a single general intelligence quotient,"[1] there is a need to compare different scores from different tests. This does create a problem because of differences between normative populations, statistical idiosyncrasies of tests (e.g., skewness), unique statistical relationships between tests, and methods for reporting test scores.

The multidisciplinary team must consider anecdotal reports, checklists, work samples, interviews, and a variety of quantitative scores and indices. However, the regulations are explicit regarding the need to compare and understand a variety of data sources when conducting an individual evaluation:

(a) In interpreting evaluation data and in making placement decisions, each public agency shall:

1. Draw upon information from a variety of sources, including aptitude and achievement tests, teacher recommendations, physical condition,

243

social or cultural background, and adaptive behavior;

2. Ensure that information obtained from all of these sources is documented and carefully considered;

3. Ensure that the placement decision is made by a group of persons, including persons knowledgeable about the child, the meaning of the evaluation data, and the placement options; and

4). Ensure that the placement decision is made in conformity with the LRE rules in §§300.550-300.554[2]

The primary task of the multidisciplinary evaluation team is three-fold: (1) to use a variety of sources to make decisions, (2) to understand and consider all information, and (3) to make a decision concerning the need for special education and related services based on the child, the data, and the possible placement options. In order to accomplish this task the multidisciplinary team must consider and compare all manner of scores, including raw scores, percentile ranks, stanine scores, grade equivalents, IQ scores, miscellaneous standard scores, and a variety of indices used to indicate the degree of test error.

Raw Scores

The raw score for a standardized test can provide useful information regarding a student's ability. For most tests, the raw score is the number of correct responses. If a student's score is substantially below the mean so that standardized scores cannot be used, the raw score will provide a description of the student's test item performance. For example, for a certain test all raw scores between 0 and 15 are all equivalent to a stanine of 1. A student might have received a stanine 1, but knowing whether the student received a raw score of 0 or 15 might be useful information concerning the student's test performance.

For objective tests, even if normative data is available, the raw score can help clarify the content mastered. A student might have received a score one standard deviation below the mean on a mathematics computation task, but adding a parenthetic statement (e.g., 12/18 or 12 out of 18 items were correctly answered) might further clarify the degree of content knowledge.

For multiple-choice tests, the raw score can provide insights as to the effects of chance in relation to score performance. On one statewide competency test comprised of over 50 items, there are a number of reported scores of 0. Because of the large number of items and the multiple-choice format, a raw score of 0 is so statistically improbable that the reason for this score should be explored. Regardless of the standardized score a student receives, knowing a student's raw score in relation to a chance score will provide a useful perspective. If a 25 item multiple-choice test is given to a student and each item has four alternatives, a chance score of 5 would warrant closer inspection.

For a multiple-choice test the mean chance score is determined by

$$\bar{X}_{chance} = (Number\ of\ Items)\ (\frac{1}{Number\ of\ Alternatives})$$

so that for a 50 item test with five alternatives per item the mean chance score is 10.[3] Whenever a student receives a score near the chance level some attempt should be made to determine whether this is the result of disinterest, test difficulty, insufficient time, a problem recording answers or some other factor.

Multiple-choice tests have been subjected to more criticism than most forms of testing and these criticisms are often well-deserved. Nonetheless, multiple-choice tests do provide a systematic and potentially useful mode of assessment, when the chance character of tests are taken into account. For students with disabilities, multiple-choice tests can be used to obtain diagnostic information, to meet specific learning needs (e.g., reduced time for certain types of multiple-choice tests), and for evaluating students with severe motor disabilities (e.g., alternative scanning).

Percentages. In order to better explicate a student's ability, a percentage can be a useful way to interpret a raw score so that for a 40 items test, a raw score of 30 would be 30/40 X 100 or a score of 75. Although a percentage can be a useful way to conceptualize data, knowing the total number of items, the number correct, the number omitted and the number attempted should also be used to evaluate multiple-choice data. For open-ended tests which result in a percentage type score, the criteria for determining the score should be readily available. For example, a five-point rating scale ranging from 1 (poor) to 5 (excellent) might be used to evaluate handwriting using the following criteria: Mechanics, Vocabulary, Syntax, Spelling and Ideation. A perfect score would be a rating of 5 on each item for a possible summated rating of 25. Finally, a percentage can be a subjective assessment of a student's performance such as when a student is given a grade of say 73 based on the teacher's evaluation of an essay. In order for this "holistic" percentage to have meaning, the criteria or basis for assigning the percentage must be known.

Criterion-referenced scores. A criterion-referenced score might be a raw score, a percentage or even a standard score. A statewide competency test might specify what the expected level of competency is in terms of raw score points so that on a particular test a student must receive a score of X or higher. This level of competency could be expressed in terms of a percentage or a standard score. The exact normative meaning of the score depends on the underlying rationale for the criterion. If the criterion for a test is a score of 20 out of 30, the rationale for the criterion of 20 might be based on the fact that this raw score is 2.0 standard deviations below the mean, and a decision was made that competency must be a z score $\geq$-2.0. Basing the level of competency on a standard score has more to do with the number of students who will be designated competent than actual competency. If a state agency only reports whether a score is above or below a criterion level, limited comparisons can be made between the raw score and other standard scores unless distribution statistics (viz., the mean and standard deviation of the raw scores) or norm tables are provided.

Rather than being based on a standard score, a criterion score of 20 correct might be based on an intuitive decision that a competent student should have a score greater than 66%. Determining a criterion for competency is arbitrary. Spache (1976, p. 314) discussed the problems associated with establishing criteria for informal reading inventories (IRI) such as 90% comprehension for independent reading, 75% for instructional reading and 50% or less indicates reading at the frustration level. The difficulty with IRI's include arbitrary criteria, lack of objective data, out-dated standards, and questions relating to validity and or reliability. Although Spache did recommend a reading comprehension level of at least 70 percent (p. 314), this seems to be more a guideline than an absolute criterion.

Prorated scores. A prorated score can be used to determine a total test score when one or more subtests have not been given, or to determine a test score when items have been eliminated. Because these are entirely different situations, a general test accommodation to "prorate scores" or "prorate credit" should not be used.

If a test is comprised of a number of subtests and one or more subtests cannot be given or should not be used in the interpretation of total test score performance, a prorated score can be determined by

$$X_{prorated} = \frac{Total\ Items}{Administered\ Items}\ (X_{obtained})$$

Assume that a test consists of five subtests, the total number of items comprising these subtests is 200, and a student is not able to take two subtests because of the format. If the subtests administered consist of 120 items and a student received a score of 60, a prorated score could be determined by (200/120) X 60 = 100. The adequacy of using a prorated score depends on the comparability and psychometric characteristics of the subtests. If the subtests have similar difficulty levels and item numbers, a prorated solution might have some merit. A test such as the PIAT-R (Markwardt, 1989) has fairly homogeneous subtests (with the exception of Written Expression), but a report of test performance would be better served if subtest scores were cited rather than a prorated total score if not all the subtests could be administered.

The need to prorate scores requires very unusual circumstances such that a subtest is clearly unsuitable or the results inaccurate (e.g., the student refused to take the subtest). Following the administration of a test, if a score must be prorated to determine a total score there should be an explicit need for deleting the subtest(s) and the number of subtests deleted should be kept to an absolute minimum so as not to provide a misleading total score.

The above formula could also be used to prorate credit for a single test or subtest but the error involved in this is usually so great that this practice should be avoided. Deleting items from a test or prorating a score based on items completed, where difficult items might have been omitted by the student, changes the difficulty of the test. If a student completes the first half of the test, and this half is comprised of easier items, prorating a score based on these items will obviously inflate the student's test score. Although prorating a test score because of deleted or omitted items might be possible if the items were randomly deleted or if the items were of equal difficulty, this is generally not how test items are answered by students or developed by test makers. Overall, prorating credit might seem an alternative to an extended time accommodation, but prorating can seriously impact a student's score and should be used only when absolutely necessary and under very special circumstances.

Redefining criteria. Redefining what is correct or incorrect is an inappropriate accommodation when used with a standardized test. For example, a writing competency test might include spelling as a criterion. Excluding this criterion because the student had difficulty spelling will give the student an unfair if spelling is an evaluation criterion. If spelling is conceptualized as an integral part of writing by the publisher, the test user cannot unilaterally delete this criterion because it does not benefit a student.

Multiple-choice Profiles

Multiple-choice tests are frequently machined scored so that the actual answer sheets are all but ignored. For students who take a test, and certainly for students being considered for special education, multiple-choice answer sheets should be scanned for salient answer patterns. Consider a student who received a score of 25 on a four-alternative 50-item multiple-choice test. If the student answered the first 25 items correctly and did not attempt the remaining 25 items, this profile might suggest that the student did not have sufficient time. There are many reasons for a specific score on a test, and a cursory look at the answer sheet might generate hypotheses for understanding test performance.

Correction for guessing. There are several methods that can be used to adjust scores for guessing. The traditional formula is to correct for guessing using the number of incorrect responses and alternatives so that

$$X_{corrected} = Correct - \frac{Incorrect}{Alternatives - 1}$$

For a 30-item multiple-choice test with five alternatives, a student who received a raw score of 22 and answered eight items incorrectly, the corrected score for guessing would be 22 - 8/(5-1) or 20. If a student guessed randomly and received a score of 6, the corrected score would be 6 - 24/(5-1) or 0. If scores are corrected for guessing, the correction must be used with all students. For standardized tests in which no correction for guessing is used (which is the case with most achievement and psychological tests), a correction for guessing formula cannot be used in the determination of normative scores.

The multiple-choice component breakdown for the scores shown in

Table 9.1 illustrates the relationship between the different multiple-choice elements. For each student, the following multiple-choice factors are shown: number of alternatives, number of items, number correct, number incorrect, number omitted, and the corrected raw score using the correction for guessing formula shown above.

Table 9.1 Multiple-Choice Score Component Breakdown.

Examples of Multiple-choice Score Components						
Student	Choices	Items	Correct	Incorrect	Omitted	Correction For Guessing
A	4	30	18	12	0	14
B	4	30	18	3	9	17
D	4	30	10	0	20	10
E	3	30	5	10	15	0
F	2	20	10	10	0	0
G	2	20	0	20	0	-20

Students A and B both received raw scores of 18, but the scores are different when corrected for guessing. Student C received a score of only 10, yet there were no incorrect responses and many items were left unanswered. This might indicate that time was a factor, the student did not understand the task, or was reluctant to guess. Of course, there is also the possibility that the student knew exactly 10 items and the score is an accurate portrayal of the student's knowledge. For students E and F, the scores are at the chance level; that is, these scores might be the result of simple guessing. The score for student G might reflect colossal bad luck, or the student deliberately answered items incorrectly.

Differentiating score patterns. For three students who all receive scores of 2 on a ten-item five-alternative multiple choice test, each score can have a unique underlying meaning. One student does not answer most of the items, a second randomly selects answers, and a third is distracted by very good distracters. The first step for differentiating these three students is to visually inspect the choices made. For one of the students, the test items might have been too difficult, there might have been insufficient time, or the student had partial knowledge but was not inclined to guess.

After inspecting the answer sheets, an attempt should be made to discern whether incorrect responses represent some type of logical error pattern. For example, given the problem 23-7, the student selects 26. This is a logical error and the response might indicate that the distracter was "working." The incorrect response might have a different meaning if the student selected an unlikely alternative such as 237. Of course, a student might have selected either of these alternatives as a result of guessing which is why a number of similar incorrect responses must be used to suggest a logical error pattern. The final step which should be used to interpret errors is to ask the student why an answer was selected. This is done after the test has been given, and the results are not used to change the students's original test responses. The student should verbally work through the problem, and an attempt should be made to determine whether the student did not know the answer, guessed, or explains why that a particular answer was selected.

The following are several factors which should routinely be considered when evaluating the multiple-choice responses of a student requiring test accommodations: multiple-marks, poorly recorded marks, poorly erased marks, random response pattern, repeated pattern, many omitted items, omitted sections, limited use of alternatives, and an unlikely error score. Cronbach's (1970) cautioned that "constant vigilance is necessary to guarantee accurate scoring (in hand scoring as much as witch machines). Errors are not frequent, but when they occur they are serious" (p. 82).

For every multiple-choice test, the examiner should visually inspect raw score answer sheets for possible unusual patterns. Table 9.2 illustrates several answer sheets where each answer is indicated by an ■ and incorrect responses by an X. Student A did not have time to attempt all the questions; student B received a score of 0 which is unlikely to occur from a purely probability standpoint; students C and E each received the same score but the manner of guessing is unique for each student; and student D had sufficient time to complete test but did not answer all items.

Table 9.2 Multiple-choice Answer Sheet Profiles.

Student				
A	**B**	**C**	**D**	**E**
B ■	B x, C ■	A ■, B x	B ■	A ■, B x
D ■	C ■, D x	A ■, D x	D x	B ■, D x
A ■	A x, B ■	A ■	A ■	A x, C ■
E ■	C ■, E x	A ■, E x	E x	D ■, E x
C ■	C x, D ■	A ■, C x	C ■	C x, E ■
	C ■, D x	A ■, D x	D x	C ■
	A x, B ■	A ■	A x	A x, C ■
	A ■, B x	A ■, B x	B ■	B ■
	A x, B ■	A ■	A ■	A ■
	B ■, E x	A ■, E x	E x	B ■, E x

Standard Scores

Standard scores are critical for interpreting a student's performance when using standardized tests. Standard scores are reported as stanine scores, IQ scores, and various scaled scores having different means and standard deviations. The *z* score is the basic unit for standardized scores and is based on the mean and standard deviation, where a *z* score indicates the number of standard deviations a score is below or above the mean:

$$z = \frac{Score - Mean}{Standard\ Deviation} = \frac{(X - \bar{X})}{SD}$$

A z score, and all corresponding standard scores, are linear transformations of scores based on the mean and standard deviation. The relationship between several of the more commonly-used transformations is as follows: where Z represents a system of z scores, each having a different mean and standard deviation, but score representing the number of standard deviations, a raw score is below or above the mean:

$$Z = \frac{(X - \bar{X})}{SD} = z(100) + 500 = z(21.06) + 50 = z(15) + 100 =$$
$$z(10) + 50 = z(3) + 10 = z(2) + 5$$

The selection of a mean and standard deviation for transforming scores is arbitrary. For example, a mean of 100 and a standard deviation of 15 is often selected for IQ-type tests because this is the approximate mean and standard deviation of ratio IQs or CA/MA(100); stanines, which have a mean of 5 and standard deviation of 2,[a] and are represented as integers (viz., 1, 2...9) can be traced to ease of recording scores on computer cards (remember?); and normal curve equivalents which have a mean of 50 and a standard deviation of 21.06 are similar in range to percentile ranks but do not have the scaling limitation inherent in percentile ranks.

Table 9.3 shows the mean and standard deviations for scores one standard deviation above and one standard deviation below the mean. When the mean is 100 and the standard deviation is 15, +1 SD (or one standard deviation above the mean) is 115 and -1 SD is 85. Expressed in terms of z scores, when the mean is 100 and standard deviation 15, a score of 115 is equal to $z=1.0$ and a score of 85 to $z=-1.0$.

Table 9.3 Standard Score Equivalents.

Mean	+1 SD	SD	-1 SD
100	116	16	84
100	115	15	85
500	600	100	400
50	71	21.06	29
10	13	3	7
5	7	2	3
0	1	1	-1

[a] Stanines were originally developed so that the stanines from 1 to 9 adhere to the following percent distribution: 4, 7, 12, 17, 20, 17, 12, 7, 4. Thus, 4% of the cases would have a stanine of 1, 12% a stanine of 3, and 20% a stanine of 5.

Using alternative standard scores. There are several reasons why either an alternative standard score might be used to interpret test performance. The first reason is one of consistency. Often the multidisciplinary team must evaluate a variety of scores and tests, and having scores which are comparable (i.e., having similar means and standard deviations) can greatly simplify the task of interpreting test scores. Second, several scores are simply difficult to interpret as is the case with percentile ranks. Third, certain transformations can be statistically and interpretatively advantageous as when percentile ranks are transformed to normalized scores, or IQ scores are transformed to z-scores.

Normalized scores. Most standardized tests provide a variety of measures for interpreting score performance. One advantage of a standard score is each score can be interpreted with respect to a known mean and standard deviation. Percentile ranks, on the other hand, are easily understood, less influenced by the shape of the underlying score distribution, and clearly show a person's rank within a distribution of scores. The following describes a very simple accommodation that can be made to better interpret a standard score by combining useful characteristics of percentile ranks and standard scores.

The primary disadvantage of percentile ranks is that the differences between different percentile ranks do not represent equal differences in terms of raw scores. A percentile rank difference near the median will generally reflect a relatively small raw score difference, while percentile rank differences farther from the median reflect larger raw score differences. This is shown in the normal distribution where the differences between percentile ranks of 50 and 16 and 16 and 2 are both one standard deviation, yet, a percentile rank difference between 50 and 16 appears to be larger (34 points) than the difference between percentile ranks of 16 and 2 (14 points).

One method for interpreting percentile ranks for comparative purposes is to use normalized scores. This is accomplished by finding the normal curve z score for a given percentile rank and then transforming this value to a distribution of scores having a known mean and standard deviation. When the mean is set to 21.06 and the standard deviation to 50, the resulting value is referred to as a normalized percentile rank (NPR) or Normal Curve Equivalent (NCE) or

$$\text{NPR} = z(21.06) + 50$$

Thus, the z corresponding to a percentile rank of 99 (which is usually the highest percentile rank available) is 2.33. When this z score is transformed using a standard deviation of 21.06 and a mean of 50, the result is 2.33(21.06)+50 = 99.07 or a normalized value of 99. Normalized percentile ranks range from 1 to 99, have a mean of 50, and look very much like a traditional percentile rank, but are actually standard scores with a set mean and standard deviation, and, unlike percentile ranks, are very useful for statistical score comparisons.

The Table 9.4 lists percentile ranks, corresponding normal curve z scores, normalized percentile ranks (NPR), normalized stanine scores and normalized IQ-type scores (i.e., scores having a mean of 100 and standard deviation of 15). Instead of using NPR's to interpret performance, percentile ranks are easily converted to normalized stanine scores (NSS) by setting the mean to 5 and the standard deviation to 2. Instead of reporting stanines as a single digit score, the normalized stanines in Table 9.4 have been carried to one decimal place which better reflect the underlying z score level than does a single digit score.

$$NSS = z(2)+5$$

Assume that percentile ranks are available for a student and the scores appear to indicate several discrepancies. As shown in Table 9.5, the student's percentile rank in Reading Comprehension is 30 but 48 in Reading Vocabulary. By converting the percentile ranks to normalized stanine scores, the scores differences might be far less dramatic. As shown, percentile rank of 30 is equivalent to a z score of -.52 and a percentile rank of 48 to a z score of -.05. The 18 point percentile rank difference (48 - 30) converts to a z score difference of less than half of a standard deviation (-.05 - -.52).

Table 9.4 Standard Score Conversion Chart.

Code: PR = percentile rank, z = score or number of standard deviations above or below the mean, NPR = normalized percentile rank (or normal curve equivalent), NSS = normalized stanine score, IQT = IQ-type score

Score	z	NPR	NSS	IQT	Score	z	NPR	NSS	IQT
99	2.33	99	9.7	134	1	-2.33	1	.3	66
98	2.02	93	9.0	130	2	-2.02	7	1.0	70
97	1.88	90	8.8	128	3	-1.88	10	1.2	72
96	1.75	87	8.5	126	4	-1.75	13	1.5	74
95	1.64	85	8.3	124	5	-1.64	15	1.7	76
94	1.55	83	8.1	123	6	-1.55	17	1.9	77
93	1.48	81	8.0	122	7	-1.48	19	2.0	78
92	1.41	80	7.8	121	8	-1.41	20	2.2	79
91	1.34	78	7.7	120	9	-1.34	22	2.3	80
90	1.28	77	7.6	119	10	-1.28	23	2.4	81
89	1.23	76	7.5	118	11	-1.23	24	2.5	82
88	1.17	75	7.3	117	12	-1.17	25	2.7	83
87	1.13	74	7.3	116	13	-1.13	26	2.7	84
86	1.08	73	7.2	116	14	-1.08	27	2.8	84
85	1.04	72	7.1	115	15	-1.04	28	2.9	85
84	.99	71	7.0	114	16	-.99	29	3.0	86
83	.95	70	6.9	114	17	-.95	30	3.1	86
82	.92	69	6.8	113	18	-.92	31	3.2	87
81	.88	69	6.8	113	19	-.88	31	3.2	87
80	.84	68	6.7	112	20	-.84	32	3.3	88
79	.81	67	6.6	112	21	-.81	33	3.4	88
78	.77	66	6.5	111	22	-.77	34	3.5	89
77	.74	66	6.5	111	23	-.74	34	3.5	89
76	.71	65	6.4	110	24	-.71	35	3.6	90
75	.67	64	6.3	110	25	-.67	36	3.7	90
74	.64	63	6.3	109	26	-.64	37	3.7	91
73	.61	63	6.2	109	27	-.61	37	3.8	91
72	.58	62	6.2	108	28	-.58	38	3.8	92
71	.55	62	6.1	108	29	-.55	38	3.9	92
70	.52	61	6.0	107	30	-.52	39	4.0	93
69	.50	61	6.0	107	31	-.50	39	4.0	93
68	.47	60	5.9	107	32	-.47	40	4.1	93
67	.44	59	5.9	106	33	-.44	41	4.1	94
66	.41	59	5.8	106	34	-.41	41	4.2	94
65	.39	58	5.8	105	35	-.39	42	4.2	95
64	.36	58	5.7	105	36	-.36	42	4.3	95
63	.33	57	5.7	104	37	-.33	43	4.3	96
62	.31	57	5.6	104	38	-.31	43	4.4	96
61	.28	56	5.6	104	39	-.28	44	4.4	96
60	.25	55	5.5	103	40	-.25	45	4.5	97
59	.23	55	5.5	103	41	-.23	45	4.5	97
58	.20	54	5.4	103	42	-.20	46	4.6	97
57	.18	54	5.4	102	43	-.18	46	4.6	98
56	.15	53	5.3	102	44	-.15	47	4.7	98
55	.13	53	5.3	101	45	-.13	47	4.7	99
54	.10	52	5.2	101	46	-.10	48	4.8	99
53	.08	52	5.2	101	47	-.08	48	4.8	99
52	.05	51	5.1	100	48	-.05	49	4.9	100
51	.02	50	5.0	100	49	-.02	50	5.0	100
50	.00	50	5.0	100	50	-.00	50	5.0	100

Table 9.5 Sample Score Interpretation.

Subtest	Percentile Rank	Z Score	NPR	NSS	IQ-type Score
Reading Vocabulary	48	-.05	49	4.9	100
Reading Comprehension	30	-.52	39	4.0	93
Word Study Skills	44	-.15	47	4.7	98
Mathematics Computation	46	-.10	48	4.8	99
Mathematics Problems	35	-.39	42	4.2	95
Spelling	28	-.58	38	3.8	92

With every profile of scores there are always fluctuations, but the above profile is fairly consistent in showing scores within the proverbial "average" range. Even for the lowest score in Spelling where the z is -.58, this is still well within one standard deviation of the mean. There is a tendency when evaluating scores of students thought to have learning problems to look for problems.

Grade Equivalents

The multitude of problems inherent with grade equivalents is readily acknowledged (Burns, 1979, pp. 59-67). Yet, not only are grade equivalents frequently used, but there are situations when a grade equivalent might be the only normative index of a student's achievement. One alternative to traditional grade equivalents is to transform a standardized score to a standardized grade equivalent by[4]

$$SGE = z(\text{Grade Level}+5)(.15) + \text{Grade Level}$$

or

$$SGE = z(CA)(.15)+CA - 5$$

where z can be determined from percentile ranks or from some other standard score (e.g., stanine scores). For a student with a z score of -1.0, the corresponding SGE using a CA of 12 is -1(.15)12+12-5 or 5.2. In other words, for a student with a CA of 12 and a z score of -1, the corresponding standardized grade equivalent is 5.2.

Although setting the grade equivalent standard deviation to a set value can be useful for interpreting individual scores (if, for whatever reason, a grade equivalent-type score is desired), this technique does not allow for the statistical treatment of standardized grade equivalents for different age groups in that the standard deviation for each age group will be different. Of course, the same restriction applies to MA scores in that the standard deviation for MA scores for one age group (e.g., CA=8) is different than the standard deviation for a different age group (e.g., CA=12).

Table 9.6 provides standardized grade equivalents for various z scores and grade levels. For a grade level of 3.5, one standard deviation below a grade level of 3.5 is a grade equivalent of 2.2; for a grade of 8.5, 1.5 standard deviations below grade level of 8.5 is 5.4.

Table 9.6 Standardized Grade Equivalents.

z score	Grade Level 1.5	2.5	3.5	4.5	5.5	6.5	7.5	8.5	9.5	10.5	11.5
3.0	4.4	5.8	7.3	8.7	10.2	11.6	13.1	14.5	16.0	17.4	18.9
2.5	3.9	5.3	6.6	8.0	9.4	10.8	12.1	13.5	14.9	16.3	17.6
2.0	3.4	4.7	6.0	7.3	8.6	9.9	11.2	12.5	13.8	15.1	16.4
1.5	2.9	4.1	5.4	6.6	7.8	9.0	10.3	11.5	12.7	13.9	15.2
1.0	2.4	3.6	4.7	5.9	7.0	8.2	9.3	10.5	11.6	12.8	13.9
.5	1.9	3.0	4.1	5.2	6.2	7.3	8.4	9.5	10.5	11.6	12.7
0.0	1.5	2.5	3.5	4.5	5.5	6.5	7.5	8.5	9.5	10.5	11.5
-.5	1.0	1.9	2.8	3.7	4.7	5.6	6.5	7.4	8.4	9.3	10.2
-1.0	0.5	1.3	2.2	3.0	3.9	4.7	5.6	6.4	7.3	8.1	9.0
-1.5	0.0	0.8	1.5	2.3	3.1	3.9	4.6	5.4	6.2	7.0	7.7
-2.0	0.0	0.2	0.9	1.6	2.3	3.0	3.7	4.4	5.1	5.8	6.5
-2.5	0.0	0.0	0.3	0.9	1.5	2.1	2.8	3.4	4.0	4.6	5.3
-3.0	0.0	0.0	0.0	0.2	0.7	1.3	1.8	2.4	2.9	3.5	4.0

Unlike standard scores, one difficulty encountered when interpreting grade equivalents is the increasing grade equivalent standard deviation as a function of age which is reflected by suggested guidelines for providing remedial reading services. Richek, List and Lerner (1983, p. 65) stated that the following are used by many remedial reading programs: Primary = .5 years; Intermediate = 1.0; Junior High = 1.5; Senior High = 2.0. Spache (1981, p. 5) stated that a retarded reader is one who is 1.0 years below at the primary level, 2.0 years behind at the intermediate level, and 3.0 years behind at the secondary level.

Using (Grade Level+5)(.15) or CA(.15) as an estimate of the standard deviation, a reasonable estimation of the increasing grade equivalent standard deviation as a function of age can be determined. Thus, for a student with a CA of 7.5, the standard deviation is 1.125; for a student with a CA of 10, the standard deviation is 1.5; and for a student with a CA of 15, the standard deviation is 2.25.

Interpreting Standard Scores

The only guideline in the regulations which even remotely concerns the interpretation of a specific standard score is that an individual must exhibit "significantly subaverage general intellectual functioning"[5] (in addition to a deficit in adaptive behavior occurring during the developmental period). Rather than making global assumptions concerning the inherent meaning of a score (e.g., a z score less than -2.0 is an index of subaverage general intellectual functioning), Table 9.7 provides a fairly general guideline for interpreting scores based on the number of standard deviations a score is below or above the mean. Here, the categories **LOW, BELOW AVERAGE, AVERAGE, ABOVE AVERAGE** and **HIGH** are arbitrary. A degree of common sense must be used when interpreting a score that straddles two categories rather than treating these labels as absolutes. There is no rational basis for stating that a student with a percentile rank of 23 is **AVERAGE** while a student with a percentile rank of 22 is **BELOW AVERAGE,** other than these scores fit the neatly defined categories created to correspond to a sequence of percentile ranks. Consideration of test score error is never more important than when dealing when associating scores with categorical labels. Based on simple test error, the true categories for an **AVERAGE** and **BELOW AVERAGE** student might well be reversed. From an interpretation standpoint, whenever a qualitative label (e.g., **BELOW AVERAGE, LOW,** etc.) is used to describe test performance, the actual standard score should be readily available to properly evaluate standardized score performance.

Table 9.7 Interpreting Standard Scores.

Category	Percentile Rank	z score	Normalized Percentile Rank	Normalized Stanine Score	IQ-Type Score
High	97	1.88	90	8.8	128
Above Average	96	1.75	87	8.5	126
	84	.99	71	7.0	114
	78	.77	66	6.5	111
Average	77	.74	66	6.5	111
	50	0	50	5	100
	23	-.74	34	3.5	89
Below Average	22	-.77	34	3.5	89
	16	-.99	29	3.0	86
	4	-1.75	13	1.5	74
Low	3	-1.88	10	1.2	72

Because stanine scores yield single digit numbers, these scores can be used to assign students to one of nine test performance levels. As shown in Table 9.8, stanine scores can be used as the frame of reference for interpreting both percentile ranks and z scores. For example, a stanine of 3 is in the Below Average category, which includes percentile ranks between 2 and 23 or z scores between -1.22 to -.74. In terms of average performance, stanine scores of 4, 5 and 6 are generally considered in the Average range.

Table 9.8 Interpreting Stanine Scores and Percentile Ranks.[b]

Stanine	Meaning	Percentile Ranks	z scores
9	Very High	96 - 99	>1.75
8	High	89 - 95	1.23 to 1.75
7	Above Average	77 - 88	.74 to 1.22
6	Slightly Above Average	60 - 76	.26 to .73
5	Average	41 - 59	-.25 to .25
4	Slightly Below Average	24 - 40	-.73 to -.26
3	Below Average	12 - 23	-1.22 to -.74
2	Low	5 - 11	-1.75 to -1.23
1	Very Low	1 - 4	<-1.75

[b]Depending upon how stanines are calculated, the exact relationship between stanines to percentile ranks and z scores will vary. The values in this table are designed to equate, as best as possible, the underlying stanine distribution (see table 9.7) with consecutive ranges of percentile ranks and z scores.

Selecting a Standard Score

With so many standard scores to choose from, developing a coherent psychometric profile for a student can be difficult. When comparing scores, the scores should have similar distribution statistics (viz., means and standard deviations). Converting percentile ranks to normalized score is a useful way to combine attributes of both types of scores. If this is not possible, simple z scores are more than sufficient for interpreting the extent a score is above or below the mean. For example, rather than saying a student has an IQ of 85, a statement might be made that the student is 1.0 standard deviations below the mean $(z < -1.0)$ on whatever test is being used. Some practitioners argue that this can be confusing and the underlying meaning of a z score is not easily understood. If the standardized concept underlying a z score is not clear, there seems little likelihood that the meaning of a standardized IQ score will be any more understood.

Using Norms

When tests are used with students with disabilities, the appropriate normative frame of reference is not always clear. National norms and local norms are often available, and there are several tests which provide normative data for specific disabilities. The American Psychological Association's Standards for Educational and Psychological Testing provide the following guideline concerning the use of regular and special norms (American Psychological Association, 1985, p. 80):

> In assessing characteristic of individuals with handicapping conditions the test user should use either regular or special norms for calculating derived scores, depending on the purpose of the testing. Regular norms for the characteristic in question are appropriate when the purpose involves the test taker's functioning relative to the general population. If available, however, special norms should be selected when the test takers' functioning relative to their nonhandicapped peers is at issue (primary).

Local norms certainly address the central issue of how a student is performing in relation to his or her peers. This peer group, however, might be above or below the general population (i.e., all students at the national level who are given the test). If this happens, national and local norms will differ. If the school or district is appreciable below the general population mean performance, local norm performance will be higher; if the school or district is appreciable above the general population mean performance, local norm performance will be lower.

Consider a test where the population raw score mean is 25 and the standard deviation is 6. For School A the mean score is 22 and for School B the mean is 28. Two students, one from each school, receive scores of 22 on the test. Using national norms, both students receive the same standard score. However, when local norms are used, the student from School A is exactly at the school mean, while the second student is 1.0 standard deviations *below* the school mean. Using national norms, both students are .5 standard deviations below the mean. However, in School A where the mean score is below the national mean score, the local norm reveals average performance; while for School B where the mean score is above the national average, the student is one standard deviation below the mean.

The decision to use local or national norms is a matter of consistency and involves a variety of issues. At the very least, test users should be consistent when using local and national norms. For example, reporting national norm-based performance to parents and then using local norms as part of the decision-making process is a questionable ethical practice. Norm consistency is extremely important when comparing different tests. Test comparisons based on different norm groups is a risky task to begin with but the task is further confounded when local and national norms are intermixed. Most individual IQ tests rely on national norms, but achievement tests might use local and/or national norms. If a school district is above average in terms of the national population and a student receives an IQ of 115, but is below average in achievement when local norms are used, a straight-forward comparison between IQ and achievement is not possible.

When comparing two scores, the solution is to use either local or to use national norms for both tests. Because IQ tests rely on national norms, achievement scores based on national norms should be used if an IQ/achievement comparison is made. Every norm group will have a certain uniqueness and unless the norm group is completely inappropriate for comparative purposes because of technical deficiencies, most scores from different groups are comparable to some degree.

Sociocultural norms. Most definitions of a learning disability exclude students with learning problems which result from "environmental, cultural, or economic disadvantage."[6] In spite of this guideline, educational performance is often related to sociocultural factors. Several tests have focused on this problem and have provided useful normative data for interpreting test performance when sociocultural factors are salient variables. The Kaufman Assessment Battery for Children (Kaufman & Kaufman, 1983) offers normative data for blacks and whites for several educational levels. For example, if a student received a score of 100 on the achievement global scale, the corresponding percentile rank would be 30 using norms for white parents with an educational background greater than 12 years and 70 for white parents with an educational background less than 12 years.

Special Norm Groups

Using norms based on a specific disability group should not be used to distort performance, or used in an inappropriate context. Norms for a reading test could be developed for students with severe reading disorders so that a student with an "average" severe disability would have an average standardized score when the disability group is the normative frame of reference. Suggesting that this student is average in reading by not describing the normative frame of reference would be misleading. For a test such as the American Association on Mental Retardation Adaptive Behavior Scale (Nihira, Leland & Lambert, 1993) which provides norms for students with and without mental retardation, the two different norms cannot be used interchangeably. If a decision is made concerning a student in a regular school environment, norms based on students without mental retardation should be used. If a decision concerns the type of special education placement, norms based on students with mental retardation might be used.

For certain disability groups, the very heterogeneity of the group precludes the selection of a "homogeneous" sample. Willingham (1988) stated that "equitable testing for learning-disabled examinees poses very difficult problems" (p. 167) for students taking the SAT and GRE primarily because "LD students form a very large and heterogeneous group." Students are classified as LD because of reading problems, language deficits, overall poor academic performance, because no other category applies or because other categories (viz., mental retardation) have an onerous connotation. In addition, disentangling factors such as "environmental, cultural, or economic disadvantage"[7] in the determination of a specific learning disability is extremely difficult.

The primary reason for using disability-related norms occurs when regular normative data is not available or usable. For example, tests given in Braille are routinely interpreted using regular normative data. The result of this may or may not benefit the student. If an assumption is made that the overall cognitive ability of this disability group is comparable to that of students in the regular population, norms derived from a Braille edition of the test might provide valuable information concerning achievement and/or ability. Likewise, a single-switch test designed for students with severe motor disabilities might be the only way to interpret ability and achievement.

However, disability norms should not be used to mask a disability when the disability is what the test purports to measure. Developing norms based on students with below average reading skills would be tantamount to reducing the difficulty of the test and the results would not reflect the student's ability. Knowing how a student is performing with respect to a specific sample of students (e.g., deaf and hard-of-hearing), can provide useful performance, diagnostic and placement information, but norms should not be used which inaccurately reflect a student's achievement or ability.

Dated norms. In addition to basic conceptual problems involving the meaning of a disability-based normative sample, these norms are often outdated. For example, the Nebraska Test of Learning Aptitude was normed in 1966, the Leiter International Point Scale in 1948, an adaptation of this scale in 1952, and the Blind Learning Aptitude Test in 1971. Bradley-Johnson stated that because of the age of the Blind Learning Aptitude Test, the "results are likely to be inflated" (1994, p. 184). The reason for this is that test performance on standardized tests of intelligence has generally increased. As a result, a student will often seem to have a high score when compared to extremely dated norms as opposed to recently normed tests.

Biased norms. Dated norms can influence standard score interpretation, and an unusual normative sample can further confound the interpretation of normative performance. For example, the Illinois Test of Psycholinguistic Abilities (Kirk, Mccarthy & Kirk, 1968) was normed using an "average" sample with a restricted IQ range of 84 and 116. The effect of this is to inflate standard scores differences as scores depart from the mean (see Burns, 1976).

Disability based norms. The ACT Research Services (1995) has developed normative data for a variety of special norm groups (e.g., dyslexic, anxiety disorder, attention deficit disorder). From a research standpoint this data is very interesting, but using this data as a frame of reference for interpreting scores is no easy task and depends largely on the type and homogeneity of the normative sample.

The Gallaudet Research Institute's Center for Assessment and Demographic Studies has developed special norms using the 8th Edition of the Stanford Achievement Test for deaf and hard-of-hearing students. One of the reasons for the development of the SAT-8 deaf and hard-of-hearing norms is that the tests, normally assigned to students based on age, are too difficult. To overcome this problem, a series of screening tests were developed (which contain 10 to 12 items per screening test) for the eight SAT-8 difficulty levels to assign students to the appropriate level.

The norm sample consisted of 6,932 students from 106 programs who were not reported as having mental retardation. One useful guideline provided by the project is the appropriateness of different SAT-8 subtests for hard-of-hearing and deaf students. The Category 1 subtests (reading, concepts of number, computation, spelling, language and study skills) are appropriate for most students. Category 2 subtests (environment, mathematics applications, social science) are appropriate for some students because the subtests are closely related to the curriculum, and Category 3 subtests (listening, word skills, reading vocabulary) are said to be inappropriate for most hard-of-hearing and deaf students because of auditory experiential factors and poor reliability.

Standard Error of Measurement

The Standard Error of Measurement

The Standard Error of Measurement [12] (SE_{meas}) is probably the most frequently-used index to interpret individual test scores and is used extensively in the interpretation of scores to provide an index of the amount of error, to establish bands of confidence, and to evaluate scores differences. As mentioned in Chapter 2, the SE_{meas} is used extensively in the interpretation of test scores, and is based on the reliability (r_{xx}) and standard deviation (SD_x). If the test reliability is .9 and the standard deviation is 15, the SE_{meas} is found by

$$SE_{meas} = SD_x \sqrt{1 - r_{xx}} = 15 \sqrt{1 - .9} = 4.74$$

The SE_{meas} is easily calculated for different standard deviations and reliability coefficients so that for a reliability of .9 when the SD is 1.0, the SE_{meas} is .32; and when the SD is 10, the SE_{meas} is 3.16 or 3.2. Table 9.9 presents different SE_{meas} values for different standard deviations and reliabilities. If the reliability of a test is .85 and the standard deviation is 21.06, the resulting SE_{meas} is 8.2. If the reliability of the test is only .75, the SE_{meas} increases to 10.5; and if the reliability is .95, the SE_{meas} is reduced to 4.7. For many tests with standard deviations of 15, the SE_{meas} will range from 3.5 to 5.5 which reflect reliabilities of .946 to .866. As can be seen, the greater the test reliability, the smaller the SE_{meas} for any given standard deviation and, therefore, the degree of error associated with the corresponding test score.

Table 9.9 SE_{meas} for Different Standard Deviations and Reliabilities

Standard Deviation	Test Reliability				
	.75	.8	.85	.9	.95
21.06	10.5	9.4	8.2	6.7	4.7
16	8.0	7.2	6.2	5.1	3.6
15	7.5	6.7	5.8	4.7	3.4
10	5.0	4.5	3.8	3.2	2.2
3	1.5	1.3	1.2	.95	.67
2	1.0	.89	.77	.63	.45
1	.5	.45	.39	.32	.22

The SE_{meas} provides some idea of the distribution of errors for test scores. If a student received a score of 70 on a test with a standard deviation of 15 and reliability of .9, the SE_{meas} is 4.7 or 5 (see Table 9.9). The meaning of this SE_{meas} is as follows: In a hypothetical situation if an individual were given the same test a large number of times, the resulting individual test scores would form a normal distribution so that 68% of the scores would be plus or minus 1.0 standard deviation, and 95% of the scores would be plus or minus 2.0 standard deviations. The standard deviation of this hypothetical collection of scores is the SE_{meas}, and the mean of these scores is the universe or true score. The score of 70 is but one score from this universe of scores, and the SE_{meas} provides an index of error associated with the universe of scores and the range in which most universe scores tend to be.

True Scores

The concept of a true score is related to the SE_{meas} and is used in several ways to interpret and compare test scores. A "true" score is the average score from a hypothetical collection of repeated administrations of the same test. Thorndike (1951) accurately described true scores when he stated that "the term is convenient but a little misleading. As we speak of it, true score is not the ultimate fact in the book of the recording angel" (p. 566). The possibility that a true score might be misleading stems from the fact that an obtained score might be substantially different from the hypothetical true score. For example, a student received a score of 70 on a test with a mean of 100, a standard deviation of 15, a reliability of .93, and a SE_{meas} of 4. Unbeknownst to all, and due to test error, the student's true score is actually 80. However, the calculated true score (see the below section) would reveal a score of 72. When the effects of regression resulting from reliability are taken into account, the result is sometimes referred to as a true score. In actuality, these are "estimated" true scores in that the truth of these scores might impart considerable less truth than the name implies. Because the general practice is to refer to these *estimated true scores* simply as *true scores,* this will be the designation given in this work. However, the practitioner must not forget that a true score has many limitations, that it is really not a *true* score, and the use of such a score does not provide a definitive answer to fundamental psychometric questions relating to both the reliability of an individual score and what an individual score measures. With this cautionary note in mind, a true score or **X'** is found by

$$X' = r_{xx}(X - \bar{X}) + \bar{X}$$

or

$$z'_x = z_x \, (r_{xx})$$

so that if a student received a score of 87, the true score is $(.9)(87 - 100) + 100 = 88.3$ or 88. For a score of 87, the corresponding z score is -.87. The estimated true z score for a z score of -.87 when the reliability is .9 is -.87(.9) or -.78. When the mean is 100 and the standard deviation 15, an estimated true z score of -.78 is equal to a score of 88.3 or -.78(15)+100.

Table 9.10 shows scores for a mean of 100 and standard deviation of 15 for reliabilities ranging from .7 to .95. As shown in this Table 9.10, as reliability decreases, the estimated true score regresses toward the mean. In the extreme case, if a student received a score of 70 and the reliability of the test were 0, the estimated true score would be 100; if the reliability were .5, the estimated true score would be 85.

Table 9.10 Estimated True Scores (Mean=100, SD=15).

						RELIABILITY							
Score	.96	.94	.92	.90	.88	.86	.84	.82	.80	.78	.76	.74	.72
100	100	100	100	100	100	100	100	100	100	100	100	100	100
99	99	99	99	99	99	99	99	99	99	99	99	99	99
98	98	98	98	98	98	98	98	98	98	98	98	99	99
97	97	97	97	97	97	97	97	98	98	98	98	98	98
96	96	96	96	96	96	97	97	97	97	97	97	97	97
95	95	95	95	95	96	96	96	96	96	96	96	96	96
94	94	94	94	95	95	95	95	95	95	95	95	96	96
93	93	93	94	94	94	94	94	94	94	95	95	95	95
92	92	92	93	93	93	93	93	93	94	94	94	94	94
91	91	92	92	92	92	92	92	93	93	93	93	93	94
90	90	91	91	91	91	91	92	92	92	92	92	93	93
89	89	90	90	90	90	91	91	91	91	91	92	92	92
88	88	89	89	89	89	90	90	90	90	91	91	91	91
87	88	88	88	88	89	89	89	89	90	90	90	90	91
86	87	87	87	87	88	88	88	89	89	89	89	90	90
85	86	86	86	87	87	87	87	88	88	88	89	89	89
84	85	85	85	86	86	86	87	87	87	88	88	88	88
83	84	84	84	85	85	85	86	86	86	87	87	87	88
82	83	83	83	84	84	85	85	85	86	86	86	87	87
81	82	82	83	83	83	84	84	84	85	85	86	86	86
80	81	81	82	82	82	83	83	84	84	84	85	85	86
79	80	80	81	81	82	82	82	83	83	84	84	84	85
78	79	79	80	80	81	81	82	82	82	83	83	84	84
77	78	78	79	79	80	80	81	81	82	82	83	83	83
76	77	77	78	78	79	79	80	80	81	81	82	82	83
75	76	77	77	78	78	79	79	80	79	80	81	82	82
74	75	76	76	77	76	77	78	78	79	79	80	81	81
73	74	75	75	76	76	77	77	78	78	79	79	80	81
72	73	74	74	75	75	76	76	77	78	78	79	79	80
71	72	73	73	74	74	75	76	76	77	77	78	79	79
70	71	72	72	73	74	74	75	75	76	77	77	78	78
69	70	71	71	72	73	73	74	75	75	76	76	77	78
68	69	70	71	71	72	72	73	74	74	75	76	76	77
67	68	69	70	70	71	72	72	73	74	74	75	76	76
66	67	68	69	69	70	71	71	72	73	73	74	75	76
65	66	67	68	69	69	70	71	71	72	73	73	74	75
64	65	66	67	68	68	69	70	70	71	72	73	73	74
63	64	65	66	67	67	68	69	70	70	71	72	73	73
62	64	64	65	66	67	67	68	69	70	70	71	72	73
61	63	63	64	65	66	66	67	68	69	70	70	71	72
60	62	62	63	64	65	66	66	67	68	69	70	70	71
59	61	61	62	63	64	65	66	66	67	68	69	70	70
58	60	61	61	62	63	64	65	66	66	67	68	69	70
57	59	60	60	61	62	63	64	65	66	66	67	68	69
56	58	59	60	60	61	62	63	64	65	66	67	67	68
55	57	58	59	60	60	61	62	63	64	65	66	67	68

Confidence Intervals

The SE_{meas} is a standard deviation which represents the degree of test error, and is often interpreted in terms of normal curve probabilities. For example, if the SE_{meas} is 4, 68% of test scores will fall within ± 4 points of the true score, or 68% (actually .6826) will be between -1 SE_{meas} and +1 SE_{meas}. To be even more confident, a 2 SE_{meas} level of confidence could be used. The area under the normal curve between -2 SE_{meas} and +2 SE_{meas} is .9544 which is equivalent to the 95% confidence level.

A statistical probability can provide some insight as to the meaning of a score or how a score might be interpreted, but the apparent statistical precision should not be misinterpreted. Kaufman's (1994) comments regarding rules-of-thumb is accurate when he stated that "I find it silly to stress precision to the nearest 10th of a point when the scaled scores are just not that accurate in the first place" (p. 127).

The SE_{meas} can be used to provide an overall index of test error for a test, and to establish confidence intervals for scores. If the SE_{meas} is 4 and a student receives a score of 30, a statement might be made that the student's score was between 26 and 34 (or plus or minus 1.0 SE_{meas}). Although Cronbach (1970, p. 164) suggested that establishing confidence intervals might lead to a false conclusion, establishing a "band of confidence" around a score using the SE_{meas} is widely used. The problem with using the SE_{meas} to establish confidence intervals concerns the use of a student's score as the center point of the interval; that is, the obtained score is interpreted as the true score. For example, assume a student's obtained and true score are significantly different. In the above example where the student obtained a score of 30, assume that this student's true score was actually 41 (or 19 or whatever). Constructing a confidence around the obtained score of 30 (when unbeknownst to all the true score is 41) would mistakingly give confidence that the obtained score was reflective of the student's ability.

Using a student's estimated true score as the basis for constructing a confidence interval as recommended by Nunnally (1967, p. 201) is an attempt to deal with this possibility, but a calculated true score as described below is nothing more than an estimation and it is not the person's "true" score in any absolute sense. Cronbach's criticism of confidence intervals is well-taken, but this technique does have the advantage of interpreting a student's test score in relation to test error.

Furthermore, confidence intervals are widely used, as well as providing the basis for several techniques to understand test score differences. With these problems in mind (see also Salvia & Ysseldyke, 1995, p. 154), confidence intervals should be interpreted with some degree of caution.

The following illustrates how confidence intervals are constructed for a student using the SE_{meas}, where z is the level of significance and the lower and upper limits of the confidence interval are determined by

$$-z(SE_{meas})+X \text{ to } z(SE_{meas})+X$$

For the 95% level of confidence, where the corresponding normal curve value is 1.96 and the SE_{meas} is 5 and the student's score is 70, the confidence interval is

$$-1.96(5)+70 \text{ to } 1.96(5)+70$$

or 60 to 80 which is equivalent to 70 ± 10.

The number of SE_{meas} units to use to establish confidence intervals is based on normal curve distribution values shown in Table 9.11. To state with 90% confidence that a score is within a specified range, a z score of 1.65 would be used so that

$$IQ_{68}= -1.65(5)+70 \text{ to } 1.65(5)+70$$

or 62 to 78 which is equivalent to 70 ± 8.

Table 9.11 Confidence Level Values.

Normal Curve z-score Values for Establishing Score Confidence Intervals		
Confidence Level	z score	Example: $SE_{meas}=5$, $X=70$
99%	2.58	70 ± 12.9
95%	1.96	70 ± 9.8
90%	1.65	70 ± 8.25
85%	1.44	70 ± 7.2
68%	1.00	70 ± 5

Most professionals recognize the need to incorporate the SE_{meas} in the interpretation of scores, but exactly which confidence level to use is a matter of judgement. As a rule of thumb, the minimum confidence level should be 68%, while a level of 95% (the counterpart of the traditional .05 level of significance) is often associated with "statistical significance."

True Score Confidence Bands

Nunnally (1967) suggested that the only reason to estimate true scores is in the determination of confidence intervals "since estimated true scores correlate perfectly with obtained scores and making practical interpretations of estimated true scores is difficult, in most applied work it is better to interpret the individual's obtained score" (p. 221). For example, if a student received an IQ of 70, and the reliability of the test is .9, the estimated true score is 73. Given a standard deviation of 15 and reliability of .9, the SE_{meas} is 5 and the confidence intervals would be

$$73 \pm 5 = 68 - 78 = 68\% \text{ Confidence Interval}$$
$$73 \pm 10 = 63 - 83 = 95\% \text{ Confidence Interval}$$

The effect of using true scores for students scoring below the mean is to provide an upward estimate of true score performance. This is probably a good idea in that it provides an upward and likely more realistic appraisal of the student's score (or at least potential score).

ENDNOTES

1.   34 C.F.R. §300.532(b)
2.   34 C.F.R. §300.533
3.   These statistics do not apply when basal and ceiling rules are used to determine beginning and ending test items.
4.   The following can be used to estimate the grade equivalent standard deviation (SD_{ge}): (Grade Level+5)(.15). The resulting grade equivalent standard deviation is similar to that of the mental ability standard when MA scores are derived from IQ scores having a mean of 100 and standard deviation of 15 or MA=(CA X IQ)/100. For a fifth grade student with a CA of 10.5, the SD_{ge} would be (5.0+5)(.15) or 1.5. In this case, if CA were used instead of Grade Level+5, the result would be the same. As the disparity between CA and Grade Level increases, so will the estimated standard deviations.
5.   34 C.F.R. §300.7(b)(5)
6.   34 C.F.R. §300.7(b)(10)
7.   34 C.F.R. §300.7(b)(10)

8. The SE_{meas} is sometimes confused with the Standard Error of Estimate (SE_{est}). In actuality, the SE_{meas} is a form of SE_{est} (See Guilford, 1965, p. 444) when test scores are predicted from true scores. Whereas the SE_{meas} is used when the goal is to understand what Mehrens and Lehman (1973) referred to as "intra-individual variability" (p. 103), the SE_{est} is used to when the goal is to estimate what degree of confidence can be placed in a predicted value. The SE_{meas} is based on test reliability, while the SE_{est} is based on the correlation between two variables.

Chapter 10

TEST SCORE COMPARISONS

Comparing test scores is an extremely important task for the multidisciplinary team when evaluating test performance and determining special education and related services. For students with specific learning disabilities, the multidisciplinary team is required to determine whether the student "does not achieve commensurate with his or her age and ability levels," and that the student "has a severe discrepancy between achievement and intellectual ability."[1] This requires a comparison between mental ability and achievement. Because this comparison is important for determining the existence of a specific learning disability, and therefore the need for special education and related services,[2] a discrepancy between mental ability and achievement can also provide the need and rationale for making test accommodations.

In addition to determining whether there is a discrepancy between mental ability and achievement, test score comparisons are used to determine specific learning needs. A student might have a specific learning disability in reading, but a determination must be made whether the problem involves language, word attack skills, reading vocabulary, comprehension, etc. Likewise, to determine whether a student has a problem involving written expression, written expression must be compared to both mental ability, verbal ability and reading.

One of the most important comparisons made concerning special education is the effectiveness of the services. If a student has a disability in reading or mathematics, comparing scores from standardized and nonstandardized tests might be to evaluate the effectiveness of instruction. The need to compare test scores is necessary and an integral part of the regulations but factors such as regression toward the mean, multitest comparisons, and the limitations of statistical significance can confound a comparison and interpretation of test scores.

Regression and Score Comparisons

In Chapter 9, estimated true scores were determined by adjusting obtained scores for the effects of regression on z scores in combination with test reliability so that the estimated true z' score is equal to $(r_{xx})z_x$. If a student received a z score of -2.0 and the test reliability was .9, the estimated true score is -2.0(.9) or -1.8. This basic concept of regression also applies when comparing different test scores; that is, when predicting one score from another, the predicted value is somewhere between the obtained value and the mean of the test and is determined by the correlation between the two tests.

Regression toward the mean can affect the interpretation of scores in several subtle, but extremely important ways. If a student is classified as mentally retarded because of a verbal deficit, nonverbal test performance will probably be greater than verbal performance. If the student's verbal z score is -3.0 and the correlation between the verbal and nonverbal test is .6, the predicted nonverbal z score is -1.8. The reverse will occur if a student is identified as gifted because of a high verbal test score so that for a student three standard deviations above the mean, the predicted nonverbal score would be a score 1.8 standard deviations above the mean.

Whenever a student is selected on the basis of a criterion, test scores will regress toward the mean in accordance with the correlation between tests and the selection criterion. This "selection criterion" is sometimes very identifiable and other times very complex and not easily recognized. Assume that a student's underlying problem is a verbal deficit, and the student has a verbal IQ of 70 which is 2.0 standard deviations below the mean, a reading score which is 1.5 standard deviations below the mean, and a nonverbal IQ which is 1.0 standard deviations below the mean. The cause for this deficit could be neurological, cultural, or socioeconomic, but the manifestation would seem to involve verbal behavior. In this hypothetical example, performance regresses toward the mean as the correlation between the test and the underlying criterion (the "selection criterion") decreases.

Predicting scores. In statistical terms, predicating a z' score from test X or z_x, is the product of z_x and the correlation between test X and test Y or r_{xy}:

$$Z'_y = z_x(r_{xy})$$

which is similar to the formula for determining estimated true scores, but the above uses the correlation between test Y and test X rather than the reliability of test X as the basis for the prediction.

When standard scores other than *z* scores are used, and the test standard deviations are the same, the predicted values are found by

$$Y' = r_{xy}(X - \overline{X}) + \overline{Y}$$

Both of the above formulas are based on the general linear regression formula for predicting a score:

$$Y' = r_{xy}(\frac{SD_y}{SD_x})(X_x - \overline{X}_x) + \overline{Y}_y$$

When the mean is 100 and the standard deviation 15 for two tests, the correlation between the tests .6, and a student received a score of 70 on test X, the predicted score on Y' is

$$Y' = .6(\frac{15}{15})(70 - 100) + 100 = 82$$

which is simplified to .6(70-100)+100 or 82.

Table 10.1 provides predicted values of Y from X when the means of both Y and X are 100 and the standard deviations 15. For example, if a student received an IQ score of 70 on a test and the correlation between the IQ and an achievement test is .6, the predicted achievement score based on IQ is 82. Rather than comparing IQ and achievement directly, achievement can be compared to predicted achievement. The reason for this is that the effects of statistical regression can incorrectly suggest that a student is over- or underachieving. A difference score of 10 between IQ and achievement for a student who received an IQ score of 75 and an achievement score of 85 might suggest a discrepancy between IQ and achievement, but a comparison of actual achievement (a score of 85) to predicted achievement which would be 85 when the score is 75 and reliability .6.

Table 10.1 Predicted Scores (Y').[a]

Score						CORRELATION							
	.30	.35	.40	.45	.50	.55	.60	.65	.70	.75	.80	.85	.90
100	100	100	100	100	100	100	100	100	100	100	100	100	100
99	100	100	100	100	100	99	99	99	99	99	99	99	99
98	99	99	99	99	99	99	99	99	99	99	98	98	98
97	99	99	99	99	99	98	98	98	98	98	98	97	97
96	99	99	98	98	98	98	98	97	97	97	97	97	96
95	99	98	98	98	98	97	97	97	97	96	96	96	96
94	98	98	98	97	97	97	96	96	96	96	95	95	95
93	98	98	97	97	97	96	96	95	95	95	94	94	94
92	98	97	97	96	96	96	95	95	94	94	94	93	93
91	97	97	96	96	96	95	95	94	94	93	93	92	92
90	97	97	96	96	95	95	94	94	93	93	92	92	91
89	97	96	96	95	95	94	93	93	92	92	91	91	90
88	96	96	95	95	94	93	93	92	92	91	90	90	89
87	96	95	95	94	94	93	92	92	91	90	90	89	88
86	96	95	94	94	93	92	92	91	90	90	89	88	87
85	96	95	94	93	93	92	91	90	90	89	88	87	87
84	95	94	94	93	92	91	90	90	89	88	87	86	86
83	95	94	93	92	92	91	90	89	88	87	86	86	85
82	95	94	93	92	91	90	89	88	87	87	86	85	84
81	94	93	92	91	91	90	89	88	87	86	85	84	83
80	94	93	92	91	90	89	88	87	86	85	84	83	82
79	94	93	92	91	90	88	87	86	85	84	83	82	81
78	93	92	91	90	89	88	87	86	85	84	82	81	80
77	93	92	91	90	89	87	86	85	84	83	82	80	79
76	93	92	90	89	88	87	86	84	83	82	81	80	78
75	93	91	90	89	88	86	85	84	83	81	80	79	78
74	92	91	90	88	87	86	84	83	82	81	79	78	77
73	92	91	89	88	87	85	84	82	81	80	78	77	76
72	92	90	89	87	86	85	83	82	80	79	78	76	75
71	91	90	88	87	86	84	83	81	80	78	77	75	74
70	91	90	88	87	85	84	82	81	79	78	76	75	73
69	91	89	88	86	85	83	81	80	78	77	75	74	72
68	90	89	87	86	84	82	81	79	78	76	74	73	71
67	90	88	87	85	84	82	80	79	77	75	74	72	70
66	90	88	86	85	83	81	80	78	76	75	73	71	69
65	90	88	86	84	83	81	79	77	76	74	72	70	69
64	89	87	86	.84	82	80	78	77	75	73	71	69	68
63	89	87	85	83	82	80	78	76	74	72	70	69	67
62	89	87	85	83	81	79	77	75	73	72	70	68	66
61	88	86	84	82	81	79	77	75	73	71	69	67	65
60	88	86	84	82	80	78	76	74	72	70	68	66	64
59	88	86	84	82	80	77	75	73	71	69	67	65	63
58	87	85	83	81	79	77	75	73	71	69	66	64	62
57	87	85	83	81	79	76	74	72	70	68	66	63	61
56	87	85	82	80	78	76	74	71	69	67	65	63	60
55	87	84	82	80	78	75	73	71	69	66	64	62	60

[a]The formula used to calculate predicted scores (Y') is the same as that used to determine estimated true scores (X') except that the former uses the correlation between X and Y and the later the reliability of X. In addition, as indicated by the range of values, reliability coefficients are generally larger than correlation coefficients.

If a student is either above or below average on an IQ test, the predicted score on a corresponding achievement test will depend on the correlation between achievement and IQ. If the correlation between achievement and IQ is .6 and the IQ z score is -2.0 or an IQ of 70, the corresponding predicted achievement z score will be -1.2 or a score of 82; and if the z score is +2.0 or an IQ of 130, the corresponding z score will be +1.2 or score of 118. This does not mean that the first student is overachieving (i.e., z scores of -2.0 and -1.2) and the second student is underachieving, but that if the IQ is the selection variable, other scores will regress toward the mean as a function of the correlation between IQ and the corresponding score.

Multitest comparisons. No matter what statistic is used, or even if a practitioner simply guesstimates scores differences, the more tests that are used, the greater the likelihood that some type of *significant* difference will be found. In an extreme case, if 100 tests have been given to a student and assuming that the student survived this psychometric onslaught, the likelihood that several of these tests would be significant is quite high. Because of this, the evaluation of all possible pairs of subtests must be approached with caution. Because the number of test scores for an individual is often quite large, considering every possible score comparison will probable yield a significant result somewhere, yet a difference which might have little practical importance.

Simply identifying a statistically significant discrepancy does not relinquish the task of interpreting the meaning of the discrepancy. For example, a student with a CA of 10 and an IQ of 130, who is achieving at grade level would have a significant discrepancy between IQ and achievement, but the need for special education services is not determined by simply comparing two test scores.

In addition, the allure of statistical precision should not mask the underlying constructs which are being compared. A significant difference might exist between a bead-stringing test and walking a balance board, but the educational import of this difference might have no meaning whatsoever. Unfortunately, the statistical essence of many test comparisons centers about reliability rather than validity.

Comparing Test Scores

There are a variety of techniques which can be used to compare test scores such as by comparing using cutoff criteria, indices of test scatter, confidence intervals, gain scores or test score differences. The methods for comparing test scores described below can provide useful insights as to test accommodations needs, but as noted by Wilson and Reynolds (1984) "diagnosis should remain a human decision process aided by relevant test data. Careful application of theoretically sound test models will produce better decisions..." (p. 487).

Confidence-interval comparisons. There are several ways in which a band of confidence can be used to interpret individual scores. One method is to create a band of confidence using the SE_{meas} for each score as discussed in Chapter 9, and then evaluating the degree of overlap between the bands of confidence (see Anastasi, 1982, p. 128). If a student received a standard score of 70 on a reading test and a score of 86 on a mathematics test, and the SE_{meas} is 3 for reading and 4 for mathematics, the 95% (i.e., z=1.96) confidence interval for each test is

$$-1.96(3)+70 \text{ to } 1.96(3)+70 \text{ (Reading) or 64 to 76}$$

and

$$-1.96(4)+86 \text{ to } 1.96(4)+86 \text{ (Mathematics) or 78 to 94}$$

In this case, there is no overlap between the bands so that the reading score is interpreted to be significantly different than the math score.

Another rule of thumb which is sometimes used to compare scores is that the difference should be at least one standard deviation. When reliabilities are in the .9 range, the one standard deviation rule of thumb is a reasonable approximation to calculating bands of confidence. In the above example where the standard deviation for both tests is 15, the difference between the scores (70 and 86) is greater than the single standard deviation rule-of-thumb.

Bivariate criteria. The regulations state that "no single procedure is used as the sole criterion for determining an appropriate educational program for a child."[3] Although there are a seemingly infinite number of ways to define a learning disability, determining an actual discrepancy is probably less-used than more general classification cutoff criteria. To be classified as having a specific learning disability, the bivariate criteria might be below average achievement (e.g., achievement $z<-1.0$), but with an IQ score above the mental retardation range (e.g., IQ $z>-2.0$). The result of using more than one criterion may or may not result in a statistical difference. For a student with an IQ $z=$

1.8 and an achievement $z = -1.5$, the difference between IQ and achievement would not be statistically significant but would meet the bivariate criteria of an IQ $z > -2.0$ and an achievement $z < -1.0$.

Gain scores. A gain score is a difference score but where a single test is administered on two occasions and where the first test represents the pretest (X_{pre}) and the second test the posttest (X_{post}) so that the gain score is

$$X_{gain} = X_{post} - X_{pre}$$

As noted in the discussion of test difference reliability, the reliability of a difference increases as the correlation between the two tests decreases. With respect to test gains, factors ranging from regression to reliability can influence pre-posttest differences. Mehrens and Lehmann (1973) stated that "gain scores are the least reliable of all difference scores" (p. 120). Cronbach and Furby (1970) provided a very negative evaluation of gain scores and suggested "gain scores are rarely useful, no matter how they are adjusted or refined" (p. 68). More important, these authors questioned the role of validity when using gain scores and stated that "the claim that an index has validity as a measure of some construct carries a considerable burden of proof" (p. 79).

If a statewide test is administered to all students within the state, and state regulations mandate that students with scores below a certain cutoff are required to have some type of remediation, the average score performance of these students on the posttest will be directly related to the correlation between the pre and posttest. The gain is not the result of an intervention, but is caused by regression toward the mean.

Most of the difficulties involving pre- posttest and gain scores center about regression toward the mean and can affect the interpretation of any score used to select students needing remediation. If students are selected on the basis of a single reading test score, this student's performance on other tests will vary in relation between the correlations between these other tests and the reading test used to select students.

Construct comparisons. Verbal and nonverbal ability are two frequently compared constructs. A student receives a verbal IQ score of 70 and a nonverbal or performance score of 85 and a comparison is made between the two scores. One of the problems with this type of comparison results from the selection criterion and regression effects. If a student was selected for evaluation because of a verbal deficit, the difference between verbal and nonverbal scores might be nothing more than a reflection of this underlying deficit and the imperfect correlation between verbal and nonverbal ability. A similar situation occurs when IQ and achievement are compared to provide an estimate of under- or overachievement. A student two standard deviations below the mean on an IQ test and one standard deviation below the mean on an achievement test is said to "overachieve," while a student two standard deviations above the mean on an IQ test and one standard deviation above the mean on a measure of achievement is said to "underachieve." In both situations, the score differences reflect the selection criterion (IQ) and the imperfect correlation between IQ and achievement. As discussed below, part of this problem can be addressed (but not eliminated) by a linear regression adjustment.

Test scatter. There are a variety of methods for evaluating test scatter or the variation among scores including comparing subtest scores, comparing subtests with an average subtest score, and comparing subtests with a score not included in the test battery. A single index of test scatter has sometimes been used as an indication of learning difficulties. Paraskevopoulous and Kirk (1969) used the sum of the absolute differences between subtest scores and the average subtest score as a index of learning ability:

$$\frac{\sum |X_{subtest} - \bar{X}|}{n}$$

Unless test scores are perfectly correlated, the mean dispersion is a function of the intercorrelation between the tests and the selection test. If the student's underlying problem is a verbal deficit, the result will be lower scores on tests which possess this ability. Because scores regress toward the mean at varying rates depending on the correlation between the test and the selection variable, there is greater dispersion for both lower and higher scores. This is not an indication of a learning disability in and of itself, but rather a statistical tautology caused by the varying intertest correlations. Looking for meaningful patterns is an essential part of every psychoeducational evaluation. Low scores in areas which require verbal skills, or low scores in just reading or math, or a mixture of high and low scores might be useful in understanding a student's needs. However, a statistical index of scatter might be one situation where a qualitative interpretation of subtest performance is more efficacious than a single quantitative index of subtest scatter.

Predicting Achievement

Criterion-related validity concerns the comparison of test scores with some criterion. The criterion might be the test scores available at the time of testing or a criterion determined some time in the future. The former is referred to as concurrent validity and might involve comparing achievement and/or IQ scores; the latter is referred to as predictive validity and might entail an IQ test to predict academic performance.

On the surface there is an intuitive appeal to "predictive" validity. Nunnally (1967) offered a compelling argument (as do developers of college admission tests) as to why predictive validity is not nearly as important as correlational analysis: "In most prediction problems, it is reasonable to expect only modest correlations between a criterion and either an individual predictor test or a combination of predictor tests. People are far too complex to permit a highly accurate estimate of their performance from any predictable collection of test materials" (p. 79).

Determining a Discrepancy

A *discrepancy* between test scores can be used to indicate whether a student is entitled to a test accommodation under IDEA or Section 504, or whether a student has a specific test accommodation need. A discrepancy between mental ability and achievement might indicate a disability and thereby qualify a student for a test accommodation which mitigate the effects of the disability (e.g., individualized testing, extended time). If a student is not disabled under IDEA, a test score discrepancy might nonetheless support the need for a test accommodation under the more inclusive Section 504 definition.[4] In addition to a score discrepancy signifying a disability, a discrepancy can indicate the need for specific test accommodations such as when a significant discrepancy is found between mental ability and reading, spelling and reading, mathematics word problems and mathematics computation, or reading and writing.

One frequently-used method for determining a score discrepancy is to compare expected achievement with actual achievement or

Discrepancy = Expected Achievement - Actual Achievement

Actual achievement is represented by a score on a group or individual achievement test, and expected achievement is usually estimated by one of the many linear regression model variations which entail the prediction of achievement from variables such as mental age (MA), chronological age (CA), grade age (GA), and/or years in school. Certainly one of the more perplexing problems in this respect is the relationship between achievement and IQ. To have a specific learning disability, a student must exhibit a severe discrepancy between mental ability and achievement, but the determination of a severe discrepancy does present several problems. First, there is the question of determining what exactly is a severe discrepancy. Although a 50% learning discrepancy is frequently cited as a criterion for a discrepancy, there is little agreement as to exactly what the 50% refers.

Second, an even more perplexing problem is determining ability. An IQ score certainly measures ability to some degree, but there are obviously many other factors which can influence an IQ score. Although the definition of a specific learning disability excludes students who have a discrepancy as a result of "environmental, cultural, or economic disadvantage,"[5] these elements are inextricably related to the assessment of ability and are difficulty to eliminate.

Predicting School Achievement

The task is to compare the student's actual achievement with the level of achievement that would be expected based on mental ability;[6] that is, an index of achievement is compared to an index of predicted achievement based on mental ability or IQ so that a severe discrepancy is defined as a difference greater than some stated criterion:

**Severe Discrepancy =
(Predicted Achievement - Actual Achievement) > Criterion,**

where the difference must be greater than some criterion value used to indicate the size of the discrepancy. If predicted achievement and actual achievement are z scores then a severe discrepancy is

$$\textit{Severe Discrepancy} = z'_y - z_x > \Delta$$

where Δ (delta) is the size of the difference needed to indicate a *severe* discrepancy.

Several formulas which have been proposed to determine expected achievement based on mental ability or IQ. All of these expectancy formulas are based on the general regression model to predict Y scores (predicted achievement) from X scores (an index of mental ability) and are based on the correlation between achievement and IQ.

The basic model was offered by Horn (1941) who provided the first and still most widely-used expectancy formula: Reading Expectancy = (2MA+CA)/3 - 5 (see Burns, 1982). This formula is based on 1941 data which revealed a correlation of .67 between reading and mental age. The general linear equation for this often-used formula is as follows:

$$\text{Reading Expectancy} = r_{ach.ma}\left(\frac{SD_{ach}}{SD_{ma}}\right)(X_{ma} - X_{ma}) + Y_{ach} - 5$$

The original intent of the Horn formula was to predict reading so that the correlation of .67, which is attained by the (2MA+CA)/3 simplification, is appropriate for reading and mental ages scores, at least in 1941, and based on the data used by Horn.

When (MA+0CA) is used as an estimate of the expected achievement of a student, no weight is given CA and the assumed correlation between mental age and achievement is 1.0. As the weighting of CA increases, the assumed correlation between mental age and achievement decreases so that in the case of (MA+2CA)/3, the assumed correlation between mental age and achievement is .33.

The formula (Mental Age + Life Age + Grade Age)/3 (see Myklebust, 1968) is a variation of a formula proposed by Monroe (1932) who used MA, CA and arithmetic computation to produce a reading index. The rationale for this was that because disabled readers sometimes do poorly on tests involving arithmetic (see Spache, 1976, pp. 139-144), the result is an assumed correlation between mental ability and MA/CA/Arithmetic somewhere between .3 and .7.

Bond and Tinker (1973) offered a formula based on Years in School (YIS) which results in an assumed correlation between reading and MA equivalent to (Years in School)/CA. For a student with a CA of 12 and who has completed six years of school, the assumed correlation between reading achievement and MA is (6/12) or .50, and for a student who has been held back, the correlation is (7/12) or .58. One advantage of this formula is that the assumed correlation between reading achievement and MA increases as a function of age; the major disadvantages are twofold: relatively low assumed correlations and assumed correlations based on years in school and CA.

The correlation used in an expectancy formula can be determined empirically using actual correlation data, based on existing research data, or estimated on a purely intuitive impression of the correlation between achievement and MA. If extant test information indicates that the correlation between MA and achievement is .65, the following can be used to weight MA and CA accordingly:[b]

$$\textit{Achievement Grade Expectancy} = r_{aa.ma}MA + (1 - r_{aa.ma})CA - 5$$

The method described in Chapter 9 to predict standard scores from one test to another is yet another method for creating an expectancy formula

$$Y'_{ach} = r_{xy}(X - \bar{X}) + \bar{Y} - 5 = r_{xy}(MA - CA) + CA - 5$$

This formula is an abbreviated version of the general linear regression formula and is easily used in association with most expectancy formulas. When a correlation between MA and achievement of .67 is used in the above formula, the result is the same as the expectancy formula (2MA+CA)/3-5 or

$$.67(MA - CA) + CA - 5 = .67MA + .33CA - 5 = \frac{2MA + CA}{3} - 5$$

For a student with an IQ of 90 and a CA of 12, MA is 10.8, or 90(12)/100=10.8, and expected achievement is

$$EA = .67(10.8 - 12) + 12 - 5 = .67(10.8) + .33(12) - 5 = \frac{2(10.8) + 12}{3} - 5 = 6.2$$

An expected achievement value of 6.2 is for an IQ of 90 and CA of 12. Table 10.2 provides MA-based expected achievement values using 2MA+CA weighting.

---

[b]The term $r_{aa.ma}$ indicates that mental ability (MA) is used to predict academic achievement (AA). Correlations with subscripts can be written r_{yx} or r_{yx} to indicate that variable x is used to predicate performance on variable y, but r or r_{xy} is often used for simplicity.

Table 10.2 (2MA+CA)/3 MA-based Expected Achievement.

					Chronological Age					
	6	7	8	9	10	11	12	13	14	15
IQ										
140	2.6	3.8	5.1	6.4	7.6	8.9	10.2	11.4	12.7	14.0
135	2.4	3.6	4.8	6.0	7.3	8.5	9.8	11.0	12.2	13.5
130	2.2	3.4	4.5	5.8	7.0	8.2	9.9	10.5	11.8	13.0
125	2.0	3.1	4.3	5.5	6.6	7.8	9.0	10.1	11.3	12.5
120	1.7	2.9	4.0	5.2	6.3	7.4	8.5	9.7	10.8	12.0
115	1.5	2.7	3.8	4.9	6.0	7.0	8.2	9.3	10.4	11.5
110	1.4	2.4	3.5	4.5	5.6	6.7	7.8	8.8	9.9	11.0
105	1.2	2.2	3.2	4.3	5.3	6.3	7.4	8.9	9.9	10.5
100	1.0	2.0	3.0	4.0	5.0	6.0	7.0	8.0	9.0	10.0
95	.7	1.7	2.7	3.7	4.6	5.6	6.5	7.5	8.5	9.5
90	.5	1.5	2.4	3.4	4.3	5.2	6.2	7.1	8.0	9.0
85	.4	1.2	2.2	3.4	4.0	4.9	5.8	6.7	7.5	8.5
80	.2	.1	1.9	2.7	3.6	4.5	5.4	6.2	7.1	8.0
75	0.	.8	1.6	2.5	3.3	4.1	5.0	5.8	6.6	7.5
70	0.	.5	1.4	2.2	3.0	3.8	4.5	5.4	6.2	7.0
65	0.	.3	1.1	1.9	2.6	3.4	4.2	4.9	5.7	6.5
60	0.	.1	.8	1.5	2.3	3.0	3.8	4.5	5.2	6.0

The 50% Discrepancy Criterion

A severe discrepancy is often conceptualized as 50% discrepancy between achievement and ability. There is no statistical basis for using a 50% discrepancy (e.g., why not a 40% or 60% level), and even conceptualizing exactly what a 50% discrepancy means is difficult. More often than not, 50% of predicted achievement is used as the criterion for a severe disability. If expected achievement is 4.0, a 50% discrepancy would be 2.0 so that a student would need to have an obtained achievement score 2.0 years below predicted achievement or

$$\text{Severe Discrepancy} = X'_{ach} - X_{ach} > (X'_{ach}).5$$

If IQ=90, CA=9, MA 8.1, actual achievement is 2.0, and predicted achievement (2MA+CA)/3-5 or 3.4 then

$$X'_{ach} - X_{ach} = 3.4 - 2.0 < 3.4(.5) = 1.7$$

For a student with a CA of 10 and an IQ of 80, the expected achievement level is 3.6 (see Table 10.2), and half of this results in a 50% discrepancy level of 3.6(.5) or 1.8. For a student whose grade level is 5.5, this is equivalent to a grade level of 3.7 or lower.

Although more controversial, a variation of the basic Horn formula to determine a 50% learning discrepancy which yields the exact same result as (2MA+CA)/3-5 (Federal Register, Nov. 29, 1976, P. 52407) is

$$CA(\frac{IQ}{300} + .17) - 2.5 = .5(\frac{CA + 2MA}{3}) - 5$$

Apparently, the reason for not using this formula stemmed from objections to the use of MA (Danielson & Bauer, 1978) so that the MA term was replaced by (CA)(IQ)/100 and the various terms rearranged. In spite of this transformation, the objections to this formula were many and related to use of a 50% criterion and IQ as a basis for determining potential.

There are certainly a host of reasons for not comparing predicted and obtained achievement values. Reynolds' (1984) noted that these formulas are "essentially meaningless and in all cases misleading" (p. 453) applies to all comparisons of predicted and obtained achievement regardless of the unit of measurement (e.g., grade equivalents, age equivalents, standard scores). In terms of use, the differences between the expectancy formulas cited above and those described below using standard scores will be somewhat different, and expectancy formulas based on standard scores should be the first choice for use, but no expectancy formula obviates the fundamental problem of determining potential based on an IQ-type index.

Empirical Regression Analysis

Cone and Wilson (1981) commented that "eventually all methods of determining academic discrepancy must be validated empirically" (p. 370). Empirically determining the relationship between MA and achievement would certainly eliminate estimating the correlation between these two variables for a given sample, as well as other sample statistics (viz., the means and standard deviations). Indeed, virtually every expectancy method used with a particular sample (when the sample correlation, mean and standard deviation differ from those associated with the specific expectancy model values) will either underpredict or overpredict the number of students identified as having a significant discrepancy.

As explained by Cone and Wilson (1981) there are a variety of practical problems when using regression analysis to determine a discrepancy such as problems associated with sampling. When tests such as the WISC-III are used to determine IQ, the ability to collect districtwide data from the general school population might be extremely limited. Although the determination of a 50% discrepancy might not be done routinely, empirical information based on districtwide or school data would provide guidance in the selection of an expectancy formula which best approximates the districtwide or school population statistical characteristics.

Expectancy formulas might provide some insight concerning individual needs (including test accommodations) if used cautiously and not as the sole criterion for determining services. As Spache (1976) so rightly stated, expectancy "formulas ignore the possible influences of socioeconomic status, race, native language, instructional method, personality disorders, any physical handicaps, or any other recognized obstacles to pupil achievement" (p. 129).

Significant Score Differences

Comparing scores is often a critical task when determining the need for special education services and test accommodations. In the previous section dealing with prediction formulas, a relatively intuitive approach for determining 50% discrepancy was discussed. In this section, several statistical criteria for evaluating the statistical significance of a discrepancy are presented. That is, instead of an arbitrary criterion such as a 50% discrepancy level, a statistical criterion entails a probability statement as to the statistical likelihood that a difference occurred by chance. If a statement could be that there is a 95% or 99% probability that an observed difference did not occur by chance, or a 5% or 1% probability that an observed difference is the result of chance, the confidence level can be used as a criterion. In other words, if a difference falls within the 95% (or whatever confidence level is specified), the difference is considered *statistically significant*.

SE_{meas}-*based Differences*

One of the most frequently-cited methods for determining test scores differences entails the use of the Standard Error of the Difference (SE_{dif}) which is determined using the SE_{meas} or

$$SE_{dif} = \sqrt{SE^2_{meas_x} + SE^2_{meas_y}}$$

or when the test standard deviations are the same by

$$SE_{dif} = SD\sqrt{2 - r_{xx} - r_{yy}}$$

Table 10.3 shows difference scores needed to be significant at z score values of z=1.0 (p=.68), z=1.96 (p=.95) and z=2.58 (p=.99) based on the SEdif. When the standard deviation is 15, the average reliability of two tests .9, a difference score of 13 (13.1) is necessary to be significant at the 95% confidence level. To illustrate the use of the values in Table 10.3, consider a student who received a score of 85 on one test and 70 on another where the means are 100 and standard deviations 15 for both tests. If the reliability was .9 for each test, the difference between 85 and 70 would be significant at the 95% confidence level or 85-70 > 13.1.

Table 10.3 Significant Score Differences.

Standard Deviation	Average Test Reliability											
	.80			.85			.90			.95		
	p_{68}^d	p_{95}	p_{99}	p_{68}	p_{95}	p_{99}	p_{68}	p_{95}	p_{99}	p_{68}	p_{95}	p_{99}
21.06	13.3	26.1	34.4	11.5	22.6	29.8	9.4	18.5	24.3	6.7	13.1	17.2
16	10.1	19.8	26.1	8.8	17.2	22.6	7.2	14.0	18.5	5.1	9.9	13.1
15	9.5	18.6	24.5	8.2	16.1	21.2	6.7	13.1	17.3	4.7	9.3	12.2
10	6.3	12.4	16.3	5.5	10.7	14.1	4.5	8.8	11.5	3.2	6.2	8.2
3	1.9	3.7	4.9	1.6	3.2	4.2	1.3	2.6	3.5	.94	1.9	2.4
2	1.3	2.5	3.3	1.1	2.1	2.8	.9	1.8	2.3	.63	1.2	1.6
1	.6	1.2	1.6	.5	1.1	1.4	.4	.9	1.2	.31	.6	.8

Learning disability indices. Myklebust (1968) used the ratio between actual achievement (AA) and expected achievement (EA) based on MA, CA and grade level to calculate an expectancy age (EA) to produce a learning quotient. A learning disability is defined as a learning quotient less than 90. This is somewhat higher than the index recommended by Monroe (1932, p. 17) where an index below .80

'Probabilities (p) are also expressed in terms of levels so that when z=1.96, the corresponding confidence level is referred to as the ".05 level" or "p=.05," and when z=2.58, the corresponding confidence level is referred to as the ".01 level" or "p=.01."

^{d}The 68% confidence level (p_{68}) is equivalent to 1 SE$_{dif}$, p_{95} to 1.96 SE$_{dif}$, and p_{99} to 2.58 SE$_{dif}$.

almost always indicates the need for remediation, and an index between .80 and .90 is said to be in the borderline range. Whatever the learning quotient measures, a quotient of 89 does not indicate 89 percent of what the student is capable of learning but is yet another comparison between IQ and achievement.

The use of all discrepancy indices of learning disabilities which do not incorporate a below-average or below-grade level restriction can identify all students, regardless of IQ, for possible identification as learning disabled. For example, if an 8-year-old student in the third grade has an IQ of 140 (and MA of 11.2), the expected age using the Myklebust formula is (8+11.2+8)/3 or 9.1. If the student is achieving at grade level, the learning quotient is 8/9.1(100) or 88. The question is not that a small number of students will have IQ scores of 130 who are achieving at grade level, but rather how a specific learning disability is conceptualized. As noted by Schuerholz et al. (1995) the use of a discrepancy between ability and achievement "is further compromised when a discrepancy is found to exist in a child whose day-to-day educational performance is not adversely affected" (.18).

Although many districts do reserve special education services for students who do have a problem with day-to-day education performance, an argument can be made not to use a criterion which systematically excludes high IQ students (see Reynolds, 1984). If high IQ students are identified as learning disabled, the need and use of test accommodations becomes very unclear. If a student is achieving at grade level in reading and has an IQ score of 150, is the student entitled to test accommodations? If so, what accommodation would be appropriate? Extended time? Individualized testing? The availability of a reader? In other words what are the "unique needs"[8] of a student with an IQ of 150 and reading at grade level?

Regression Prediction Discrepancy

Schuerholz et al. (1995) cited a regression analysis used by the Maryland State Department of Education to determine a "severe discrepancy" between ability and achievement. For a student with an IQ greater than 130, an achievement standard score less than or equal to 100 is said to be a severe discrepancy; for an IQ in the 100 to 109 range, an achievement score less than or equal to 82 is a severe discrepancy.

The State of Washington[9] also uses a regression approach to generate severe discrepancy criterion scores. For example, when both IQ and achievement are expressed as having distributions means of 100 and standard deviations of 15, a student with an IQ of 100 would need an achievement score equal to or less than the criterion score of 82. The formula for determining discrepancy criterion scores is based on the SE_{est}:

$$Criterion\ Score = IQ - (z)SD \sqrt{1 - r^2_{xy}}$$

so that for an IQ of 100, if a discrepancy is defined as a z of 1.5 and the correlation between IQ and achievement is .6, the score needed for a severe discrepancy (i.e., the criterion score) would be 100-(1.5)12=82 or 82.

$$Criterion\ Score = 100 - (1.5)15 \sqrt{1 - .6^2_{xy}} = 82$$

Reynolds (1984) and Wilson and Reynolds (1984) discussed several models for defining a learning disability and recommended the following:

$$Y' - Y_i \ge (2\ SD_y \sqrt{1 - r^2_{xy}}) - 1.65\ SE_{y'\cdot y_i}$$

Which is found by:

$$Y' - Y \ge 1.96\ SD_y \sqrt{1 - r^2_{xy}} - 1.65\ SD_y \sqrt{r^2_{xy}(1 - r_{xx}) + (1 - r_{yy})}$$

Using the above formula, the WIAT (Psychological Corp, 1992) manual (p. 190) gives an example for reliabilities of .91 and a correlation .of 47. When predicted achievement is calculated by .47(90-100)+100 (or 95.3) and compared to actual achievement of 74, the resulting difference of 21.3 is significant at the 95% confidence level or 21.3 (difference) > 17.75 (critical value).[e]

Using the difference between obtained IQ and achievement, or 90 - 74 = 16, and the SE_{meas} method to determine the critical region, the 16 point difference also exceeds the critical region of 6.36(1.96) = 12.47 or 16 (difference > 12.47 (critical region).

$$Critical\ Value = (1.96)\ SD \sqrt{2 - .91 - .91} = 12.47$$

The following BASIC computer program will determine the statistical significance of a discrepancy using the model recommended by Reynolds (1984, p. 461). The test reliabilities are specified in line 140,

---

[e]The exact same statistical decision will be reached if standardized grade equivalents are used where achievement is determined by $(X_{ach} - 100)/15(CA(.15)) + CA-5$, predicted achievement by $r_{xy}((X_{iq} - 100)/15(CA(.15)))+CA - 5$, and the standard deviation by $CA(.15)$.

the correlation between tests in line 150, and the standard deviations in line 160.

Table 10.4 Predicted Achievement Computer Program.

```
10 REM PREDICTED-ACHIEVEMENT REGRESSION ANALYSIS
20 REM
30 CLS
40 PRINT "PREDICTED-ACHIEVEMENT REGRESSION ANALYSIS:"
50 PRINT
60 PRINT "Enter two scores X,Y or RETURN to quit:"
70 PRINT
80 INPUT "Input X(IQ): ",X$
90 IF X$="" THEN 500
100 INPUT "Input Y(achievement): ",Y$
110 IF Y$="" THEN 500
120 X = VAL(X$): Y = VAL(Y$)
130 IF X = 0 THEN 500
140 RX = .91: RY = .91
150 RXY = .47
160 SDX = 15: SDY = 15
170 PRINT
180 PRINT "Test Statistics:"
190 PRINT
200 PRINT "Reliability: Test X ="RX,"Test Y = "RY
210 PRINT "Standard Deviation: Test X = "SDX,"Test Y = "SDY
220 PRINT "Correlation: = "RXY
230 PRINT
240 PRINT "Predicted-Achievement Regression Analysis:"
250 PRINT
260 SDRESID = SDX*SQR(1-RXY^2)
270 RELRESID = (RY+RX*RXY^2-2*RXY^2)/(1-RXY^2)
280 SERESID = SDX*SQR(RXY^2*(1-RX)+(1-RY))
290 PRINT "Standard Deviation (residual) = "SDRESID
300 PRINT "Reliability (residual) = "RELRESID
310 PRINT "Standard Error (residual) = "SERESID
320 PRINT
330 SD95 = 1.96*SDX*SQR(1-RXY^2)-1.65*SERESID
340 PRINT "Severe Discrepancy (.95 level) = "SD95
350 SD99 = 2.58*SDX*SQR(1-RXY^2)-2.33*SERESID
360 PRINT "Severe Discrepancy (.99 level) = "SD99
370 PRINT
380 PRINT "Observed Difference: "X"(IQ) -"Y"(ACH) = "X-Y
390 PACH = RXY*(X-100)+100
400 PADIF = PACH-Y
410 PRINT "Predicted - Actual Achievement ="PACH" - "Y" = "PADIF
420 IF PADIF < SD95 THEN PRINT "Not Significant": GOTO 450
430 IF PADIF >=SD99 THEN PRINT "Significance = .99 level": GOTO 450
440 PRINT "Significance = .95 level"
450 PRINT
460 PRINT "Press ENTER for more or Q to quit:";
470 R$=INKEY$: IF R$="" THEN 470
480 IF R$ = "Q" OR R$="q" THEN 500
490 GOTO 30
500 END
```

If the standard scores for IQ and achievement are transformed to standardized grade equivalents, the z statistics to test the hypothesis that $(Y'-Y) > z$ is exactly the same (regardless of what CA is set to in line 161 shown below) as when standard scores values are used with means of 100 and standard deviations of 15. The above program is easily modified to display results in a standardized grade equivalent form by these changes:

> 161 CA = 10
>
> 162 SDX = CA*.15: SDY = SDX
>
> 191 PRINT "CA = "CA
>
> 390 PACH = RXY*(X-100)/15*CA*.15+CA-5
>
> 391 Y = (Y-100)/15*CA*.15+CA-5

The above changes result in a predicted grade equivalent of 4.53 and an obtained achievement standardized grade equivalent of 2.4. The difference (4.53-2.4=2.13) is greater than the 95% confidence critical value of 1.775.

Professional Judgement

When all is said and done, a purely statistical decision based on statistical significance should not be used to determine the severity of a discrepancy between achievement and ability. In the end, the multidisciplinary team must rely on a combination of quantitative indices and qualitative reports[10] when providing written documentation[11] explicating the existence of a severe discrepancy between achievement and ability.

Certainly for those with the statistical perseverance, the formula provided by Reynolds (1984) offers a very thoughtful rationale for identifying a severe discrepancy. This formula can be used with IQ and achievement scores in standard form or with standardized grade equivalents as previously discussed. Unfortunately, whether a relatively simple formula or elaborate regression equation is used, every IQ-based formula is faced with the underlying validity problems associated with every index of IQ. As shown by "overwhelming opposition" (see Danielson & Bauer, 1978) to the (2MA+CA)/3 formula for determining a severe discrepancy, one of the primary criticisms concerns the very meaning of an IQ score and what an IQ score reflects.

The professional judgement of the multidisciplinary team, and not a statistical formula, must make the final decision as to the need for special education services and test accommodations. In the State of Washington, discrepancy tables for determining severe discrepancy levels are published, but when

> the evaluation results do not appear to accurately represent the student's intellectual ability and where the discrepancy between the student's intellectual ability and academic achievement does not initially appear to be severe upon application of the discrepancy tables, WAC 392-172-130, the multidisciplinary team shall apply professional judgment in order to determine the presence of a severe discrepancy. In this event, the multidisciplinary team shall document in a written narrative an explanation as to why the student has a severe discrepancy.[12]

Even if there is not a statistical discrepancy between mental ability and achievement, this does not preclude the need for test accommodations. If a student has a specific learning disability involving listening comprehension,[13] an IQ score might reflect this disability and mask actual mental ability, a case might be made that there is indeed a discrepancy between mental ability and achievement. If a student is below average in an achievement area (e.g., $z < -1.0$)) regardless of the student's IQ score, the student might benefit from a test accommodation even though the scores do not indicate a discrepancy. For example, a student who is two standard deviations below the mean on IQ and achievement tests, might need an accommodation to mitigate the effects of the disability as defined by either IDEA or Section 504 even though the discrepancy between mental ability and achievement is not statistically significant. A discrepancy between IQ and achievement, or between any two test scores, can only indicate and not preclude the need for a test accommodation if no discrepancy is found.

ENDNOTES

1. 34 C.F.R. §300.541(a)
2. 34 C.F.R. §300.7(a)(1)
3. 34 C.F.R. §300.532(d)
4. 34 C.F.R. §104.3(j)
5. 34 C.F.R. §300.7(b)(10)

6.   See 34 C.F.R. §300.541 for the criteria for determining the existence of a specific learning disability.

7.   The 68% confidence level (p_{68}) is equivalent to 1 SEdif, p_{95} to 1.96 SEdif, and p_{99} to 2.58 SEdif.

8.   34 C.F.R. §300.17(a)(1)

9.   Washington Administrative Code, 392-172-132, 1995.

10.   34 C.F.R. §300.542 which requires an observation of the student academic performance by "at least one team member other than the child's regular teacher..."

11.   34 C.F.R. §300.543

12.   Washington Administrative Code, 392-172-130, 1995.

13.   34 C.F.R. §300.541(a)(2)(ii)

APPENDIX A

Abbreviations

Whether it be a law, regulation, or a general article relating to special education and testing, abbreviations can make reading virtually uninterpretable. The following provides a guide to several of the more commonly-used abbreviations which relate to special educating, testing and test accommodations.

α -	Coefficient Alpha (a reliability coefficient)
ACT -	American College Testing program
ADD -	Attention Deficit Disorder
ASL -	American Sign Language
AP -	Appropriate Placement
AU -	Administrative Unit
CP -	Cerebral Palsy
CAP -	Corrective Action Plan
CASE -	Council for Administrator of Special Education
CAT -	California Achievement Test
CBA -	Curriculum-based Assessment
CBM -	Curriculum-based Measurement
CEC -	Council for Exceptional Children
CFR -	Code of Federal Regulations, C.F.R., CFR
CLD -	Council for Learning Disabilities
CTBS -	Comprehensive Test of Basic Skills
DIQ -	Deviation IQ
EAHCA -	Education for All Handicapped Children Act of 1975
ED -	Emotional Disturbance
EDGAR -	Education Department General Administrative Regulations
EHA -	Education of the Handicapped Act
EMH -	Educable Mentally Handicapped
EMR -	Educable Mental Retardation, Educable Mentally Retarded
EHA -	Education of the Handicapped Act
ESEA -	Elementary and Secondary Education Act
ESL -	English as a Second Language
FAPE -	Free Appropriate Public Education

GE -	Grade Equivalent
GEPA -	General Education Provisions Act
GORT -	Gray Oral Reading Test
IAP -	Individualized Accommodation Plan
IAP -	Individualized Assessment Plan
IDEA -	Individuals with Disabilities Education Act
IEP -	Individualized Education Program
IEU -	Intermediate Educational Unit
IFSP -	Individualized Family Service Plan
IRI -	Informal Reading Inventory
ITBS -	Iowa Test of Basic Skills
KR-20	Kuder-Richardson Formula #20 (a reliability coefficient)
IQ -	Intelligence Quotient
LD -	Learning Disabilities
LEA -	Local Educational Agency
LEP -	Limited English Proficiency
LID -	Low Incidence Disability
LM -	Language Minority
LRE -	Least Restrictive Environment
μ -	Mean
M -	Mean
MA -	Mental Age
MAT -	Metropolitan Achievement Test
Md	Median
MR -	Mental Retardation
MDT -	Multidisciplinary Team
NAEP -	National Assessment of Educational Progress
N -	Number of persons in a group
NCEO -	National Center on Educational Outcomes
OCR -	Office of Civil Rights
OSEP -	Office of Special Education
PIAT -	Peabody Individual Achievement Test
PPVT -	Peabody Picture Vocabulary Test
PR -	Percentile Rank
r_{kk} -	Test Reliability
r_{xy} -	Correlation, r
REI -	Regular Education Initiative
σ -	Standard Deviation
σ^2 -	Variance
S-B -	Stanford Binet Intelligence Scale
SE -	Standard Error, S.E., SE
SEA -	State Educational Agency
SEM -	Standard Error of Measurement
SOP -	State Operated Programs
SAT -	Scholastic Assessment Test

SAT -	Stanford Achievement Test
SD -	Standard Deviation, S.D., SD, σ
SD -	Severe Disability
SEA -	State Education Agency
SE_{est} -	Standard Error of Estimate
SE_{meas} -	Standard Error of Measurement
SH -	Severely Handicapped
SRA -	Survey of Applied Skills
SOP -	State Operated Programs
t'-	Estimated True Score
TOLD -	Test of Language Development
TOWL -	Test of Written Language
TMR -	Trainable Mental Retardation, Trainable Mentally Retarded
USC -	United States Code (also (U.S.C.)
V -	Variance, Var, V, SD^2, σ^2
WISC -	Wechsler Intelligence Scale for Children
WISC-R -	WISC-Revised
WISC-III -	WISC-Third Revision
WRAT -	Wide Range Achievement Test
WRMT -	Woodcock Reading Mastery Test
$\bar{x}$ -	Mean
z -	Value indicating the number of SD's below or above the mean

APPENDIX B

Assistive Technology Applications

The programs shown below are designed to illustrate how various test items, content and tasks can be modified via a single-switch format. All the programs can be used by means of a switch connected to a game port) or by using any keyboard key. The amount of time allowed to activate a switch before the next item is scanned is determined by variable **DELAY** which is contained in line 30 or 40. The value in **DELAY** represents seconds so that when **DELAY** $= 2$, the length of time each alternative is scanned is two seconds.

Single-switch tasks can be created using a puff switch, tread switch, or virtually a switch device involving an intentional muscle movement. The single-switch task involves scanning a series of alternatives so that when the desired alternative is scanned, the student activates the switch. The task is essentially the same as when a teacher scans a series of items by pointing, and the student indicates a choice by an intentional behavior (e.g., blinking, hand movement or any other intentional movement).

All of the programs shown below can be enhanced to incorporate features such as synthesized speech, techniques for improving item display characteristics, the complexity of the item task (e.g., using Morse Code), and monitoring performance. The following programs are intended to illustrate how a single-switch task can be used to accommodate a student's testing needs. As is the case with all testing accommodations, a single-switch tasks requires considerable individualization and ongoing evaluation.

Discrimination. Before modifying an academic task for a student requiring a single-switch format, the ability of the student to intentionally use a single-switch format must be determined. The basic single-switch scanning task is demonstrated by the **DISCRIMINATION** program shown below. The task is to engage the switch when the scan moves beneath the shape that is different. The activation of the switch is detected in line 20. In the program listing, the item shapes are generated beginning in line 680.

A single-switch scanning task can be created for most mathematics items. Nonetheless, because of the multiple-choice character of the task, care must be taken to differentiate random from intentional responses. Determining the intentionality of behavior cannot be made solely on the basis of the number of correct and incorrect responses, but is also assessed closely by evaluating such factors as the alternative selection, immediacy of response, possible multiple-responses, response latency.

```
10 REM DISCRIMINATION
20 REM
30 DIM LATENCY(100),ANSWER$(100)
40 DELAY = 2
50 CLS
60 STRIG ON
70 KEY OFF
80 SCREEN 1
90 RANDOMIZE TIMER
100 NS = 9
110 X = 50: Y = 80
120 N = N+1
130 RC = INT(RND(1)*8+1)
140 RI = INT(RND(1)*8+1)
150 IF RI = RC THEN 140
160 RP = INT(RND(1)*3+1)
170 FOR PL = 1 TO 3
180 GS = RI: IF RP = PL THEN GS = RC
190 IF PL = 2 THEN X = 130
200 IF PL = 3 THEN X = 210
210 COLOR 1,3
220 ON GS GOSUB 680,710,750,780,800,830,850,870
230 NEXT PL
240 SP = 47: P = 1
250 LINE (SP,130) - (SP+30,138),2,BF
260 START = TIMER
270 IF STRIG(1) < 0 THEN 260
280 IF INKEY$>"" THEN 260
290 IF TIMER - START <.5 THEN 270
300 START = TIMER
310 IF TIMER - START > DELAY THEN 360
320 IF STRIG(1) < 0 THEN 400
```

```
330 KY$ = INKEY$: IF KY$ = "" THEN 310
340 IF ASC(KY$) = 27 THEN 560
350 GOTO 400
360 LINE (SP,130) - (SP+30,138),0,BF
370 SP = SP+80: IF SP > 220 THEN SP = 47
380 P = P+1: IF P > 3 THEN P = 1
390 GOTO 250
400 LATENCY(N) = TIMER - START
410 IF RP = P THEN 470
420 ANSWER$(N) = "INCORRECT" + STR$(P)
430 LINE (SP,130) - (SP*30,138),0,BF
440 GOTO 530
450 REM
460 REM
470 LOCATE 21,15
480 ANSWER$(N) = "CORRECT" + STR$(P)
490 PRINT "CORRECT!"
500 SOUND 659,3
510 SOUND 1046,7
520 C = C+1
530 START = TIMER
540 IF TIMER - START > DELAY THEN 40
550 GOTO 540
560 SCREEN 0
570 WIDTH 80
580 LOCATE 7
590 N = N - 1
600 PRINT "Number = "N
610 PRINT "Correct = "C
620 PRINT: PRINT "Item latency Values"
630 PRINT
640 FOR K = 1 TO N
650 PRINT "Item #"K" = "LATENCY(K)" "ANSWER$(K)
660 NEXT K
670 END
680 FOR K = 1 TO 25
690 LINE (X,Y+K) - (X+25,Y+K)
700 NEXT K: RETURN
710 LINE (X,Y) - (X,Y+30)
720 LINE (X,Y+30) - (X+30,Y+30)
730 LINE (X+30,Y+30) - (X,Y)
740 RETURN
750 FOR K = 0 TO 25
760 LINE (X,Y) - (X+K,Y+25)
770 NEXT K: RETURN
780 LINE (X+6,Y) - (X+18,Y+25),1,BF
790 RETURN
800 FOR K = 1 TO 25
810 LINE (X+12-K,Y+K) - (X+12+K,Y+K)
```

```
820 NEXT K: RETURN
830 CIRCLE (X+12,Y+15),25
840 RETURN
850 LINE (X,Y) - (X+25,Y+25),2,BF
860 RETURN
870 CIRCLE (X+12,Y+15),25,2
880 PAINT (X+12,Y+15),2
890 RETURN
```

The summary data for the above program includes a latency analysis. For each item, the length of time to engage the switch when an alternative is scanned is displayed, followed by the correctness of the item, and the position of the alternative when scanned. The following is an example of the type of latency values provided:

Item # 1 = .609375	INCORRECT 1
Item # 2 = 0	INCORRECT 2
Item # 3 = .4882813	CORRECT 1
Item # 4 = .328125	CORRECT 2
Item # 5 = 0	INCORRECT 1
Item # 6 = .046875	CORRECT 1
Item # 7 = .3320313	CORRECT 1

SENTENCE CLOZE. The following reading sentence cloze program can be used to develop or assess content area skills using a single-switch format. Each item is contained in **DATA** statements beginning in line 960. Each item is comprised of the stem (where the = sign indicates the missing word), one correct alternative, followed by a series of incorrect alternatives.

```
10 REM SENTENCE CLOZE
20 REM
30 DELAY = 2
40 STRIG ON
50 KEY OFF
60 RANDOMIZE TIMER
70 WIDTH 40
80 DIM Q$(50),Q(50)
90 ON ERROR GOTO 130
100 SN = 1
110 READ Q$(SN)
120 SN = SN+1: GOTO 110
130 SN = SN-1
140 FOR Q = 1 TO SN
150 RQ = INT(RND(1)*SN+1)
160 IF Q(RQ) = 1 THEN 150
170 Q(RQ) = 1
```

```
180 LOCATE ,,0
190 CLS
200 P$(0) = "": QP = 0
210 GOSUB 930
220 PRINT "SENTENCE "Q
230 VL = 5
240 LOCATE VL
250 FOR CH = 1 TO LEN(Q$(RQ))
260 L$ = MID$(Q$(RQ),CH,1)
270 IF L$ = "/" THEN 310
280 P$(QP) = P$(QP)+L$
290 IF CH = LEN(Q$(RQ)) THEN 310
300 GOTO 330
310 QP = QP+1: P$(QP) = ""
320 IF QP = 7 THEN 340
330 NEXT CH
340 QP = QP-1: LOCATE ,1
350 FOR CH = 1 TO LEN(P$(0))
360 L$ = MID$(P$(0),CH,1)
370 IF L$ = " " THEN 420
380 IF L$ = "=" THEN L$ = "___"
390 U$ = U$+L$
400 IF CH = LEN(P$(0)) THEN 420
410 GOTO 490
420 IF LEN(U$)+P+1 > 39 THEN 460
430 U$ = U$+" ": PRINT U$;
440 P = P+LEN(U$)
450 U$ = "": GOTO 490
460 PRINT: PRINT U$" ";
470 P = LEN(U$)+1: U$=""
480 VL = VL+1
490 NEXT CH: P = 0
500 VL = VL+2
510 FOR K = 1 TO QP
520 A(K) = 0: NEXT K
530 FOR QA = 1 TO QP
540 RN = INT(RND(1)*QP+1)
550 IF A(RN) = 1 THEN 540
560 A(RN) = 1: PC(QA) = RN
570 IF RN = 1 THEN CP = QA
580 LOCATE VL+QA*2,10
590 PRINT P$(RN)
600 NEXT QA
610 SP = 1
620 LOCATE VL+SP*2,8
630 PRINT CHR$(219)
640 START = TIMER
650 IF TIMER - START > DELAY THEN 700
660 IF STRIG(1) < 0 THEN 740
670 KY$ = INKEY$: IF KY$ = "" THEN 650
```

```
680 IF ASC(KY$) = 27 THEN 860
690 GOTO 740
700 LOCATE VL+SP*2,8
710 PRINT CHR$(32)
720 SP = SP+1: IF SP <= QP THEN 620
730 SP = 1: GOTO 620
740 LOCATE VL+SP*2,1: PRINT STRING$(40,32)
750 LOCATE VL+SP*2,12
760 PRINT P$(PC(SP))
770 GOSUB 930
780 IF SP = CP THEN 800
790 GOTO 830
800 LOCATE VL+CP*2,1
810 PRINT "CORRECT!"
820 C = C+1
830 GOSUB 930
840 N = N+1
850 NEXT Q
860 WIDTH 80
870 CLS
880 LOCATE 7
890 PRINT "Number = "N
900 PRINT "Correct = "C
910 PRINT "Percent = "INT(C/N*100+.5)
920 END
930 START = TIMER
940 IF TIMER - START > DELAY*.25 THEN RETURN
950 GOTO 940
960 DATA WHAT=IS IT?/TIME/SAW/GO/LUNCH
970 DATA HE IS A VERY TALL=./MAN/GIRL/WOMAN/SHORT
980 DATA I=HUNGRY./AM/IS/ARE/HE
990 DATA Binghamton is approximately=miles from
    Albany./150/50/350/500/900
```

SCANSPELL. Many single-switch tasks use a multiple-choice format to scan a set of items so that a switch is used to make a selection. Variations of this technique can be expanded to produce very complex responses. The **SCANSPELL** program uses a matrix scan technique to scan and select letters of the alphabet (see Chapter 8). The alphabet is displayed using five screen lines. Each matrix row is scanned to first select an array of characters. A second scan is then used to select the specific letter or character in that array. Thus, to select a character two switch movements must be made: row selection and then the specific character selection. Although row/element scanning is fairly efficient, the task can be difficult for some individuals to conceptualize. One obvious alternative to row/element scanning, but a procedure which can be time-consuming, is to sequentially scan every matrix element until the specified element (viz., letter) is scanned and selected. A similar technique is discussed in Chapter 8.

After a character is selected, the letter is displayed at the bottom of the screen. The program can be enhanced with a speech synthesizer, as well as additional punctuation. Press the keyboard *c* key to clear the current screen message and the *Esc* key to exit the program.

```
10 REM SCANSPELL
20 REM
30 DELAY = 2
40 STRIG ON
50 KEY OFF
60 WIDTH 40
70 SCREEN 0
80 COLOR 7,1
90 L$(1) = "A   B   C   D   E   F"
100 L$(2) = "G   H   I   J   K   L"
110 L$(3) = "M   N   O   P   Q   R"
120 L$(4) = "S   T   U   V   W   X"
130 L$(5) = "Y   Z   .   ?"
140 CLS
150 LOCATE ,15: PRINT "SCANSPELL"
160 VP = 1
170 FOR D = 1 TO 5
180 LOCATE VP+D*3,9
190 PRINT L$(D): NEXT
200 LOCATE VP*3+1,9,0
210 COLOR 1,7
220 PRINT L$(VP)
230 COLOR 7,1
240 GOSUB 590
250 IF SW = 1 THEN SW = 0: GOTO 340
260 LOCATE VP*3+1,9
270 PRINT L$(VP)
280 VP = VP+1: IF VP > 5 THEN VP = 1
290 LOCATE VP*3+1,9
300 COLOR 1,7
310 PRINT L$(VP)
320 COLOR 7,1
330 GOTO 240
340 LOCATE VP*3+1,9
350 PRINT L$(VP)
360 LOCATE VP*3+1,9
370 COLOR 1,7
380 PRINT MID$(L$(VP),1,1)
390 COLOR 7,1
400 HP = 9
```

```
410 GOSUB 590
420 LOCATE VP*3+1,HP
430 PRINT MID$(L$(VP),HP-8,1)
440 IF SW = 1 THEN 530
450 HP = HP+4
460 IF HP > 29 THEN HP = 9
470 LOCATE VP*3+1,HP
480 COLOR 1,7
490 PRINT MID$(L$(VP),HP-8,1)
500 COLOR 7,1
510 GOTO 410
520 SW = 1
530 C$ = MID$(L$(VP),HP-8,1)
540 M$ = M$+C$
550 LOCATE 20,1: PRINT M$
560 START = TIMER
570 IF TIMER - START > 1 THEN 160
580 GOTO 570
590 IF STRIG(1) < 0 THEN 590
600 START = TIMER
610 IF TIMER - START > DELAY THEN 670
620 IF STRIG(1) < 0 THEN 680
630 KY$ = INKEY$: IF KY$ = "" THEN 610
640 IF ASC(KY$) = 27 THEN 710
650 IF ASC(KY$) = 99 THEN 700
660 GOTO 680
670 SW = 0: RETURN
680 SW = 1
690 RETURN
700 CLEAR: GOTO 30
710 WIDTH 80
720 COLOR 7,0
730 CLS
740 END
```

MORSE CODE. The ability to use Morse Code requires not only the ability to conceptualize the relationship between a series of dots, dashes and letters, as well as a degree of reading proficiency, but also the physical ability to use a switch to enter the necessary dots and dashes. The following is a relatively simple program which illustrates one of many techniques which can be used to respond via single-switch Morse Code. The essence of the program is a timing loop which records the presence and duration of a keyboard response. If a keyboard key is engaged (e.g., the spacebar), a timing loop is initiated to determine whether the response is a dot or dash: quickly releasing the key will produce a dot, and holding the key slightly longer will produce a dash. The **c** key is used to start a new word and **Esc** to exit the program. Although some experimentation is required in order to become accustomed to the task, this is a relatively simple program and many enhancements could be added such as synthesized speech, individualized timing adjustments, and word processing features.

```
10 REM MORSE CODE
20 REM
30 CLEAR
40 CLS: WIDTH 40
50 DIM L$(26)
60 FOR K = 1 TO 26
70 READ L$(K): NEXT K
80 DATA .-,-...,-.-.,-..,.
90 DATA ..-.,--.,....,..,.---
100 DATA -.-,.-..,--,-.,---,.--.
110 DATA --.-,.-.,...,-,..-,...-
120 DATA .--,-..-,-.--,--..
130 LOCATE 2,15,0
140 PRINT "MORSE CODE"
150 LOCATE 8,6: PRINT ">"
160 START = TIMER
170 IF TIMER - START > 2.5 THEN 340
180 KY$ = INKEY$: IF KY$ = "" THEN 170
190 KY = ASC(KY$): IF KY = 27 THEN 410
200 IF KY$ = "c" THEN 30
210 KY$ = ""
220 STARTLET = TIMER
230 IF TIMER - STARTLET > 2.5 THEN 260
240 KY$ = KY$ + INKEY$
250 GOTO 230
260 IF KY$ = "" THEN 280
270 GOTO 300
280 L$ = L$ + "."
290 SOUND 750,3: GOTO 320
300 L$ = L$ + "-"
310 SOUND 650,6
320 LOCATE 8,10: PRINT L$
330 GOTO 160
340 FOR K = 1 TO 26: IF L$ = L$(K) THEN 360
350 NEXT K: GOTO 380
360 M$ = M$ + CHR$(64+K)
370 LOCATE 12,1: PRINT M$
380 L$ = ""
390 LOCATE 8,1: PRINT STRING$(30,32)
400 GOTO 150
410 WIDTH 80: CLS
420 END
```

REFERENCES

American Association for the Advancement of Science. (1991). *Barrier-free in brief: laboratories in science and engineering.* Washington, DC: Author.

American College Testing Program. (1995). *Reference norms for Spring 1995 ACT tested H.S. Graduates.* Iowa City, IA: Author.

American College Testing Program. (1995). *Preparing for the ACT assessment: special edition.* Iowa City, IA: Author.

American College Testing Program. (1995-96). *Taking the ACT assessment for special and arranged testing.* Iowa City, IA: Author.

American Council on Education. (1991). *1990 statistical report. GED. Tests of general educational development.* Washington, DC, General Educational Development testing Service. ERIC No. ED 330 405.

American National Standards Institute. (1986). *Providing accessibility and usability for physically handicapped people.* New York: Author.

American Printing House for the Blind. (1994). *APH catalog of accessible books for people who are visually impaired.* Louisville, KY: Author.

American Printing House for the Blind. (1994). *APH catalog of instructional aids, tools, and supplies.* Louisville, KY: Author.

American Psychiatric Association. (1994). *Diagnostic and statistical manual of mental disorders (DSM-IV).* Washington, DC: Author.

American Psychological Association. (1985). *Standards for educational and psychological testing.* Washington, DC: Author.

Anastasi, A. (1982). *Psychological testing (5th ed.).* New York: Macmillan.

Ballard, J., Ramirez, Zantal-Warner, K. (1987). *Public Law 94-142, Section 504, and Public law 99-457: understanding what they are and are not.* Reston, VA: Council for Exceptional Children. ERIC No. ED 295 392.

Barraga, N, and Erin, J. (1992). *Visual handicaps and learning.* Austin, TX: Pro-Ed.

Baumeister, A. (1964). Use of the WISC with mental retardates: a review. *American Journal of Mental Deficiency, 69,* 183-194.

Bennett, R.E., Rock, D.A., & Jirele, T. (1986). *The psychometric characteristics of the general test for three handicapped groups.* Princeton, NJ: Educational Testing Service.

Bennett, R.E., Rock, D.A., & Kaplan, B.A. (1985). *The psychometric characteristics of the SAT for nine handicapped groups.* Princeton, NJ: Educational Testing Service.

Bigge, J. L. (1982). *Teaching individuals with physical and multiple disabilities.* Columbus, OH: Charles E. Merrill.

Biklen, D. (1990). Communication unbound: autism and praxis. *Harvard Educational Review, 60,* 291-314.

Biklen, D. (1993). *Communication unbound: how facilitated communication is challenging traditional views of autism and ability/disability.* New York: Teachers College Press.

Bond, G., and Tinker, M. (1973). *Reading difficulties: their diagnosis and correction (3rd ed.).* New York: Appleton-Century-Crofts.

Bradley-Johnson, S. (1994). *Psychoeducational assessment of students who are visually impaired.* Austin, TX: Pro-Ed.

Braun, H, Ragosta, M., & Kaplan, B. Predictive validity. (1988). In W.W. Willingham, M. Ragosta, M., R.E. Bennett, H. Braun, H., D.A. Rock, & D.E. Powers, *Testing handicapped people* (pp. 109-132). Boston, MA: Allyn & Bacon.

Brigance, A.H. (1977). *Brigance Diagnostic Inventory of Basic Skills.* North Billerica, MA: Curriculum Associates.

Brigance, A. H. (1983). *Brigance Diagnostic Assessment of Basic Skills - Spanish Edition.* North Billerica, MA: Curriculum Associates.

British Columbia. (1996). *Special education services: a manual of policies, procedures and guidelines.* Victoria, B.C.: Author.

Brown, L., Sherbenou, R.J. & Johnsen, S.K. (1990). *Test of Nonverbal Intelligence-revised.* Austin, TX: Pro-Ed.

Burns, E. (1976). Effects of restricted sampling on ITPA scaled scores. *American Journal of Mental Deficiency, 80,* 394-400.

Burns, E. (1979). *The development, use and abuse of educational tests.* Springfield, IL: Charles C Thomas.

Burns, E. (1982). Bivariate normal distribution estimates of the prevalence of reading disabilities. *Journal of Special Education, 16,* 431-437.

Burns, E. (1982). Linear regression and simplified reading expectancy formulas. *Reading Research Quarterly, 17,* 446-453.

Campbell, D. & Fiske, D. (1959). Convergent and discriminant validation by the multitrait-multimethod matrix. *Psychological Bulletin, 56,* 81-105.

Carr, A. (1989). *Visual impairments.* Reston, VA: Council for Exceptional Children.

Centra, J. (1986). Handicapped student performance on the Scholastic Aptitude Test. *Journal of Learning Disabilities, 19,* 324-327.

Chalfant, J. C. & Van Dusen Pysh, M. (1980). *The compliance manual: a guide to the rules and regulations of the Education for All handicapped Children Act Public Law 94-142.* New Rochelle, NY: Penn Press.

Choate, J.S., Enright, B.E., Miller, L.J., Poteet, J.A. & Rakes, T.A. (1995). *Curriculum-based assessment and programming (3rd ed.).* Boston: Allyn and Bacon.

Cole, M., John-Steiner, V., Scribner, S., & Souberman, E. (Eds.). (1978). *L. S. Vygotsky—Mind in society: the development of higher psychological processes.* Cambridge, MA: Harvard University Press.

College Entrance Examination Board. (1982). *Scholastic Aptitude Test: braille edition and large print edition.* Princeton, NJ: Author.

College Entrance Examination Board. (1986). *10 SATs.* Princeton, NJ: Author.

College Entrance Examination Board. (1994a). *SAT services for students with disabilities: information for students with special needs.* Princeton, NJ: Author.

College Entrance Examination Board. (1994b). *SAT services for students with disabilities: information for counselors and admission officers.* Princeton, NJ: Author.

Cone, T.E. and Wilson, L.R. (1981). Quantifying a severe discrepancy: a critical analysis. *Learning Disability Quarterly, 4,* 359-371.

Connecticut State Education Department. (1996). *Guidelines for administering the Connecticut mastery test (CMT) and the Connecticut Academic performance Test (CAPT) to students receiving special education or Section 504 services.* Hartford, CT: Author.

Connolly, A. (1988). *Keymath - Revised.* Circle Pines, MN: American Guidance Service.

Conoley, J.C. & Kramer, J.J. (Eds.). (1989). *The tenth mental measurements yearbook.* Lincoln, NE: University of Nebraska Press.

Council of Administrators of Special Education. (1992). *Student access: a resource guide for educators. Section 504 of the Rehabilitation Act of 1973.* Albuquerque, NM: Author. ERIC No. 349 769.

Cronbach, L.J. (1970). *Essentials of psychological testing (3rd ed.).* New York: Harper and Row.

Cronbach, L J. & Furby, L. (1970). How we should measure change—or should we? *Psychological Bulletin, 74,* 68-80.

Danielson, L.C. & Bauer, J.N. (1978). A formula-based classification of learning disabled children: an examination of the issues. *Journal of Learning Disabilities, 11,* 163-176.

Davis, F.B. (1959). Interpretation of differences among averages and individual test scores. *Journal of Educational Psychology, 50,* 162-170.

Diamond, J., & Evans, W. (1972). An investigation of the cognitive correlates of test-wiseness. *Journal of Educational Measurement, 9,* 145-150.

Doe. vs. Withers. (1993). *Individuals with Disabilities Law Report, 206,* p. 422-427.

Donner, M. (1981). *How to beat the SAT.* New York: Workman.

Dunn, L. M. (1968). Special education for the mildly retarded—Is much of it justifiable? *Exceptional Children, 35,* 5-22.

Dunn, L. M. & Dunn L. M. (1981). Peabody Picture Vocabulary Test—Revised. Circle Pines, MN: American Guidance Service.

Dunn, L. M. & Markwardt, F.C. (1970). *Peabody Individual Achievement Test.* Circle Pines, MN: American Guidance Service.

Educational Testing Service. (1996). *GRE 1996-97 information and registration bulletin.* Princeton, NJ: Author.

Friend, M, & Bursuck, W. (1996). *Including students with special needs: a practical guide for classroom teachers.* Boston: Allyn & Bacon.

Gajria, M., Salend, S., & Hemrick, M. (1994). Teacher acceptability of testing modifications for mainstreamed students. *Journal of Learning Disabilities, 94,* 236-243.

Gallaudet Research Institute. (1989). *Administering the 8th edition Stanford Achievement Test to hearing impaired students.* Washington, DC: Author.

GED Testing Service. (1990). *1990 statistical report.* Washington, DC: American Council on Education. ERIC No. ED 335 405.

Goldberg, S.S. (1982). *Special education law.* New York: Plenum Press.

Greenberg, L. (1980). *Test development procedures for including handicapped students in new jersey's state assessment program.* Trenton, NJ: New Jersey State Department of

Education, Division of Operations, research, and Evaluation. ERIC No. ED 187 767.

Grise, P., Beattie, S., & Algozzine, B. (1982). Assessment of minimum competency in fifth grade learning disabled students: test modifications make a difference. *Journal of Educational Research, 76,* 35-40.

Guilford, J.P. (1954). *Psychometric methods (2nd ed.).* New York: McGraw-Hill.

Guilford, J.P. (1965). Fundamental statistics in psychology and education. New York: McGraw-Hill.

Hallahan, D.P. & Kauffman, J.M. (1997). *Exceptional learners (7th ed.).* Boston: Allyn & Bacon.

Hampton-Brown Company. (1991). *Spanish Assessment of Basic Education, Second Edition.* Monterey, CA: CTB\MacMillan\McGraw Hill.

Hargrove, L., & Poteet, J. (1984). *Assessment in special education.* Englewood Cliffs, New Jersey: Prentice-Hall.

Harris, A. (1970). *How to increase reading ability (5th ed.).* New York: McKay.

Hiskey, Marshall S. (1966). *Hiskey Nebraska Test of Learning Aptitude.* Lincoln, NE.

Holt, J.A. & Hotto, S.A. (1994). *Demographic aspects of hearing impairment: questions and answers (3rd ed.).* Washington, DC: Gallaudet Research Institute.

Holt, J.A., Traxler, C.B. & Allen, T.E. (1992). *Interpreting the scores: a user's guide to the 8th edition of the Stanford Achievement Test for educators of deaf and hard of hearing students.* Washington, DC: Gallaudet Research Institute.

Horn, A. (1941). The uneven distribution of the effects of special factors. *Southern California Education Monograph,* (No. 12).

Individual with Disabilities Education Act Amendments of 1997, P.L. 105-17, (H.R. 5 & S. 717). Signed into law by President Clinton on June 4, 1997.

Jastak, S. & Wilkinson, G. (1984). *Wide Range Achievement Test-Revised.* Wilmington, DE: Jastak Associates.

Joint Committee on Testing Practices. (1988). *Code of fair testing practices in education.* Washington, DC: Author.

Jones, J. W. (1961). *Blind children: degree of vision mode of reading.* Washington, DC: United States Department of Health, Education & Welfare.

Kaufman, A.S. & Kaufman, N.L. (1983). *Kaufman Assessment Battery for Children.* Circle Pines, MN: American Guidance Service.

Kaufman, A.S. (1994). *Intelligent testing with the WISC-III.* New York: John Wiley.

Kerlinger, F.N. (1973). *Foundations of behavioral research (2nd ed.).* New York: Holt, Rinehart and Winston.

Kirk, S., McCarthy, J., & Kirk, W. (1968). *Illinois Test of Pyscholinguistic Abilities (Rev. ed.).* Urbana, IL: University of Illinois Press.

Lambert, N. Nihira, K., & Leland, H. (1993). *AAMR Adaptive Behavior Scales: school (2nd ed.).* Austin, TX: Pro-ed.

Lauer, V.K. & Smith, G.A. (1994). A reply to Goodman and Bond. *Journal of Special Education, 28,* 106-108.

Lawrence, I. & Dorans, N. (1994). *Optional use of calculators on a mathematical test: effect on item difficulty and score equating.* Princeton, NJ: Educational Testing Service. ERIC No. ED 382 656.

Learner, J. (1988). *Learning disabilities (5th ed.)*. Princeton, NJ: Houghton Mifflin.

Leiter, Russell G. (1966). *Leiter International Performance Scale*. Wooddale, IL: Stoelting.

Lyon, M.A. (1995). A comparison between WISC-III and WISC-R scores for learning disabilities reevaluations. *Journal of Learning Disabilities, 28,* 253-255.

Markwardt, F.C. (1989). *Peabody Individual Achievement Test-Revised*. Circle Pines, MN: American Guidance Service.

Massachusetts Department of Education. (1995). *Question and answer guide on the new special education educational plan (IEP) and related chapter 766 regulations*. Malden, MA: Author.

May, G., & Braswell, J. SAT I. (1994). *Test development procedures for students with disabilities*. Paper presented at the Annual Meeting of the National Council on Measurement in Education, New Orleans, LA. ERIC No. ED 375 544.

McKinney, J.D. (1983). Performance of handicapped students on the North Carolina minimum competency test. *Exceptional Children, 49,* 547-550.

McLoughlin, J. & Lewis, R. (1990). *Assessing special students (3rd Ed.)*. Columbus, Ohio: Merrill.

McNemar, Q. (1942). *The revision of the Stanford-Binet scale, an analysis of the s t a n - dardization data*. Princeton, NJ: Houghton Mifflin.

Mehrens, W. A. & Lehmann, I.J. (1973). *Measurement and evaluation in education and psychology*. New York: Holt, Rinehart & Winston.

Meyen, E., & Skrtic, T. (1995). *Special education and students disability (4th ed.)*. Denver, CO: Love.

Monroe, M. (1932). *Children who cannot read*. Chicago: University of Chicago Press.

Myklebust, H. R. (Ed.). (1968). *Progress in learning disabilities (Vol. 1)*. New York: Grune & Stratton.

National Braille Association. (1973). *NBA manual for large type transcribing*. Rochester, New York: Author.

National Center on Educational Outcomes. (1993). *Accommodating students with disabilities in national and state testing programs*. (Brief report No. 9). Minneapolis, MN: Author. ERIC No. ED 373 504.

New York State Education Department. (1995). *Test access and modifications for individual with disabilities*. Albany, NY: Author.

New York State Education Department. *New York State guidelines for educational interpreting*. Albany, NY: Author.

New York State Education Department. (1994). *High school equivalency diploma and GED testing*. Albany, NY: Author.

New York State Education Department. (1996). *Registration bulletin 1996-97*. Albany, NY: Author.

Nunnally, J. (1967). *Psychometric theory*. New York: McGraw-Hill.

Ohio Department of Education. (1996). *Standards for Ohio schools*. Columbus, OH: Author.

Paraskevopoulous, J. & Kirk, S. (1969). *Development and psychometric characteristics of the revised Illinois Test of Psycholinguistic Abilities*. Urbana, IL: University of Illinois Press.

Phillips, S. (1993). *Legal implications of high-stakes assessment: what states should know.* Oak Brook, IL: North Central Regional Educational Laboratory.

Psychological Corporation. (1992). *Stanford Achievement Test (8th ed).* San Antonio, TX: Harcourt Brace Jovanovich.

Psychological Corporation. (1992). *Aprenda 2: La Prueba de Logros en Espanol.* San Antonio, TX: Harcourt Brace Jovanovich.

Psychological Corporation. (1992). *Wechsler Individual Achievement Test.* San Antonio, TX: Harcourt-Brace Jovanovich.

Psychological Corporation. (1993). *Miller Analogies Test: candidate information booklet.* San Antonio, TX: Harcourt-Brace Jovanovich.

Ragosta, M. & Wendler, C. (1992). *Eligibility issues and comparable time limits for disabled and nondisabled examinees.* New York: College Entrance Examination Board.

Registry of Interpreters for the Deaf, Inc. *Code of Ethics.* Silver Spring, MD: Author.

Reid, D.K., Hresko, W.P. & Hammill D. (1989). *Test of Early Reading Ability (2nd ed.).* Austin, TX: Pro-ed.

Reynolds, C.R. (1984). Critical measurement issues in learning disabilities. *Journal of Special Education, 18,* 451-476.

Richardson, M.W. & Kuder, G.F. (1939). The calculation of test reliability coefficients based on the method of rational equivalence. *Journal of Educational Psychology, 30,* 681-687.

Richek, M., List, L, & Lerner, J. (1983). *Reading problems: diagnosis and remediation.* Englewood-Cliffs, NJ: Prentice-Hall.

Riverside Publishing Company. (1994). *Riverside Performance Assessment Series, Spanish Edition.* Chicago, IL: Author.

Rothstein, L. F. (1990). *Special education law.* New York: Longman.

Rothstein, L. F. (1995). *Special education law (2nd ed).* New York: Longman.

Salvia, J. & Ysseldyke, J.E. (1995). *Assessment (6th ed.).* Boston: Houghton Mifflin.

Sattler, J. M. (1972). *Assessment of children's intelligence. Philadelphia: W.B.* Saunders Company.

Schildroth, A. (1990). *Achievement testing of deaf students: the 8th edition Stanford Achievement Test.* Washington, DC: Gallaudet University.

School, B.A. & Cooper, A. (1981). *The IEP primer and the individualized program.* Novato, CA: Academic Therapy Publications.

Schuerholz, L.J., Harris, E.L., Baumgardner, T.L., Reiss, A.L., Freund, L.S., Church, R.P., Mohr, J. & Fenckla, M.B. (1995). An analysis of two discrepancy-based models and a process-deficit approach in identifying learning disabilities. *Journal of learning Disabilities, 28,* 18-29.

Schulz, J.B., Carpenter, C.D. & Turnbill, A.P. (1991). *Mainstreaming exceptional children: a guide for classroom teachers.* Boston: Allyn & Bacon.

Shane, H.C. (Ed.). (1994). *Facilitated communication: the clinical and social phenomenon.* San Diego, CA: Singular Publishing Group.

Shriner, J., Spande, G, & Thurlow, M. (1994). *State special education outcomes, 1993: a report on state activities in the assessment of educational outcomes for students with disabilities.* Minneapolis, MN: National Center on Educational Outcomes. ERIC No. ED 372 558.

Slakter, M.J., Crehan, K.D. & Koehler, R.A. (1975). Longitudinal studies of risk taking on objective examinations. *Educational and Psychological Measurement, 75,* 97-105.

Smith, S. (1990). Comparison of individualized education programs (IEPs) of students with behavioral disorders and learning disabilities. *Journal of Learning Disabilities, 24,* 85-100.

Smith, T., Polloway, E., Patton, J., & Dowdy, C. (1995). *Teaching children with special needs in inclusive settings.* Boston: Allyn and Bacon.

Spache, G. (1976). *Investigating the issues of reading disabilities.* Boston: Allyn & Bacon.

Spache, G. (1981). *Diagnosis and correcting reading disabilities (2nd ed.).* Boston: Allyn & Bacon.

Terman, L.M. and Merrill, M.A. (1973). *Stanford-Binet Intelligence Scale.* Boston: Houghton-Mifflin Company.

Texas Education Agency. (1994). *Texas student assessment program technical digest of the academic year 1994-1995.* Austin, TX: Author.

Texas Education Agency. (1997). *Frequently asked questions.* Austin, TX: Author.

Thorndike, R.L. (1951). *Reliability.* In Educational Measurement. E.F. Lindquist, Washington, DC: American Council on Education.

Thurlow, M., Ysseldyke, J., & Silverstein, B. (1993). *Testing accommodations for students with disabilities: a review of the literature.* (Synthesis Report No. 4). Minneapolis, MN: National Center on Educational Outcomes. ERIC No. ED 358 656.

Thurlow, M.L., Ysseldyke, J.E. & Silverstein, B. (1995). Testing accommodations for students with disabilities. *Remedial and Special Education, 16,* 260-270.

United States Department of Education, Office of Special Education and Rehabilitative Service, the Assistant Secretary Memorandum (September 16, 1991) *Clarification of policy to address the needs of children with attention deficit disorders within general and/or special education.*

United States Department of Education. (1993). *Implementation of the individuals with disabilities act: fifteenth annual report to congress.* Washington, DC: Author. ERIC No. ED 363 058.

United States Department of Education. (1994). *Implementation of the individuals with disabilities act: sixteenth annual report to congress.* Washington, DC: Author. ERIC No. ED 373 531.

United States Department of Education. (1995). *Implementation of the individuals with disabilities act: seventeenth annual report to congress.* Washington, DC: Author. ERIC No. ED 386 018.

United States Department of Education. (1996). *Implementation of the individuals with disabilities act: eighteenth annual report to congress.* Washington, DC: Author.

United States General Accounting Office. (1994). *Social security: rapid rise in children on SSI disability rolls follows new regulations.* Washington, DC Author. GAO/HEHS-94-225 Rapid Rise in Children on SSI.

Vaughn, S., Bos, C.S., & Schumm, J.S. (1997). *Teaching mainstreamed, diverse, and at-risk students in the general education classroom.* Boston: Allyn and Bacon.

Walker, J. (1961). *Blind children: degree of vision mode of reading.* Washington, DC United States Government Printing Office.

Washington State Administrative Code (Chapter 392-172). *Rules for the provision of special education to special education students.* Olympia, WA: Author.

Wechsler, D. (1974). *Manual Wechsler Intelligence Scale for Children: Revised.* San Antonio, TX: Psychological Corporation.

Wechsler, D. (1991). *Manual Wechsler Intelligence Scale for Children: Third Edition.* San Antonio, TX: Psychological Corporation.

Wendler, C. & Wright, N. (1994). *Reactions of students with disabilities to the new SAT.* Paper presented at the Annual Meeting of the National Council on Management in Education, New Orleans, LA. ERIC No. ED 375 543.

Wiederholt, J.L., and Bryant, B. R. (1992). *Gray Oral Reading Tests, Third Edition.* Austin, TX: Pro-Ed.

Wild, C., & Durso, R. (1979). *Effect of increased test-taking time of test scores by ethnic groups, age, sex.* Princeton, NJ: Educational testing Service. ERIC No. 241 570.

Wilkinson, G. (1984). *The Wide Range Achievement Test-Revised.* Wilmington, DE: Jastak Associates.

Wilkinson, G. (1993). *The Wide Range Achievement Test-3.* Wilmington, DE: Jastak Associates.

Willingham, W.W., Ragosta, M., Bennett, R.E., Braun, H., Rock, D.A., & Powers, D.E. (1988). *Testing handicapped people.* Boston: Allyn & Bacon.

Willingham, W.W. (1988). Discussion and conclusions. In W.W. Willingham, M. Ragosta, M., R.E. Bennett, H. Braun, H., D.A. Rock, & D.E. Powers, *Testing handicapped people* (pp. 143-186). Boston: Allyn & Bacon.

Willingham, W.W. (1988). Introduction. In W.W. Willingham, M. Ragosta, M., R.E. Bennett, H. Braun, H., D.A. Rock, & D.E. Powers, *Testing handicapped people* (pp. 1-16). Boston: Allyn & Bacon.

Wilson, V.L. & Reynolds, C.R. (1984). Another look at evaluating aptitude-achievement discrepancies in the diagnosis of learning disabilities. *Journal of Special Education, 18,* 477-487.

Winer, B. (1971). *Statistical principles in experimental design (2nd ed.).* New York: McGraw-Hill.

Wisconsin Department of Public Instruction. (1996). *The testing of students with disabilities (exceptional educational needs students), handicapped students under section 504, and limited-English speaking students: DPI guidelines for non-discriminatory testing.* Madison, WI: Author.

Woodcock, R. (1973). *Woodcock Reading Mastery Tests.* Circle Pines, MN: American Guidance Service.

Woodcock, R. (1987). *Woodcock Reading Mastery Tests-Revised.* Circle Pines, MN: American Guidance Service.

Wright, N. & Wendler, C. (1994). *Establishing timing limits for the new SAT for students with disabilities.* Paper presented at the Annual Meeting of the National Council on Management in Education, New Orleans, LA. ERIC No. ED 375 542.

Ysseldyke, J., Thurlow, M., McGrew, K., & Shriner, J. (1994). *Recommendations for making decisions about the participation of students with disabilities in statewide assessment programs: a report on a working conference to develop guidelines form statewide assessments and students with disabilities.* (Synthesis Report No. 15). Minneapolis, MN: National Center on Educational Outcomes. ERIC No. ED 375 588.

INDEX